Clan Fabius, Defenders of Rome

For Olivia

Clan Fabius, Defenders of Rome

A History of the Republic's Most Illustrious Family

Jeremiah McCall

PEN & SWORD
HISTORY

First published in Great Britain in 2018
by Pen & Sword History
An imprint of Pen & Sword Books Limited
47 Church Street
Barnsley
South Yorkshire
S70 2AS

ISBN 978 1 47388 561 5

A CIP catalogue record for this book is
available from the British Library

Typeset in Ehrhardt
by Mac Style

Printed and bound in the UK
by TJ International Ltd, Padstow, Cornwall

Pen & Sword Books Limited incorporates the imprints of Atlas,
Archaeology, Aviation, Discovery, Family History, Fiction, History,
Maritime, Military, Military Classics, Politics, Select, Transport,
True Crime, Air World, Frontline Publishing, Leo Cooper,
Remember When, Seaforth Publishing, The Praetorian Press,
Wharncliffe Local History, Wharncliffe Transport,
Wharncliffe True Crime and White Owl.

For a complete list of Pen & Sword titles please contact
PEN & SWORD BOOKS LIMITED
47 Church Street, Barnsley, South Yorkshire, S70 2AS, England
E-mail: enquiries@pen-and-sword.co.uk
Website: www. pen-and-sword.co.uk

Contents

Chapter 1   Introduction   1

Chapter 2   Shadows of the Past: The Fabii and the Fledgling Republic   10

Chapter 3   The First Fabius Maximus, Rullianus and the Samnite Wars   33

Chapter 4   The Battle of Sentinum   67

Chapter 5   Fabius Maximus Cunctator and the War against Hannibal   86

Chapter 6   The Fabian Strategy and the End of the War   115

Chapter 7   Spanish Wars, Gallic Wars, Civil Wars and the End of the Line   149

Appendix A: Roman Names   170
Appendix B: Glossary of Some Technical Terms   171
Appendix C: Glossary of Major Sources for the Republic   173
Appendix D: Online Sources of Ancient Authors in Translation   175

Notes   177
Bibliography   195
Index   198

Chapter 1

Introduction

For centuries after the event, the Romans told tales of a noble clan, the Fabii, whose men sacrificed their lives for the good of the Republic.[1] As the ancient stories had it, for a span of years, 485–479 BC by our reckoning, the three sons of Kaeso Fabius – Kaeso the younger, Quintus and Marcus – had reached the pinnacle of political power in the early decades of the Republic.[2] Each had served more than once as one of the two yearly consuls, the powerful magistrates who commanded Rome's legions and executed its laws.[3] Under their command, Roman armies had successfully defended the fledgling Republic from ever-present foes in central Italy: the tribes of Aequi, Volsci and Hernici, and the rival Etruscan city-state of Veii. Yet despite Roman successes, these enemies continued to threaten from all sides. Powerful Veii posed a special threat. The Veientes forded the Tiber River into Roman territory with impunity, raiding herds and carrying off loot. The Roman Army, slow to muster and needed elsewhere, could not respond to the constant threat. Hence the Fabii, loyal Roman

Ancient Italy.

aristocrats – descended, tradition had it, from a romance between Hercules and a nymph, and standing alongside Romulus when the city was founded – offered their services to the nascent Republic.[4] At their own expense and from their own family, they would muster a warband, build a fort on the far side of the Cremera River and punish the Veientes for their crimes. The tales differ at this point: either the Fabii alone, some 300 men, built the fort that was to be a thorn in Veii's side, or they brought along their loyal retainers and clients, some 4,000, to assist. But the effect was clear. The Fabii watched the frontiers and took their own vengeance on Veii, raiding its lands and plundering its herds. For some time, the Roman border with Veii was quiet, well protected by Fabian arms.

And then, disaster. The Veientes baited a trap, leaving some prime flocks ostensibly untended while gathering their forces just out of sight. The Fabii, bold from their many successful raids, approached the flocks without scouting the surrounding environs: a mistake. Veientine warriors burst out of hiding and surrounded the valiant Fabii. Herders no more, now the Fabii were themselves herded into a cramped space. Though they fought mightily, the tale-tellers told, they died where they stood, overwhelmed. Three hundred and six Fabii died that day, all the men in the family. The Fabian clan would have been extinguished forever, except that one youth, named Marcus, escaped the massacre. He became the progenitor of what would eventually become the Fabius Maximus clan, the father of a family of heroes who would serve the Republic well indeed over the centuries.

These tales of the three brothers and the disaster at the Cremera mark the first discoverable appearance of that famous Fabian clan in the history of the Roman Republic. To understand that tale and consider what historical reality may be behind it, however, requires some background in the early history of the Romans. According to the accounts later Romans wrote, the city was founded on some hills south of the Tiber less than 20 miles from the sea by the legendary king Romulus in the middle of the eighth century BC.[5] Six subsequent kings ruled the nascent state, tradition told, each contributing important religious, political, military and legal customs and institutions. As Rome developed internally, it also grew in power and prestige in the region of central Italy called Latium. After a couple of centuries under beneficent masters, however, the Romans came to be ruled by a malevolent Etruscan king, Tarquinius Superbus, 'Tarquin the Proud'. His oppressive rule, and his son's rape of the virtuous Lucretia, wife of an influential young man, pushed the Roman aristocracy past the breaking point, and, in the late sixth century, those aristocrats eradicated the monarchy and replaced it with a new form of government, the Republic. The name itself in Latin is *res publica* and means 'public affairs' or 'public matters'.

Historians have frequently challenged the details of this ancient narrative. The basic picture that the city of Rome began as a monarchy is plausible enough, as is the creation of a Republic. It seems clear, however, that the Republican form of government did not simply spring fully formed from the murdered monarchy. Rather, its offices and their powers and interactions, the rules of politics, developed slowly over the centuries.[6] Still, since the historical Fabii were, first and foremost, aristocrats of the Roman Republic, it is worth briefly examining the basic components of that Republic.

The Workings of the Roman Republic

Polybius is the starting point for those investigating the classical Republic of the second century BC.[7] A citizen of Greek Megalopolis, he became a politician and military leader for the Achaean League of city-states to which his city belonged. That League ran afoul of the Romans early in the second century BC. In 167, following Rome's crushing victory over king Perseus of Macedonia, the Roman Senate opted to arrest prominent Achaean citizens, Polybius among them. Deported to Rome, they served as hostages for the League's good behaviour. Polybius was luckier than most of his fellow-captives. He met the young Roman aristocrat Publius Cornelius Scipio Aemilianus and became the boy's tutor and friend. Enabled by this friendship over the years to access Roman political and military workings, Polybius decided to investigate the Romans and write an account – some of which still survives – of Roman institutions and how Rome had come to dominate the Mediterranean over the course of the second century BC. His work offers the most thorough description of the Republic as it ostensibly functioned in the second century, an account that is supplemented and corroborated by all manner of references in the ancient sources.[8]

Polybius, who wrote in Greek for an audience not wholly familiar with Roman customs, suggests three political organs shared power in the Roman Republic.[9] The consuls were the chief magistrates. Elected in pairs that held office for one year only, the consuls were the chief executives and military commanders. They held by right of their office *imperium*, a term that translates roughly as 'power'. That power included the right to levy and command armies and have one's commands obeyed. Though Polybius does not mention them in his basic account, there were other magistrates in the Roman government: among others, praetors who served as judges and, by the middle Republic, governors of territories under Roman control, aediles, who maintained the temples and held public games, and censors, who were responsible for managing the lists of citizens and their corresponding military obligations.

The second critical government body was the Senate. Until perhaps 300 BC, the Senate was little more than a group of distinguished elders selected first by the kings and later by the chief magistrates to provide counsel. The informality of membership in the Senate meant the body of senators fluctuated from year to year. Under these circumstances, the Senate did not fully function as a regular governing body. Over time, however, the custom developed that it might be a more permanent body consisting of lifelong members. This custom was put into law, perhaps, by the *lex Ovinia* of the later fourth century BC.[10] This legislation, as the much later Roman grammarian Festus preserved it, called for the censors to 'enroll in the Senate the best men from all ranks', with a result that 'senators who were passed over and thus lost their place, were held in dishonour'.[11] So unlike today, where senators in the United States are elected officials, senators in the Republic were those whom the censors deemed the best men. In practice, this meant those who had held political office. From this time on, those Romans honoured with senatorial status retained that status for life, so long as they conducted themselves appropriately and were not struck from the list of senators by a disapproving censor. This shift dramatically enhanced the prestige of senatorial status. By Polybius' day the Senate wielded a great deal of informal, but very real, power. It was the body that assigned provinces of action to the military commanders of the year, consuls and, sometimes, praetors. It received the growing number of foreign envoys and conducted diplomacy. Most importantly of all, perhaps, the Senate effectively controlled the state funds and their use. As convention had it, the Senate also deliberated issues before putting proposals before the citizen assemblies for a vote.

Though Rome was not a true democracy, it had democratic elements in the form of the citizen assemblies, the third critical element of the Republic. The Romans assembled citizens in various ways to hold elections, declare wars and pass laws. Different assemblies were organized differently, like, for example, the *comitia centuriata*, or centuriate assembly. This assembly, which ranked citizens by wealth and gave more voting power to those with the greatest means, elected consuls and praetors, and declared wars, among other functions.

The other main assembly of the Republic was the tribal assembly. Here citizens were organized not by wealth but by tribes, the basic organizational units of Roman citizens. This assembly ratified laws and elected the tribunes of the plebs. Special mention must be made of these tribunes. In the middle Republic, ten of these officials were elected every year. They had a set of powers that enabled them to serve as defenders of the plebeians, the Roman commoners. First, they could stop an assembly cold with their power of veto, effectively blocking elections and legislation. They could also, as magistrates, propose bills to the tribal assembly for passage into law. Finally, they were sacrosanct while in office. This last item amounted to a formal guarantee of safety by the plebeians, the majority at Rome, as a whole: any aggressors harming a tribune in office would unleash the punitive power of the entire plebs on their heads.[12]

In the fifth century BC, when the Fabii sons held their string of consulships, the institutions of the Republic were still taking shape and not fully in the form they took in Polybius' day. How different their forms were is difficult to say, and it does not help that some of our sources write as if the early Republic functioned just as it would in later years. Still, some differences appear. To mention just a few, at the very beginning of the Republic, the chief magistrates, consuls for practical purposes, may have been termed praetors, and it is not entirely clear that there were two magistrates equal in power.[13] Praetors in their later sense, the special judicial magistrates with less *imperium* than the consuls, did not exist until the early fourth century BC. The Senate was still an advisory body with a fluid membership. There were multiple tribunes, two or five most likely, but not ten.[14]

It was in this Republic that the Fabii and, eventually even more famously, the Fabii Maximi, came to play a critical role. The first Fabii to hold the highest political offices at Rome – let's call them consulships for sake of convenience – did so within a few decades of the very start of the Republic, traditionally dated to 509 BC. From then until the collapse of that Republic in the late first century BC, Fabii were part of the political and military elite. First bearing the family name Fabius Vibulanus, some descendants split off and took the name Fabius Ambustus to distinguish themselves from other branches of the clan. These Fabii Ambusti later became the Fabii Rulliani. Then Quintus Fabius Rullianus in 304 BC received the epithet of Maximus, 'the Greatest'. Without question, the Fabii Maximi were by far the politically and militarily most important of the Fabian clan. Generation after generation, the ancestors of the Fabii Maximi held numerous consulships, steered the ship of state from the advisory body of the Senate, commanded armies and prosecuted criminals. Indeed, the ancestors of the Fabius Maximus family witnessed and participated as the Republic developed its institutions. They were there during the wars through which the Republic came to dominate central Italy, the peninsula and, finally, the Mediterranean. The political importance of the family outlasted, just barely, the Republic. But the collapse of the Republic with its arena of political competition for aristocrats, and its replacement by a monarchy in the form of emperors, the Fabii Maximi quickly declined. Once champions in the competitive sphere of Republican politics, in the Empire the Fabii could only rest on the laurels of their great ancestors, a tenuous position at best. And so the rise and fall of the Fabius Maximus family, in a real sense, parallels the rise and fall of the Roman Republic itself. Investigating the Fabii Maximi gives us a chance to glimpse that rise and fall of the Republic, itself a fascinating story.

Considering the Sources: The Historians of the Republic

But how can one track the Fabius Maximus family over the centuries of the Republic, from the shadowy legends of the fifth century BC to the more brightly lit anecdotes of the first? It is a critical point to consider. Unlike the histories of the modern world, say, the twentieth and twenty-first centuries, the evidence for the Romans of the Republic is paltry, fragmentary and scattered. Roman and Greek historians, poets and antiquarians wrote about the Republic often centuries later than the events and customs they described. A few of their writings were preserved, almost never completely, by medieval monks who copied this or that text. In the process they left out sections that they found uninteresting, introduced copying errors and made the sources from the Roman period, already conjectural, even more hazy. These are the conditions that anyone investigating the Roman Republic, indeed investigating almost any era of the Greco-Roman world, must accept. They are daunting, but cannot be avoided by anyone who hopes to glimpse most any part of the Republic.

So, leaving in the critical background the problem of the ancient sources and their transmission to the present, what can be said about our evidence for the Republic? First, the evidence appears stronger beginning in the late fourth century BC. It is difficult to know, however, what to make of the surviving historical accounts for the fifth-century Republic, not least of all the span of years where the sources insist the Fabii were significant actors in war and politics. The main sources for this period, the Greeks Diodorus Siculus and Dionysius of Halicarnassus and the Roman Livy (Titus Livius), have issues concerning their credibility. The most significant problem for historians hoping to use these sources in their reconstruction of the early Republic is the problem of the historical tradition itself. Our two most important sources for the early Republic were composed at the very end of the first century BC as the Republic was supplanted by an emperor. Though some Greek historians mention early Rome, those mentions provide precious few clues about the Republic. The first Romans to write historical accounts – organized narratives – did so at the very end of the third century BC or the very beginning of the second. At that time Roman power, though certainly tested by the Carthaginian Hannibal's invasion of Italy, was on the rise. Rome now dominated Italy, and once the Carthaginian invaders were expelled from the peninsula, Rome began to dominate the Mediterranean. At this point, the first Roman historians, Quintus Fabius Pictor and Lucius Cincius Alimentus, investigated the origins of their state. Though their accounts are long lost, references to these authors in later writers like Livy and Dionysius indicate that they were important sources for later accounts of early Rome.[15]

These first historians could hardly have viewed the earliest Republic, over two centuries prior, very clearly, simply due to the limited nature of Roman documentary evidence. So how did Livy, Dionysius and their sources reconstruct the span of early years when the first Fabians were consuls? The skeleton of events was available to them through the *Fasti Consulares*, a list of the consuls for each year since the beginning of the Republic. Since the consuls of each year gave their names to the year, maintenance of these lists would have been critical early in Rome's history for keeping any kind of historical records, making their accurate transmission more likely. Four versions of the consular fasti (generally just referred to as the fasti) have survived through the millennia. Three, the historians Diodorus Siculus, Dionysius of Halicarnassus and Livy preserved in the course of their narratives. The fourth, now known as the *Fasti Capitolini*,

Augustus ordered carved in stone and placed in the Forum. Before 300 BC the versions do not always agree, but mostly do when it comes to the names of the magistrates and the order in which they held office.[16]

But a simple list of office holders and military victories, while helpful in constructing a few points of political and military narrative for the early Republic, was hardly sufficient for Dionysius, Livy or their sources to provide the details they do for these years. Episodes like the trial of Spurius Cassius and the details of the battles between Romans and Volsci did not come from the fasti. Perhaps the historians these first-century writers consulted contained these details, but the question remains: where did those earlier writers get the details? What other than the fasti could later Romans draw from when constructing these early accounts?

A critical documentary source of information for the fifth century BC, available to Roman historians from the third to first centuries, were the *Annales Maximi*, 'the Greatest Annals'. These were a list of important events for each year maintained by Rome's chief priest, the *pontifex maximus*. The first-century BC statesman Cicero describes them this way:

'From the beginning of Roman affairs to the chief pontificate of P. Mucius [130–115 BC] the chief pontiff used to write down all matters year by year, publicized them on a whitened board, and placed the table in front of his house, that the people could learn from it. Even now they are called the Chief Annals. This form of writing has been followed by many who have left behind unembellished records of mere dates, persons, places, and deeds.'[17]

Very little else is known about these records, but they provided records of important public events: significant defeats and victories that earned their commanders that spectacular military celebration the Romans called a triumph; important religious events; records of omens from the gods; legislation; public works projects and so on.[18] The consulships of the Fabii and their colleagues and the bare narrative of victories and defeats fell under this. So too, presumably, would the trial and execution of a major public figure like Spurius Cassius.

It seems, however, that the *Annales Maximi*, especially for the earliest Republic, were simple lists lacking the details that made their way into later writers' accounts. Sources that, while problematic, probably provided such details about the past were the family histories the great aristocratic families of the Republic constructed to add lustre to their lineages. These histories often took the form of eulogies dusted off and delivered during the funerals of distinguished Roman family members. Polybius suggests that in his day at least it was common to present a litany of ancestral deeds whenever celebrating the life of a newly deceased Roman aristocrat.[19] Even the ancient Romans, however, were fully aware of the potential of these family tales to distort the events of the past. Cicero notes:

'Speeches in praise of the dead are indeed extant; for families kept them as a sort of honour and a record, in order to preserve the memory of the achievements of the family and document its nobility. Of course the history of Rome has been falsified by these speeches; for there is much in them which never happened – invented triumphs, additional consulships, false claims to patrician status, and so on.'[20]

Livy, too, notes the difficulties brought on by spurious additions to the family records:

'The record has been falsified, I believe, by funeral eulogies and fictitious inscriptions on portrait busts, when families try to appropriate to themselves the tradition of exploits and titles of office by means of inventions calculated to deceive. This has led to confusion both in individual achievements and in public records of events.'[21]

There were few, if any, authoritative records available to curb the embellishments that may have made their way into the family accounts. Theoretically, outlandish claims for one family probably could be checked against details in other family accounts. It is not clear at all, however, how frequently Livy or his sources engaged in that level of source criticism.

To these other sources can be added the unfortunately vague category of stories and legends. Roman culture, like essentially all ancient cultures, was an oral one. History, story, legend and myth were preserved in their telling and retelling, and the four blended together. There is some evidence that Roman aristocrats would employ singers at their banquets who might sing about the events of the ancestors. On top of this, beginning in the mid-third century BC, the Romans began to craft plays dealing with current and historical events.[22] All of this combined to form conventional wisdoms about the past that were handed down to historians of later generations.

Still, there are details that seem unlikely to have come from any of these sources. These are the rhetorical flourishes that make these ancient historians' narratives come alive: the exact words of actors, the detailed descriptions of how people felt in this or that predicament, and so on. These were the artifacts of the historian's craft that made the narrative compelling but lacked any foundation of solid evidence.

Livy continues to be our major source for the fourth century BC, and though he has closed the gap from fifth-century events, he is still separated from his subjects by centuries and must rely on the sources that have been discussed above. The closer we get to the time when the first historians actually began to write about Rome, the more reliable the sources likely become. But even then, certainty is often impossible. So, while it will not do to blindly follow the much-later sources for the earlier Republic, there was sufficient available evidence to allow these writers to capture critical details.

When crossing over to the period after, say, 300 BC, and even more so after 200 BC, the quality of our evidence improves considerably. The first historians, writing around 200 BC, would have had better access to records and details in the prior century, solid knowledge, however biased, of events experienced by their grandparents and parents, and first-hand knowledge of many events that they described from their own time. Sources continue to accumulate for the second and first century, and many of the sources wrote during events or less than a century after, not hundreds of years distant as with the early Republic. This situation only improves in the final century of the Republic, the first century BC, when even more primary sources exist from statesmen like Cicero and Caesar, and even bits from the Emperor Augustus.

But again, even in the best-documented periods of the Republic more is hidden than known, and very few, if any, events can be pinned down with any certainty. Debates continue among modern historians for most every assertion made about the Republic. In the interests of the story, however, this book will forego persistently reminding the reader of the tenuous lines of evidence the historians had, but that uncertainty is still always present. A history like the present book is most honestly treated as a mystery, an investigation into an often shadowy past accessed by interrogating and comparing sources and teasing out what can reasonably be said. And so, as detectives, it is time to investigate the rise and decline of the Fabii in the politics, military and political culture of the Republic.

Chapter 2

Shadows of the Past:
The Fabii and the Fledgling Republic

The First Fabii of the Republic: Quintus, Kaeso and Marcus Fabius Vibulanus

Go back far enough into the mists of legend, some said, and the Fabius clan descended from Hercules. That divine hero, so the story went, stole the cattle from Geryon, a monster sporting three bodies. But as he herded the spoils and journeyed back to Greece, Hercules happened to meet a king's daughter on the spot where Rome would someday stand. One thing led to another, and the first Fabius was born.[1] So the Fabii claimed descent from Hercules, a connection that was trumpeted throughout their illustrious history. Somewhat later, but hardly less misty or legendary, a Fabius was said to have been the general of Romulus, that legendary first king of Rome. Perhaps this Fabius was the one who murdered Romulus' brother, though other traditions accused the king himself of that crime.[2] A less impressive, but not mutually exclusive, legend was that the progenitor of the Fabii had been the first Roman to construct pit-traps for catching animals, and that the name Fabii was a modification of the original Fovii or Fodii, which meant 'to dig'.[3]

While these tales do nothing to help us find the first historical Fabii, they do emphasize the distinction the family claimed. Certainly, they were counted among the *gentes maiores*, the 'greater clans' that the Romans considered to be the most distinct, the most aristocratic. But by their reckoning, Fabii were at Rome before the city had been founded, and were also there when the Roman Republic began.

The early years of the Republic itself, however, are shrouded in secrets, so long in the past, and the centuries-later writers about the period may have fabricated a great number of details to make their histories pleasant to read. Thus, it is difficult to have confidence when pinning down details of the first historical Fabii who appear in the evidence. Let's begin with what seems relatively certain: the names of the consuls, the pair of chief magistrates elected yearly to command Rome's armies and lead its government. The consulship was the pinnacle office of the Republic, held only by a minority of the aristocracy – two every year. Since Romans of the Republic named their years according to the consuls – for example, 'The year of Quintus Fabius and Servius Cornelius, consuls' – they must have kept chronological lists of these offices, which modern historians call the *fasti*. Several ancient writers relayed these *fasti* and the first emperor, Augustus, inscribed them in stone when the Republic was no more.[4] According to the *fasti*, a Fabius held the consulship every year between 485 and 479 BC.[5] To put this in perspective, this may be the most substantial stretch of the consulship held by a single family in the Republic, by three brothers no less.[6] So clearly the early Fabii were prominent at Rome. Why exactly this was the case is anyone's guess. They presumably must have had land and status that enabled them to be among the ranks of early Rome's leading aristocratic households. The rest is unclear.

Beyond this list of consuls, the total accuracy of which modern historians still dispute, the surviving sources from the late Republic leave narrative details that flesh out these office holders' tenures. Certainly embellished, likely with inaccuracies, these narrative snippets are all there is to go from for the first political Fabii of the Republic.

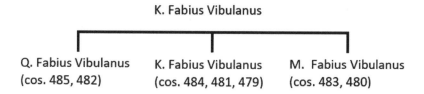

K. Fabius Vibulanus

Q. Fabius Vibulanus	K. Fabius Vibulanus	M. Fabius Vibulanus
(cos. 485, 482)	(cos. 484, 481, 479)	(cos. 483, 480)

The Consulship of Q. Fabius Vibulanus and Conviction of Spurius Cassius (485 BC)

Livy and Dionysius of Halicarnassus, both writing some four centuries later, relate that the first Fabian consul, Quintus Fabius Vibulanus, held office alongside Servius Cornelius in 485 BC. The meaning of the *cognomen* 'Vibulanus' is not clear – perhaps it comes from a geographical reference? In any event, Quintus Fabius' brother, Kaeso the younger, also appears as a young prosecutor this year, charging the three-time consul Spurius Cassius for harbouring plans of tyranny. During his final consulship in 486 BC, Cassius had proposed the Republic distribute certain tracts of state-owned land – the *ager publicus*. The beneficiaries would be the Roman plebeians – who as noted earlier, roughly speaking, were the Roman commoners – as well as Rome's Latin allies and the newly defeated and now allied tribe of the Hernici. Concern arose that Cassius might leverage this favour to allies and citizen farmers to seize sole power in Rome, and his measure was opposed.[7] At the end of 486, when Spurius Cassius' term as consul had expired, the young Kaeso Fabius, a newly elected minor magistrate called a quaestor, banded together with a colleague and prosecuted Cassius for treason.[8] One wonders how strong the evidence was, but apparently it sufficed. Convicted and condemned to die, Cassius was hurled from that cliff the Romans used for such purposes, the Tarpeian Rock.[9]

As for the consul, Quintus Fabius, it was time for a war. War was the primary activity of the consuls almost every year of the Republic. Wars of plunder, wars of conquest, wars of revenge: year after year the Romans fought with the peoples and cities surrounding them. At this early stage, the fledgling Republic's primary rivals were the Etruscans, especially those in the nearby rival city of Veii, and the tribes of Aequi and Volsci, whose territory bounded the frontiers of Rome and its Latin allies. In 485 BC, the consuls fought against these foes. According to Dionysius, Cornelius' legions raided Veii's territory and hauled off a great deal of loot, forcing the city into a truce, while Fabius' forces campaigned against the Aequi and Volsci, pillaging the lands of the latter. While the Roman soldiers were scattered, pilfering the Volscians' movable loot, the Volsci attempted a surprise attack. Fabius' scouts detected the strike, reports Dionysius, and,

> 'by a prompt recall [Fabius] drew in his men, then dispersed in pillaging, and put them back into the proper order for battle. As for the Volscians, who were advancing contemptuously and confidently, when the entire army of the enemy unexpectedly appeared, drawn up in orderly array, they were struck with fear.'[10]

What 'proper order' meant for the fifth-century Roman army will be considered later. In any event, the dismayed Volsci fled the battlefield. Rather than letting his soldiers keep their plunder, Quintus Fabius sold the captured loot and deposited the money in the state treasury, adding a nice bit of shine to his reputation.[11] Livy has little to add for 485 BC. He mentions the defeat of Volsci and Aequi, and agrees Fabius commandeered his soldiers' loot and deposited it in the public treasury. Ever interested in class conflict, Livy adds that this move incensed Fabius' soldiers.[12]

The Consulship of Kaeso Fabius (484 BC)

The consuls for 484 BC were, as usual, elected at the end of the prior year. For this election, Dionysius and Livy agree, the earliest Roman nobility, called the patricians, ordered Kaeso Fabius to run for consul alongside Lucius Aemilius. The city boiled with hostilities and resentment between the noble and privileged patricians and the plebeians. Dionysius asserts the plebeians wanted grants of farmland, but the senators, wealthy patricians, did not wish to comply. Both historians agreed, however, that when the threats of outside enemies loomed, both patrician and plebeian rallied together to defend the Republic. The Volscians chose war this year and continued their fight against the Romans, mustering two armies. One would drive into the lands of Rome's allies, Latins and Hernici; the other would defend their own lands from the inevitable Roman counter-attack. The Romans similarly divided their forces. The consuls of the year drew lots to determine their commands – the Romans used chance to decide these matters, among many others. Kaeso Fabius drew the defence of Rome's allies, while it fell to Aemilius to attack the Volscian town of Antium. There, Roman and Volscii soldiers clashed. The consul Aemilius, Dionysius narrates,

> 'led out his army. Before they engaged, [Aemilius] exhorted and encouraged his troops at length, and then ordered the trumpets to sound the charge; and the soldiers, raising their usual battlecry, attacked in close array both by cohorts and by centuries. After they had used up all their spears and javelins with the rest of their missile weapons, they drew their swords and rushed upon each other showing equal intrepidity and eagerness for the struggle.'[13]

Ultimately, the Volsci snatched victory through a ruse and pursued the Romans to their camp. Though the Volsci were eager to deliver the killing stroke, Aemilius' troops remained safe within the camp fortifications. Word soon reached Kaeso Fabius that Aemilius' troops were essentially under siege. He quickly dispatched contingents of his best soldiers to aid Aemilius. Bolstered by these men, the Romans burst free of their fort, drove off the Volscians and plundered their fields.[14] Livy's terse account, in contrast, gives no details of the battle: Aemilius simply defeated the Volsci and Aequi.[15] Either way, if these accounts are accurate, Kaeso experienced no noteworthy conflict with Rome's enemies during this year.

The Election of M. Fabius Vibulanus (483 BC) and the Conflict of the Orders

As Dionysius and Livy tell the story, when 483 BC arrived, Marcus Fabius served as consul, the third Fabian brother in as many years. The season's campaigns had a rocky start. Dionysius, as usual, provides more internal details. The Roman poor still waited for a law that would give them public land to farm, and the wealthy senators still resisted. A tribune of the plebeians, Gaius Maenius, attempted to force the senators into action by blocking the troop levies with his veto. The consuls essentially ignored the veto, however, went to the Campus Martius, the plain outside the city where troops were normally mustered, and proceeded to enroll soldiers. Maenius, whose tribune's powers did not extend outside the perimeter of the city, could do nothing but sputter in protest. Valerius took the new recruits to reinforce the army in Volscian territory while Fabius, as the lot dictated, commanded the army defending the Latins and Hernici.

This is the third time in as many years the sources assert that contention between patricians and plebeians, or – and this was not always the same thing – rich and poor, interfered with the operations of the Republic. This belief in a unified and protracted struggle between social classes, called the Conflict of the Orders, greatly influenced later historians' accounts of politics in the early Republic. Early Republican Rome, so the first-century BC historians passed along, was divided into two distinct social groups: the patricians, those whose distinguished status allegedly was inherited from King Romulus' select body of advisors, the first Senate; and the plebeians, those who lacked that distinguished patrician ancestry. When the Republic began, the patricians dominated the political and religious offices at Rome. Plebeians had grievances. The wealthier ones wanted access to the offices and honours the patricians held, especially the consulship. The poorer plebeians – presumably the majority – wanted protection from unwritten, and thus arbitrary, debt laws, particularly those that allowed a plebeian debtor to be forced into slavery to make good on their debt. Some poorer plebeians also sought land grants so that they could be successful subsistence farmers. The patricians, however, were famously unwilling to make any concessions to plebeian demands. Accordingly, the accounts say, the plebeians, who essentially were the infantry of the Roman army, began to refuse military service to pressure the patricians. This began with the Secession of the Plebs, traditionally in 494 BC, when the plebeians simply removed themselves from patrician Rome, strolled to the area around the nearby Aventine hill and refused to serve in the army. The patricians folded and compromised, creating the tribunes of the plebs, the ten magistrates whose task was to protect the plebeians from decrees of the Senate or assemblies that were harmful to their interest.

Though not incessantly, conflicts continued for another 200 years. By the early third century BC, however, the plebeians had eroded patrician political, military and legal privilege. The wealthiest of the plebeians won the legal right to hold almost every political and religious office, whilst plebeians of more modest means enjoyed all manner of legal and political rights. Gradually, the ruling aristocracy of Rome transformed from a patrician-dominated clique to a larger coterie of patricians and plebeians who held political office and gained access to positions in the Senate, that distinguished political body in the Republic.[16]

Historians have raised all manner of objections to traditional accounts of this conflict. The neat original division of Roman society into two classes, patrician and plebeian, does not seem adequately to characterize the social complexity of the archaic Republic. The ranks of the patricians, for example, appear to have been quite fluid initially, and only over time did patrician status become exclusive and distinctive. The consular *fasti*, for example, list a number of consuls in the fifth century – the first years of the Republic – whose family names are demonstrably plebeian later in the Republic. But the historical accounts insist that plebeians did not hold the consulship until the patrician monopoly was broken in 367 BC. Perhaps a greater weakness in the formulaic Conflict of the Orders is the idea that the plebeians were the sole source of Roman infantry. If this had been the case, it is difficult to see how the patricians could ever have resisted the demands of a much larger group of irate and well-armed people. Overall, it seems far too simplistic to suppose, as the narrative sources do, that every conflict in Rome in the period 500–300 BC was part of one great struggle between overweening patricians and oppressed plebeians struggling for power and land. That social and political conflicts existed in early Rome is reasonably certain. Debts and food shortages were problems for some time. A desire for access to public land also must have existed, along with a desire for written laws and procedures and, for some, access to high offices. Different plebeians sought improvements in these conditions at different times and places. Ultimately, wealthy plebeians did seek and gain access to essentially all the critical magistracies of the state such as the consulship. Plebeians did acquire their own specific magistrates, the tribunes, and their own legislative power through the plebeian assembly. Laws were fixed in writing. So the conflicts did happen to some degree, but lumping all the frictions and upsets into a unified incessant struggle excessively simplifies the matter.[17] So, when Livy and Dionysius assert almost yearly that struggles continued between patricians and plebeians, they are probably exaggerating, conforming to the traditions in their sources.

The Consulship of Marcus Fabius Vibulanus (483 BC)

Whatever the exact social and political struggles at the time were, the political system rolled along. Marcus Fabius and Lucius Valerius drew lots for their consular commands. Fabius received the army defending Rome's allies, while Valerius received the army attacking the Volscians. Dionysius describes the battle between the Romans under Valerius' command in some detail. Since the warfare of the Republic was one of the main concerns of Fabian politicians and, thus, of this book, his account is worth considering:

'When the Romans also came out and drew up their forces, a sharp engagement ensued, not only of the horse, but of the foot and the light-armed troops as well, all showing equal ardour and experience and every man placing his hopes of victory in himself alone. At last, however, the bodies of the dead on both sides lay in great numbers where they had fallen at the posts assigned to them, and the men who were barely alive were even more numerous than the dead, while those who still continued the fight and faced its dangers were but few, and even these were unable to perform the tasks of war; for their shields, because of the multitude of spears that had stuck in them, weighed down their left arms and would not permit them to sustain the enemy's onsets, and their daggers had their edges blunted or in some cases were entirely shattered and no longer of any use, and the great weariness of the men, who had fought the whole day, slackened their sinews and weakened their blows, and sweat, thirst, and want of breath afflicted both armies, as is wont to happen when men fight long in the stifling heat of summer.'[18]

After the dramatic account, however, Dionysius remarks that the outcome was indecisive. Once again, a Fabius consul was positioned to defend the allies and no noteworthy conflicts appear in the first-century sources.

Roman Armies in the Early Republic

Now that we have encountered several of Dionysius' battle descriptions, what can be said about the Roman armies of the fledgling Republic? For the Greeks, many of whom lived in colonies in the southernmost part of Italy – termed Magna Graecia by the Romans – a critical military evolution took place beginning in the eighth century BC.[19] A new type of warrior, the hoplite, came to be distinguished by a new panoply of wargear. The shield stood out most of all. Circular, roughly 3ft in diameter and concave like a shallow bowl, the hoplite shield had two grips, one a band that crossed the forearm positioned on the inside of the shield, the other a hand grip on the edge. A heavy bronze helmet with narrow openings for mouth, nose and eyes was also important. Bronze body armour, called by moderns the bell corselet because it flared out at the warrior's waist not unlike a bell, and bronze greaves to guard the legs completed the full panoply. Over time these hoplites came to group themselves in a close order formation known as a phalanx. The warriors stood in organized rows and columns so that each occupied approximately 3ft of space. This proximity allowed the hoplites on either side of a soldier to lend him extra protection with their shields. Any enemy facing the front of the phalanx would encounter a formidable wall of shields and thicket of spears thrust out from the first two ranks. The depth of the columns – eight men deep was apparently a common arrangement – lent comfort and courage to those fighting in the front.

Archaeological finds in graves and artistic depictions demonstrate that hoplite gear had made its way to the Etruscans, Rome's powerful northern neighbours, by the mid-seventh century BC. Unfortunately, the archaeological record in Rome and Latium from this period is quite poor in comparison, but historians suppose that Roman warriors also adopted hoplite gear around the same time as the Etruscans. Many historians have supposed that adopting hoplite gear necessitated fighting in the close order of the phalanx. This depends on the premise that hoplite gear was essentially useless for any other style of fighting. More recently, however, Van Wees has revised the picture of the early phalanx. Even in the Greek home of the hoplite, phalanxes for centuries consisted of a variety of warriors with all manner of arms. Wealth played a significant factor in this. Since hoplites generally had to supply their own gear, the wealthy could afford complete panoplies, while those of more modest means might only afford shield and helmet. Those poorer still might have only owned a javelin or some other inexpensive weapon, and thus served as 'light' infantry, who harassed and threw projectiles but tended to avoid hand-to-hand combat with enemies.[20]

For quite some time, battles between hoplites in the Greek world have been cast as organized chaos. Each army formed its hoplites into the organized ranks and files of the phalanx, each hoplite uniformly armed with melee weapons and armoured with shield, helmet and breastplate. They fought in close formation against their opponents, dealing wounds and death until one or the other side grew too disrupted. Then the mighty phalanx would break apart and its soldiers flee the battlefield. Recent analyses of the Greek phalanx, however, point out from the available evidence that this was an idealized form of phalanx battle. In reality, the heavy infantry of the phalanx was regularly accompanied by light infantry; the prejudice of Greek writers that the hoplite was the superior form of soldier often caused them to neglect these light troops in their accounts. In the earliest years of the hoplite phalanx, light troops seem to have fought intermingled with the lines of heavy infantry phalanx. Later they fought alongside the phalanx in separate units. Whatever the exact arrangement of troops, Greek hoplite battles were composed of a more diverse array of soldiers than has often been supposed.[21]

If this was true for Greeks in the age of hoplite warfare (roughly 700–300 BC), it seems to have been equally so for the Romans of the fifth century BC. As later Roman writers had it, King Servius Tullius bound military service to political participation at Rome by creating the *comitia centuriata*, the centuriate assembly. In the Republic, this body had significant powers: the ability to elect high magistrates such as consuls, praetors and censors, and the right to pass or reject laws proposed by magistrates. The assembly was made up of centuries, voting units that, confusingly enough, did not always consist of 100 men as the name would suggest. The centuries of cavalry were listed first on the voting rosters. Then 188 centuries of infantry were grouped into five classes based on their property. The members of each property class had to supply themselves with specific kinds of military equipment. Livy and Dionysius both preserve the list of classes and their specific equipment obligations. They have some minor variations between them, but essentially record the same classes and required equipment. Whether the sometimes trivial variations in equipment they recorded really distinguished certain property classes is debatable, and the specific property owned by members of each class cannot be absolutely verified. Still, the basic picture of soldiers supplying their own equipment is valid for the end of the monarchy and beginning of the Republic. Warriors armed in many different ways answered Rome's calls to war.[22]

So what did fifth-century BC Roman warfare look like, and did the first-century historians capture it? Livy and Dionysius paint fifth-century battles in very broad brush strokes that, when not too general, are nevertheless probably anachronistic. In their accounts, Rome fields many legions at a time, fortified formal camps like those in later centuries are a regular part of military life, and Rome fought full pitched battles with their enemies. This military picture is certainly true of the middle and late Republic, but it is not clear at all that it applies to the cloudy fifth century BC.[23] In these particular years with Fabian consuls, Livy offers very few details about battles. Dionysius, as noted, offers several battle descriptions. He refers to the Roman soldiers under Quintus Fabius in 485 BC as being in 'the proper order for battle', and 'in orderly array'. He suggests Lucius Aemilius' forces in 484 'attacked in close array both by cohorts and by centuries'. Statements like these are quite general, however, and it is by no means clear that Dionysius or his source accurately envisioned the Roman hoplite and light infantry forces of the fifth century when using these terms. His descriptions could apply equally well to the Roman manipular army that succeeded the hoplite army in the late fourth century BC or the uniform soldiers in the cohort legion of the late Republic.

Some things Dionysius includes make little sense. His reference to cohorts and centuries is a bit nonsensical. A cohort was a larger unit consisting of several centuries. Though they may have existed earlier administratively, cohorts did not really start to function as tactical units until the very end of the third century BC. If anything, the second account noted above, perhaps only coincidentally, reflects a little more of the mix probably found in a fifth-century Roman hoplite battle. It suggests that there was not simply a clash of heavily armoured troops in two monolithic phalanxes, but different types of fighters and a combination of missile and melee weapons. This fits with the centuriate division of Roman citizens described above with its variety of armour and weapons.

Returning to tracking the Fabii, it appears that during 483 BC no significant military developments took place in the field. Troubles, however, brewed at Rome. A detail in the sources, perhaps gleaned from the *Annales Maximi*, asserts that all manner of signs that year – bird patterns and the entrails of sacrificial animals – suggested the gods were displeased. Opimia, one of those Vestal Virgins charged with keeping the sacred fire to the goddess of the hearth burning, was a virgin no longer. In an execution that can only be regarded as horrific to modern readers, she was buried alive and the two men who had lain with her were scourged and executed.[24] Livy essentially concurs that nothing of great military significance occurred in 483. In his version of domestic events, however, the Vestal virgin was named Oppia, and he offers no details about her punishment.[25]

The Second Consulships of Quintus and Kaeso Fabius (482–481 BC)

When the time came to elect new consuls for 482 BC, relates Dionysius, the feuds between consuls and tribunes reached the point that no assembly could be held, and thus no new consuls elected. The Senate appointed an interrex – literally 'king in-between' – the title of a temporary figure who administered the elections of consuls when there was an extraordinary gap in their terms. Political turmoil persisted, so when his brief term ended, a second interrex followed. The conflicts subsided just enough for the second interrex to summon the centuriate assembly. The centuries voted and named Gaius Julius and Quintus Fabius as the new consuls.

The north-eastern borders of Roman land were porous: Aequi raided, seizing slaves and cattle in the east, while the people of hostile Veii marauded in the north-east. The Senate opted to strike at Veii first. The Aequians, however, took advantage of the lack of attention and stormed the Latin town of Ortona, roughly opposite Rome on the Adriatic coast. Meanwhile, Roman ambassadors investigated the border raids near Veii. They condemned Veii as an aggressor and declared war on the city-state.[26] Livy, as is often the case in this period, spares only a few words: the Aequi and Veientes invaded Roman territory.[27]

New consuls took office for 481 BC: Kaeso Fabius, for the second time, and Spurius Furius. Another tribune of the plebs, named Icilius, Sicilius or perhaps even Licinius, obstructed the levy of soldiers until the Senate addressed plebeian demands for land.[28] Other tribunes more willing to work with the senatorial leadership were found to check the troublesome tribune, however, and the state prepared again for war. Kaeso Fabius drew the command against Veii and any Etruscan allies the city might attract; Furius was assigned the Aequi. Furius' forces met no resistance. The Aequi huddled safely behind their town walls while the Romans looted their territory. Kaeso's command was more difficult. His soldiers were quite irked that he had prosecuted Spurius Cassius several years before, and now took revenge. When the legions routed an Etruscan army, through the efforts of the cavalry alone says Livy, the Roman infantry refused to hammer the victory home and pursue the defeated. They even refused to loot the enemy camp; perhaps they reasoned the consul would just give the loot to the treasury. Though they had technically won the battle, Kaeso experienced little less than a mutiny. He had no choice but to return to Rome with his recalcitrant soldiers.[29]

The Second Consulship of Marcus Fabius (480 BC)

Aspects of the campaigns in 480 BC received great detail from both Livy and Dionysius. As usual, the historians allege that a tribune, this one named Pontificius, stirred up trouble at Rome, agitating for a land-distribution law. Now, however, the senators had found an effective counter. They again persuaded agreeable tribunes to block Pontificius and moved forward with the levy. Both consuls, Marcus Fabius and Gnaeus Manlius, led their armies to Veii. When they arrived in Etruscan territory, however, the consuls refused to engage in battle, both sources say, because they could not trust their plebeian army to fight well. The Etruscans tried to cajole the Romans out of their camp and into a pitched battle, but to no avail. Finally, when the humiliation of refusing battle pushed the Roman army to breaking point, Marcus Fabius summoned the soldiers and rebuked them, accusing them of abandoning the consul of the prior year, his brother. Dionysius ostensibly records a speech for Fabius that is quite substantial – ironically perhaps, because his evidence for the words of such a speech was likely completely insubstantial.[30] Following the speech, Fabius extracted an oath from the soldiers that they would defeat their enemy or die in the endeavour. Both sources suggest that a particularly admirable centurion, Marcus Flavoleius, initiated the oath and the infantry followed suit. With the gods guaranteeing the oath, the Romans clashed with their Etruscan foes.

The surviving battle descriptions are detailed and dramatic. On the right wing, the Romans, including the soldiers of the Fabian clan led by former consuls Quintus and Kaeso, drove back the Etruscans. In the midst of victory, an Etruscan impaled Quintus on his sword, ending his life. The soldiers around him panicked, terrified by losing their commander. Just then, the consul Marcus Fabius reached his slain brother's side and reminded the soldiers of their oath to the gods. With the help of brother Kaeso, the two rallied the wing and personally led the charge back to battle. Manlius, the consul on the other wing, did not fare so well. Though his soldiers drove the Etruscans back, the consul suffered critical wounds and had to leave the fight; he soon perished. Marcus Fabius, however, transferred the infantry lines from his victory on the right to the left wing, inspiring the faltering troops there to rally.[31] The battle was won, and Fabius led the victorious army home. The Senate, both sources say, wished to grant him a triumph, but he refused. Livy, ever ready to trumpet exemplary behaviour, loyally notes that his refused triumph gained him more fame than celebrating one would have.[32]

Putting it Together (485–480 BC)

So what is reasonably certain about this period? Several features of Livy and Dionysius' account of the years 485–480 BC stand out:

- One of the three Fabius brothers holds a consulship in each of these years.
- The Romans engaged in war with their neighbours most frequently at this point: the Aequi, Volsci and Etruscans.
- Underlying all the accounts of military campaigns and political manoeuvring at Rome are the social struggles that seemed to plague the city at this point.

Though the situation was often dire and Roman armies came close to dissolving under the forces of class conflict, the Romans nonetheless prosecuted a series of wars against Volscians, Aequians and the people of the nearby city of Veii. Livy and Dionysius describe the campaigns, sometimes in a few words, sometimes in longer passages.[33] They do not always agree on the details, and both tell some dramatic tales about Fabian consuls in battle. They both agree, nevertheless, that this period had a run of Fabii consuls and regular conflicts between Romans and their nearest foes, Volscians, Aequians and the city of Veii. These details are reasonably certain.

Rome and Central Italy in the Fifth Century

Historians like Dionysius and Livy present a picture of geopolitics in central Italy that is largely accepted in its outlines if not always in specific details. Rome and the Latin city-states came to outright war at the end of the sixth century. At the watershed Battle of Lake Regillus (494 BC), the Romans defeated the Latins and imposed the Cassian Treaty (*Foedus Cassianum*) on them. The terms of the treaty, as Dionysius claimed to have cited them, obligated the Latins to follow Rome's lead in foreign policy and engage in no wars in or outside Latium without Roman approval. They were also bound to supply troops as needed to support the Romans in war. This treaty suggests that the Romans had a significant degree of control over Latin military resources at an early point. Some historians have doubted this arrangement, suggesting that Rome may have been one of many equal partners with other Latin cities. Still, it is reasonably safe to say that whatever the exact details, Romans and Latins worked closely together in military operations of the fifth century BC.[34] Together, they confronted the threat of the mountain folk of the Apennines, the Aequi and Volsci. These tribes' advances into Latium were part of a general migration of mountain tribes into the plains of central and southern Italy in the fifth and fourth centuries.[35] During the first half of the fifth century, Roman historians asserted, Romans and Latins clashed

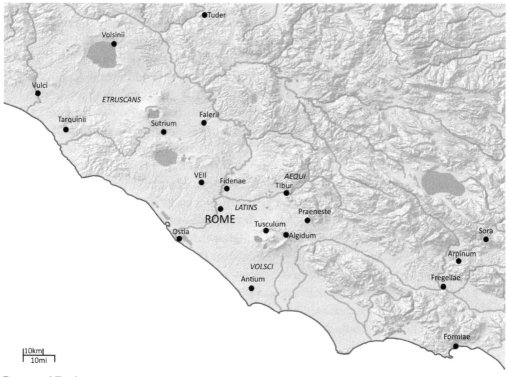

Rome and Environs

with Volsci, Aequi or both almost yearly. Records of these conflicts are exactly the sort of skeletal details that were likely preserved in the *Annales Maximi*, and there is no compelling reason to doubt the general trend of conflict. On top of these struggles, the Romans contested the lower Tiber region with the Etruscan city of Veii, on the northern side the river some 10 miles distant.

Disaster at the Cremera (479 BC)

This chain of consulships and significant Fabian contributions to military affairs came to a halt with the disaster at the Cremera, an event inscribed into Roman histories until the end of the Republic and beyond. Unchecked by any setbacks from Marcus Fabius' victory, Veii, bitter rival of Rome, continued to raid the Roman frontier. Essentially, Livy says, they practised piracy on land, preying upon Roman farms and livestock when the timing was right, then, when challenged by any Roman force, flowing back to the safety of their city walls.[36] Though Livy patriotically avoids mentioning it, the Romans likely practised similar depredations on Veii's farms and flocks. Carrying on in this manner, Veii kept a steady pressure on the Romans, who were already in danger of war with other nearby foes from central Italy: Volsci, Aequi, Sabines and Etruscans.

A permanent frontier garrison was needed, but the nascent Roman Republic lacked the funds and warriors to meet the need. The Fabii clan rose to the occasion. In 479 BC, when Kaeso held his third and final consulship, the leading Fabii offered to strike at Veii personally, to wage war against the foe with a private army. This was not the most radical suggestion. The surviving evidence hints that Rome's fifth-century armies were not much more organized beyond warbands that included the various powerful families of the city and their followers. In the battle of 480 mentioned above, for example, the sources suggest the army had a contingent of Fabian family members and followers under the command of the two former consuls, Kaeso and Quintus. It may be that personal armies of noble families and their followers not infrequently took on independent duties. Exactly who would accompany that Fabian army, however, was not entirely clear in the sources. Dionysius has the Fabii pledge themselves and their friends and clients, a force several thousand strong. More dramatically, but perhaps less plausibly, Livy suggests that the Fabii alone shouldered this burden.[37] Both agreed that the members of the Fabian family engaged in this expedition numbered 306. The larger force would surely have been more appropriate for guarding against a powerful neighbour, but that is not a decisive point for accepting Dionysius' figures. Whatever the case may have been, the Senate enthusiastically endorsed the plan. The Fabii would make private war on Veii for the public good of Rome.

Dionysius asserts that the Fabii and their clients approached the Cremera River with a Roman army in tow. Strengthened by their support, the Fabii constructed a fort complete with enclosing ditch and towers. Once the fort was complete, the consul, Kaeso Fabius, drove the strike force deep into Veientine territory, seized all manner of supplies, and deposited the lot in the fort. Then the army receded and the Fabian warband began their watch on the borderlands. Livy adds nothing, simply noting that a fort was constructed.[38] Protected by this strongpoint, the Fabian band preyed on Veii's herds.

Time passed; new consuls took office for 478 and the Fabii continued their vigil. But disaster struck the clan. Dionysius reports two competing tales about the end of the Fabii. In one version, the time had come for the Fabian men to perform a sacrifice to the gods, always a critical business for the Romans, and they left the fortress for Rome without properly scouting their way back to the city. Though he reported it, Dionysius would have none of this tale. Instead he preferred the tale that Livy essentially offers. The Veientes fashioned an ambush. Flocks and herds were gathered to lure the Fabii to a place where the Veientes could surprise them. The Fabii took the bait, descended upon the Veientes' livestock and found themselves surrounded.[39]

Each writer crafted a battle scene worthy of the legend. Livy says that javelins rained upon the Fabii, and now the Veientes herded men, not livestock. The Fabii collapsed into a circle, pressed close by the weight of the enemy numbers. Desperately, they abandoned the circle, formed a wedge, and carved their way to a small rise in the terrain. On the high ground they rallied and drove back their foes. But it was all for naught. Another force of Veientes crested the hilltop and took the Fabians from behind. The slaughter was complete. Three hundred and six warriors, all the men of the Fabian clan, died that day, leaving the fate of the family to the one boy who survived.[40] Dionysius' tale is no less dramatic and takes place over more than a single day. The Fabii fought their way to a hill, as in Livy, and gained a night's respite from their secure position. Word reached the fort of the dire situation, but the Veientes cut down the relief troops once they left the safety of the walls. No help would come. Hope gone, hungry and thirsty, the Fabii on the hillside mustered a final charge. They hacked and stabbed, warding off disaster, until their swords grew blunt and their shields were notched and rent, 'and the men themselves were for the most part, bled white and overwhelmed by missiles and their limbs paralyzed by reason of the multitude of their wounds'. The Fabii surged forward at the very end, using hands where swords no longer served.[41] They met their end bravely.

Reportedly, only a single Fabian male, a boy named Quintus, son of the two-time consul Marcus Fabius, survived this disaster. Livy eulogizes: 'Three hundred and six men perished … one who was little more than a boy in years survived to maintain the Fabian stock, and so to afford the very greatest help to the Roman people in its dark hours, on many occasions, at home and in the field.'[42] Dionysius was incredulous. How could it be, he railed, that every single Fabian male was at the Cremera, none with sons too young to participate in the battle? He thought it preposterous. He solved the dilemma by suggesting that

Quintus was not the sole survivor of the Fabii at Cremera, but simply the only Fabius from that generation who subsequently won fame and had a successful political career. With only one distinguished Fabius left, the mistaken belief took root that all the other Fabii had been slaughtered.[43]

Throwing a wrench into the works as he often does, Diodorus Siculus, another Greek historian of the first century BC, preserves a wholly different version of the Cremera: a regular pitched battle.

> 'In Italy war broke out between the Romans and the Veiians and a great battle was fought at the site called Cremera. The Romans were defeated and many of them perished, among their number, according to some historians, being the three hundred Fabii, who were of the same gens and hence were included under the single name.'[44]

But Diodorus swam against the tide. The tragic end of the 300 Fabii – the extra six were rounded off – was memorialized even when the Republic had faded away and emperors ruled the state. Recounted in later Roman histories, biographies and epic poems, the sacrifice of the 300 Fabii was embedded as a historical contribution of the Fabian clan, a mark of their greatness.[45] Whether the slaughter at the Cremera happened that way is open to debate. Historians have noted for quite a long time, for example, that the death of the Fabii in both number and timing is suspiciously parallel to the more famous and historically grounded death of the 300 Spartans at Thermopylae against an overwhelming Persian horde, also in 479 BC.[46] Could Roman writers, hoping to give Rome a deeply rooted and heroic history to rival their cultural competitors the Greeks, have fabricated the story? Perhaps. When tracking the fortunes of the Fabian clan, however, the strict accuracy of accounts is probably not as important as the decisive evidence that, for the Romans, the Fabii did fight and die at Cremera. That deed fused to the Fabian legacy, adding lustre to the family and, no doubt, serving as a goad to stir later Fabii to achieve comparable greatness.

The Fabius brothers carved a premier niche for their family in the politics of the early Republic with their string of seven consecutive consulships, capped by the self-sacrifice of the 300, a story whose fixed position in Roman historical writing demonstrates its success. They commanded forces to considerable victories over foes such as the Aequi and Volsci that threatened the strength and stability of the early Republic. Their glory was great. Accordingly, the pressure for the later scions of the Fabii to make their mark, to earn a place among the political and military elite, must have been considerable.

Sole Survivor: Quintus Fabius Vibulanus

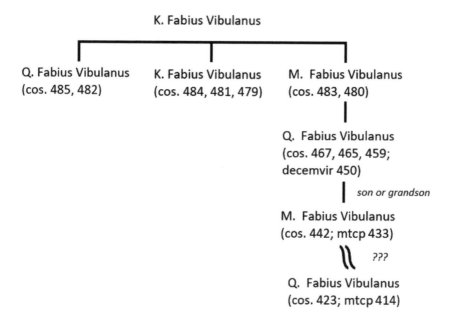

Whether because he alone survived the Cremera or only he achieved political distinction, Quintus Fabius Vibulanus, son of the consul Marcus Fabius Vibulanus who died at the Cremera and the next Fabius in the historical record, seems to have lived up to the ideals set by his progenitors. He held the consulship three times in 467, 465 and 459 BC. As usual for the fifth century, Livy and Dionysius provide most of the details for these years. Quintus Fabius won his first consulship in 467 alongside Titus Aemilius. That year some friction reportedly divided the consuls, for Titus Aemilius supported the plebeian desires for land distributions and, accordingly, antagonized the Senate. Quintus Fabius engineered a compromise. Rather than seize land from Romans for redistribution, he proposed that land recently commandeered from the Volscian town of Antium could be settled as a colony by interested Roman citizens. Reportedly, however, the poorer Romans rejected this option. They desired land within Roman territory, not what they thought of as foreign land. Ultimately, the Senate followed through with the colony but opened settlement to Latins and Hernici to make up for the small numbers of Roman citizens willing to join the venture. In this year too, apparently, Quintus Fabius campaigned against the Aequi, driving into their territory and compelling them to seek peace rather quickly.[47] Livy and Dionysius' narrative of the next couple of years conflicts on the timings of events. As Livy has it, 466 BC – the year Quintus Servilius and Spurius Postumius were consuls – passes almost without note, some illness plaguing the Roman army. Quintus Fabius was again elected consul for 465 and also declared a special ambassador of sorts to treat with the Aequi. The Romans reasoned that his recent military victory over the Aequi would add further weight to the embassy and make the Aequi more submissive. They were mistaken. The Aequi did not desist, but sent an army to fight the Romans. Fabius and his consular colleague Quinctius led legions to check the Aequi and drove them out of Roman territory.[48]

Dionysius dates things a little differently. He places Fabius' delegation to the Aequi in the consulship of Postumius and Servilius (466 BC) and gives a more elaborate account of the diplomacy, adding that Fabius spied on the Aequi during his mission and uncovered preparations for war. Essentially, however, he agrees with Livy's short notice, adding that some form of pestilence afflicted many Romans that year and made it impossible to do much in the way of military preparations.[49] He also agrees with Livy that the significant campaigns against the Aequi took place when Quintus Fabius and Titus Quinctius were consul in 465 BC. In his more elaborate battle narrative, Fabius met the Aequian army at the border of their territory and fought an indecisive battle. Another force of Aequi warriors, meanwhile, raided Roman territory. Fabius left his oldest soldiers in their camp to check the battlefield force and marched to drive the raiders out of Roman territory, ending the season with a raid to capture loot and slaves from the Aequi.[50] Despite the conflicts in chronology, the sources agree that Fabius served as an ambassador (or spy) and won a victory over the Aequians.

When Quintus Fabius next appeared in the sources he was the prefect of the city in 462 BC. A group of what appear to have been Volscian raiders penetrated Roman territory. Quintus Fabius, as the authority in the city, prepared the defences, arming the young men who were not off with the army and securing the city.[51] The wars against the Aequi and Volsci lumbered on, and Fabius seems to have played a minor role against them until he won his third consulship.

Turmoil in Rome and Quintus Fabius' Third Consulship (460–459 BC)

The years between Fabius' consulships were far from peaceful. Instead of the normal wars against the seemingly implacable Volsci and Aequi, internal conflicts rocked the Republic; the Conflict of the Orders had again reared its ugly head. Livy reports that a series of tribunes moved to draft laws that would limit the seemingly boundless authority of the consuls and that some riots broke out in the process. A youthful aristocrat, Kaeso Quinctius, stood accused of plotting a coup d'etat and was ultimately exiled on a murder conviction. Perhaps most dramatically, the Sabine Appius Herdonius seized the Capitol, the citadel at the heart of Rome's defences, with a force of slaves and discontents; only an armed effort by the Roman citizenry could recapture it.[52]

But affairs in the city seemed to have settled for a while when Fabius and his colleague, Lucius Cornelius Maluginensis, took office in 459 BC. Livy and Dionysius' accounts for the year amply demonstrate the difficulties of establishing solid details of Rome's fifth-century wars. Both agree that the Volsci and Aequi continued to threaten Rome; beyond that little is certain.

Livy and Dionysius offer different timelines for 459. Livy notes:[53]

1. Reports first reached Rome that the Volsci had led an army to Antium; there was some concern the colony might defect.
2. Fabius commanded the army bound for Antium while Cornelius defended Rome.
3. Fabius levied his force, marched to Antium, and surrounded the fortified camp of the Volsci there.
4. The Romans stormed the camp, and the panicked Volsci fled, many of them cut down by Roman cavalry. Then word reached Fabius that the Aequi had surrounded Rome's ally Tusculum.
5. Fabius and his force marched to Tusculum, north of Antium and some 10 miles south-east of Rome. They drove off the Aequi there, and then with Cornelius, pillaged the lands of Volsci and Aequi yet again.

Livy, however, reveals at the end of his account:

> 'I find in a good many sources that the people of Antium revolted in this year and that the consul Lucius Cornelius conducted that war and took the town. I would not dare to confirm this as a certainty because there is no mention of this event in the older sources.'[54]

Dionysius could not have been one of those sources, for he wrote mostly after Livy, but he did preserve such an alternate account. His version is as follows:[55]

1. The Romans first heard news of the Aequian seizure of Tusculum, then heard word of the Volsci at Antium.
2. Fabius relieved Tusculum first, then met the Volsci and Aequi not at Antium but at Algidum, some 20 miles from Antium. Fabius personally led the charge against the camp at Algidum, scattered the enemy, then raided and pillaged Volscian territory.
3. Whilst Fabius was engaged in these operations, Cornelius campaigned against those Volsci who had seized rebel Antium. The Romans stormed the town, and Cornelius swiftly scourged and executed the ringleaders of rebellion.

Both consuls, says Dionysius, earned a triumph for their deeds, and the surviving list of triumphs corroborates this.

So what did happen? The events of 459 BC are not particularly critical to our understandings of Roman history, but Livy and Dionysius' conflicting accounts here illustrate the problems faced regularly by investigators of fifth-century

Rome. Did the Romans campaign against the Volsci and Aequi? Almost certainly. Not only does this make sense of what is known about Roman relations with these peoples, but the sources say so, and the *fasti* seem to record – the text is a little fragmented – triumphs for both consuls. Did Cornelius remain at Rome during his year as consul? Probably not, because Dionysiyus and the *fasti* say he triumphed over the Volscians at Antium. So Fabius, it would seem, likely relieved Tusculum and fought both Volsci and Aequi.

Quintus Fabius Vibulanus did not hold the consulship again, but he had done his part to contribute to the legacy of the Fabian family. His final years, however, appear to have been quite ignominious. His last position of note was as a member of the ten-man committee – the decemviri – charged by the Romans to draft a set of laws that would be binding on the whole state, patrician and plebeian. Ultimately, as the accounts had it, the second set of decemviri, Fabius included, grew tyrannical and held on to their power past the original termination point. Something of a revolution ousted the ten men and they left in exile.[56]

Quintus Fabius Vibulanus, the honourable consul turned disgraced decemvir, then disappears from the records. His shared reputation for tyranny did not taint the family name in any lasting sense. The Fabii continued to be well represented among the political elite of the later fifth and early fourth century BC. It becomes essentially impossible, however, to construct with any confidence a precise genealogical connection from Quintus Fabius Vibulanus to the Fabii Maximi of the mid-fourth century. Sometimes, when examining the ancient world, earlier modern historians did the best jobs, as in this case where the clearest genealogy in English comes from William Smith's *Classical Dictionary*, first published more than 150 years ago.[57] Between the ancient sources and this reconstruction of family relationships, the following outline emerges.

The Next Generation: Marcus Fabius Vibulanus (442–433 BC)

Marcus Fabius Vibulanus may have been the son or grandson of Quintus. He won a consulship for 442 alongside Publius Aebutius Cornicen, but seems to have done little of note – little that has survived at any rate beyond a reference to some administrative details about the new Roman colony at Ardea. He appears again a few years later. Veii reared its head under King Lars Tolumius. Tolumius allied with the colonists at Fidenae who broke with Rome. In a most heinous diplomatic breach, the Fidenates murdered the Roman ambassadors sent to investigate the defection. War broke out against Fidenae and Veii. Marcus Geganius Macerinus and Lucius Sergius Fidenas – Livy supposes the latter got his *cognomen* from the battle – were elected consul in 437. The Romans, commanded at least by Sergius and perhaps by both consuls, defeated their foes but suffered severe casualties as well. In a moment of military crisis, the Senate appointed a dictator, Mamercus Aemilius, the same year. In turn, the dictator selected Titus Quinctius Capitolinus and Marcus Fabius Vibulanus to serve as his lieutenants. Mamercus marched the Roman army to Fidenae and prepared to meet the Etruscan forces in battle. The Etruscans under Lars Tolumnius also acquired the services of the Faliscans, residents of Falerii, and brought them to the battle. The battle took place in a plain between the two armed camps. This particular conflict took an epic tone in later accounts because the military tribune, Aulus Cornelius Cossus, slew the Etruscan King Tolumnius in single combat, a rare achievement. Fabius, however, was relegated to an important but far less heroic position. During the battle, he defended the Roman encampment. When the Etruscans attacked, Fabius sallied out of one of the gates and drove off the enemy.[58]

A few years passed. Tribunes of the plebs blocked the election of the consuls for 433 BC. The Senate countered by electing military tribunes with consular power, Marcus Fabius among them. The office was quite similar to the consulship, and its origins and use need not delay our investigation. Though Fabius held a military command, the plague struck Rome and its environs again, and there was apparently very little political or military activity while the Romans struggled with the disease. In 431 the Republic elected consuls again: Titus Quinctius Cincinnatus, son of the famous Cincinnatus,

Q. Fabius Vibulanus
(cos. 467, 465, 459;
decemvir 450)

| *son or grandson*

M. Fabius Vibulanus
(cos. 442; mtcp 433)

⫫   ???

Q. Fabius Vibulanus
(cos. 423; mtcp 414)

and Gaius Julius Mento.[59] The Aequi and Volsci kept centre stage as enemies. When they took to the field, however, the Senate decided the Republic really needed a dictator, especially with the disruption and casualties the recent plague had caused. Livy also suggests the two consuls bickered too much, making the Senate fear they could not work together. The consuls reportedly resisted the appointment, but ultimately were forced to name a dictator, Aulus Postumius Tubertus. In the ensuing battle against the Aequi, Marcus Fabius served as one of the dictator's legates, commanding the cavalry. The tradition Livy preserves indicated that all the Roman leaders were wounded in action. Except for one with a fractured skull, all remained in the fight, including Fabius, whose thigh, Livy says, was almost pinned to his horse by a javelin. The Romans fought on, stormed the enemy camp and won the day.[60]

But Marcus Fabius Vibulanus is never heard from again.[61] Did he die from the sepsis caused by an ugly puncture wound? Did his health continue to hold in later years? Did he add to his reputation but the surviving sources failed to notice or the records have long since disappeared? We simply do not know. Ultimately, from the standards of political competition at Rome, Marcus Fabius had a distinguished career. Both consul and military tribune with consular powers, he had achieved the pinnacle of a political career and earned additional feathers as a legate to two dictators. Arguably, as a prominent politician, he had been a senator at least some of the time too, though in that period membership in the Senate shifted regularly with the changes of officials. From the standpoint of historical posterity, however, he was relatively obscure; only scraps can be gleaned of his doings from the historical records.

Name Change: From Fabius Vibulanus to Fabius Ambustus (late fifth century BC)

After Marcus Fabius Vibulanus, the Fabii Vibulani largely disappear from the sources. Quintus Fabius Vibulanus surfaces briefly in the historical record, in 423 BC, when he was elected consul alongside Gaius Sempronius Atratinus.[62] He was perhaps the right age to be Marcus' son, but the lack of the consular *fasti* for the years 449–423 BC make any connection tenuous. Sempronius received the command against the Volsci, while Quintus Fabius stayed to defend Rome. The Roman forces with Sempronius battled bravely all day, and by night it was not clear which army had actually won the battle. Rumours fluttered to the city, however, that the Romans had been defeated. It fell to Fabius as the consul at Rome to organize a defence. He seems to have done so and at least effectively enough that the Romans survived.[63] This Quintus Fabius held a few other offices. After his first consulship in 423, he served as a military tribune with consular powers in 414, then he served as interrex. Then Quintus Fabius Vibulanus too slipped into the fog of the past, and the Fabii Vibulani disappeared after dying off, losing political significance or changing their *cognomen*.

Regardless, the branch of the Fabii Vibulani that would produce the Maximus line adopted a new *cognomen* in the late fifth century. In 412 for the first time, a new shoot of the Fabian family appears in the person of Quintus Fabius Ambustus

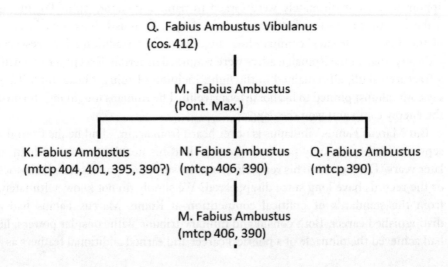

Q. Fabius Ambustus Vibulanus
(cos. 412)

M. Fabius Ambustus
(Pont. Max.)

K. Fabius Ambustus   N. Fabius Ambustus   Q. Fabius Ambustus
(mtcp 404, 401, 395, 390?)   (mtcp 406, 390)   (mtcp 390)

M. Fabius Ambustus
(mtcp 406, 390)

Vibulanus.[64] Perhaps he was the same as the Quintus Fabius Vibulanus who held the consulship in 423, but that is far from clear. Livy makes no mention of the origin of the *cognomen*; he rarely does. Ambustus means 'burnt', and that alone is provocative enough. A fondness for fire? An interesting birthmark? An unfortunate accident? Sadly, there is no way of knowing. But from this Ambustus came a son, Marcus, who kept the new *cognomen*. The only recorded post he held was that of chief priest, *pontifex maximus*. How long he held the position and whether he held any magistracy is not known. Marcus seems to have had at least three politically successful children: Kaeso, Numerius and Quintus. Livy mentions Kaeso most often, but only to note his offices and posts. Kaeso held office as military tribune with consular powers four times. The first time, in 404 BC, he commanded the Roman siege of Veii. It was the last great struggle with that Etruscan rival that would ultimately subject it to Rome.[65] The siege is generally dated as lasting from 406–396 BC, though the ten years may have been conjured to mimic the legendary Trojan War or simply to increase the epic aspect of the siege. Though the city would not fall to Kaeso, no doubt he felt at least somewhat satisfied to help subjugate the city that had massacred his ancestors some seventy-five years ago.

Three new Fabian Brothers and the Sack of Rome (390 BC)

The three brothers won a more lasting place in the historical tradition for their involvement in the disaster that permeated the accounts of the early fourth century: the Gallic sack of Rome. The story went as follows. The Senonians, a Gallic tribe in northern Italy, newly migrated from parts further north, invaded the lands of Clusium in central Etruria. Clusium begged aid from the Republic. The city had no formal relationship with Rome, however, and the Romans opted not to form one and aid Clusium. However, the three Fabii – Kaeso, Numerius and Quintus – were dispatched to treat with the Gauls and deliver a message: do not attack any allies or friends of the Roman people, and be at peace with us. Livy and Dionysius assert the three were instructed to conduct open diplomacy; Diodorus Siculus suggests the three were sent to spy on the Gauls. The two missions were not necessarily in conflict: treating with the Gauls and observing their dispositions could, if all went well, be accomplished at the same time.

Once the three Fabii delivered Rome's message, they went on to spark a bit of a diplomatic incident. Viewing Clusium as a friend, the three Fabii joined forces with Clusium and fought against the Gauls at the forefront of the Etruscan army. Perhaps even then they might have escaped notice doing so, but Quintus Fabius managed to slay a Gaul of some importance – a chieftain or a general, the accounts vary – and despoiled the corpse. The Gallic army withdrew from Clusium with vengeance on their mind. Soon their envoys travelled to Rome protesting that the Fabii's actions constituted an illegal act of war and demanding that the Republic either surrender the three sons of Fabius for punishment or risk outright war.[66]

The Senate took the matter seriously. Dionysius asserts that they hemmed and hawed, wearing away the Gauls' patience. Diodorus suggests the Senate sought to pay the Gauls to compensate for the injury. When the Senones refused, the Senate opted to surrender Quintus Fabius. At this point, Quintus' father, Marcus Fabius, appealed to the people, and the popular assembly in turn rejected the Senate's decision. This version sounds suspiciously like the appeal to the people another Fabius father would make on behalf of his son seven decades later, however, and perhaps Diodorus or his source were simply fabricating this episode based on the later one. Livy may have had it right. In his view, the Senate did wish to turn over the Fabii, but the men were far too influential to just summarily betray. Instead the Senate sought to reduce its culpability in the affair by deferring the matter to the assembly. The assembly not only voted to keep the Fabii safe, but went further and elected the three of them military tribunes with consular powers for 390 BC.[67]

Regardless of the exact details, the Senones declared war and marched on Rome. The Fabii brothers, along with three additional tribunes with consular powers, levied a mighty army of four legions, double the size of the normal levies for a year. Still, they proved no match for the Senones, who routed the legions at the Allia River and then for good measure occupied the city of Rome itself. Only the citadel on the Capitoline remained intact against the invaders.[68] Although Livy spends considerable space narrating the Gallic sack of the city and the eventual ransoming of the city, the event was likely not nearly as catastrophic as later sources would have it.[69] Rome survived and the Gallic sack proved little or no obstacle to its ability to dominate central Italy and beyond during the fourth century.

Yet the sack tarnished the reputation of Rome and the Fabii who had commanded its armies at the Allia. None of the three held office again. But both the Republic and Fabian clan would recover from this dark moment. The Fabii Ambusti went on to produce that most distinguished band of the Fabii, the Fabii Maximi. The Republic would go on, aided by the Fabii, to dominate much of Italy in the fourth century BC.

Chapter 3

The First Fabius Maximus, Rullianus and the Samnite Wars

The Growth of Roman Power in Central Italy

As the monarchy crept toward the republican revolution, Rome rose to prominence as the largest city in Latium. Trade sped its growth as the city opportunely straddled the routes connecting Etruria and Campania and provided a seaport to land goods destined for the hilly interior of Italy east of the city. Struggles with the territorially smaller but still formidable Veii played an important role in Roman foreign policy in the fifth century BC, as did frequent war against the Volsci and Aequi tribes around Latium. Ultimately, Rome defeated its rival Veii at the beginning of the fourth century. It would take considerably longer to subjugate the Volsci. Still, by the beginning of the fourth century, Rome was powerful, though not so large compared to contemporary Mediterranean states that sought to dominate their environs: Sparta and Athens, Syracuse and Carthage. Even in Italy, the magnificent cities of Capua to the south and Tarentum in the instep of the Italian boot were larger and controlled more territory. But Rome had formed an important alliance with the members of the Latin League – the other cities and peoples of Latium – and this allowed it access to critical reserves of manpower. Rome also seems to have benefited from a growing population, evidenced in an increase of those liable to serve in the army in the mid-fifth century. From that point the Romans may have fielded 4,000 men annually instead of 3,000, and the cavalry in service may have doubled. The Gallic sack of Rome was a minor setback at best. The Gauls, luckily for the Romans, were out to plunder, not conquer, and Rome recovered quite soon after the defeat.[1]

Marcus Fabius Ambustus

Along with the Volscians, the Republic continued to battle central Italian foes like the Etruscans and even enemies closer to home, such as the Tiburtines of Latium. In these wars of the mid-fourth century, the next of the Fabii Ambusti appears in the sources: Marcus Fabius Ambustus. He was the son of the Numerius Fabius who had helped usher in the Roman defeat at the Allia River, and the subsequent Gallic sack of Rome. The fortunes of his father and uncles, all involved with the Gallic sack, did not prevent his rise to political prominence: Marcus Fabius would hold three consulships within the span of seven years. Yet though this record testifies to his political importance, he makes little splash in Livy's narrative for these years, the main surviving account.

Around 367 BC, the Hernici, loyal or at least peaceful allies of Rome for the better part of the century, broke with the Republic.[2] This did not inspire Livy to comment, for 367 was also the year when the plebeian Lucius Sextius won election to the consulship by forcing down the patricians' throats a law permitting plebeians to hold the consulship – a critical step in the Conflict of the Orders.[3] The Hernici were apparently still in revolt for several years, and in 360 Marcus Fabius Ambustus held his first consulship and drew by lot a command against them. Livy spends his time discussing the far more serious threat of Tibur. This Roman ally in Latium made common cause with the Gauls in 361 and posed a significant threat to Roman control of Latium, its heartland. When Gauls and Tiburtines preyed on Rome's allies in Latium, the Republic named a dictator to handle the threat, Quintus Servilius Ahala. Servilius won a striking victory over the foes, driving the Gauls back from the very gates of Rome. As they retreated to allied Tibur, the consul Poetilius took over the offensive, herding the Gauls along to the city and defeating them, along with some Tiburtines for good measure.[4]

But what of the consul, Marcus Fabius? Livy simply notes that he too trounced the Hernici, skirmishing at first and then landing a hammer blow in a pitched battle. Where Poetelius earned a triumph, however, Fabius earned the lesser military celebration called an ovation.[5]

Livy's minimalist treatment of Marcus Fabius' consulship looks positively epic compared to the account of his brother, Gaius Fabius Ambustus. Elected consul for 358, it fell to Gaius Fabius to punish the Etruscan Tarquinians, who had raided Roman lands along the frontier with Etruria. His colleague, Gaius Plautius, campaigned against the not-quite-beaten Hernici.[6] Livy's narrative for the year focuses on the dictator, Gaius Sulpicius Peticus, who defeated another Gallic force. The consul Plautius apparently landed another victory against the Hernici. As for Gaius Fabius, Livy's notice seems to be the final word:

> 'Fabius' battle against the Tarquinienses was marked by lack of caution and circumspection on Fabius' part. Nor was the disastrous outcome for the Romans confined to the battlefield; 307 Roman soldiers were taken prisoner and offered in sacrifice by the Tarquinienses, and the humiliation of the Roman people was considerably heightened by this unspeakable form of punishment.'[7]

Perhaps unsurprisingly, Gaius Fabius – getting one's soldiers sacrificed to the gods is no ringing endorsement – never won another consulship. His brother, Marcus, was left to exact vengeance against Tarquinii. In 356, Marcus Fabius held his second consulship. His army's first clash with the Tarquinienses was singularly inauspicious. The enemy's priests led the army, says Livy, 'like Furies, bearing blazing torches and snakes before them, and throwing the Roman soldiers into disarray with the bizarre sight. And these [Romans], like men stupefied and out of their minds, ran back to their own fortifications in a panic-stricken crowd.'[8] Marcus Fabius and his officers reportedly rebuked and rallied the Romans, who smashed the Tarquinian army. Consul one final time in 354, Marcus Fabius served alongside Titus Quinctius. War against Tibur continued, and the war against Tarquinii had spread to a general rebellion of the Etruscans. This year, Livy remarked, saw two patrician consuls; even though the plebeians had gained the right to hold the consulship, there was, as yet, no law that one consulship would be reserved for them. War against the Tiburtines and Tarquinienses continued. Notably, a Roman army defeated the Tarquinienses and, in retaliation for the horrific sacrifice of a few years prior, picked 358 nobles from the defeated forces, then publicly flogged and decapitated them in the Forum.[9] It is not clear from Livy, however, the exact role each consul played in the year's operations.

This was essentially the end of Marcus Fabius' time in the sun. He was named dictator in 351, but only for holding elections.[10] Objectively, he was a successful aristocrat. He made it to the pinnacle of power as consul not once, but three times. He won several victories over his foes and won an ovation for one of them. Yet he would be eclipsed in the historical record by his far more successful son, the first Fabius Maximus: Quintus Fabius Maximus Rullianus.

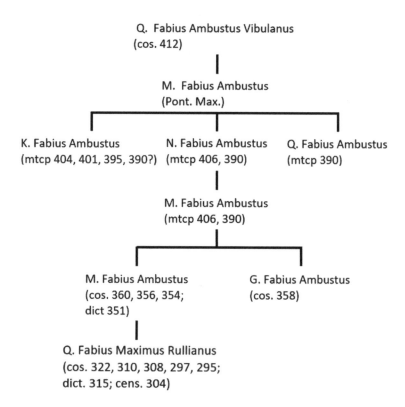

Quintus Fabius Rullianus and the First Samnite War

In the second half of the fourth century, the time when Fabius Rullianus first earned the epithet-turned-family-name Maximus, events transpired that pushed Rome to dominate central Italy. There were three wars during the later fourth century the Romans fought against the Samnites, the hardy mountain folks of the Appenines south and east of Rome. Organized into four tribes in a loosely joined republic, these Samnites were largely poor subsistence farmers and herders who eked out a living in the rugged mountain lands between Campania and Apulia. With no coastal access and poor mineral resources, Samnium had few towns but many agrarian villages. Yet these rural folk were formidable fighters who posed a clear challenge to Roman power in the southern part of the peninsula.[11]

The steadily growing population of Samnite farmers and herders regularly sought new land, as did the slowly expanding Republic. An eventual conflict between the two was probably always likely. The First Samnite War, as it happened, sparked in 343 BC over conflicting Roman and Samnite influence in Campania, the fertile plain south-east of Latium dominated by the city of Capua. Capua's petition to Rome in 343 was the decisive moment. The city was magnificent by the standards of the time in Italy, and Livy asserts it was then the most prosperous Italian city. Still, Capua and the fertile Campanian plain it dominated could not check the increasing incursions of the Samnites. Capua sought Roman aid, and the Romans agreed.[12] Beyond aiding Capua, the precise causes of the first war against the Samnites are not entirely clear, particularly when Livy goes out of his way to make the Romans appear as an injured party. Regardless, after a reasonably short conflict, Samnite influence in Campania was blunted for a time.[13]

Little more than a decade would pass before tensions between the two peoples kindled a second war. In the meantime, the members of the Latin League, Rome's allies, rebelled against Rome in the years from 340–338, a conflict known as the Latin War. The precise causes are not clear in this case either, but it is reasonable to suppose one factor was a growing fear among the Latins that their independence would eventually be swallowed by growing Roman power. Though probably with difficulty, the Romans managed to defeat their erstwhile allies in this civil war of sorts and imposed a new legal, political and military settlement that proved critical to the Romans' later expansion. Of the smaller Latin states, Rome absorbed both the citizens and the territory. Rome also seized some of the land of the two large Latin states of Tibur and Praeneste but left them with the status of Latin allies. The core legal rights for Latin allies were the ability to trade and intermarry with Roman citizens and the ability to move to Rome and adopt full Roman citizenship. The core obligations were to follow Roman foreign policy and supply troops to Roman armies. These rights collectively became known as 'Latin Rights', and the label 'Latin' transformed from strictly an ethnicity to a legal status in Roman law. The colonies that Rome founded after this point that were not citizen colonies possessed Latin rights. Around this time, Rome also forged special bonds with the people of Campania. The citizens of Capua and other critical towns in the plain were given *civitas sine suffragio*, 'citizenship without the vote'. This status was apparently not remarkably different, for practical purposes, from Latin status. These citizens had all the legal rights and responsibilities of Roman citizens except for the vote, and they could migrate to Rome to gain full citizenship status. The absorption of territory and citizens, and extension of rights to Latins and citizens without the vote, both increased Roman territory and secured even larger supplies of manpower for Roman armies in future wars.[14]

Quintus Fabius Rullianus and the Second Samnite War

After the Latin War, the Second Samnite War broke out. It was in this last third of the fourth century, when the Latins were quelled and the Samnites threatening, that Quintus Fabius Rullianus, perhaps the greatest Fabii ever to hold office, first appeared. His grandfather was a Numerius Fabius Ambustus, perhaps one of the three Fabii who served as consular tribunes the year the Senones sacked Rome. If so, Ambustus did not last long as a *cognomen*. Quintus Fabius assumed the *cognomen* Rullianus for reasons long lost. Before he was done, though, he and his descendants would be known by the *cognomen* Maximus, 'the greatest'.

Quintus Fabius Rullianus first appears in the sources as curule aedile in 331 BC. The curule aediles, elected annually in pairs, had a range of duties. They leased contracts to maintain civic constructions like temples and sewers and sponsored the public games that lent excitement to everyday existence. They also, not infrequently, investigated and prosecuted, bringing suspected criminals to trial. So it was with Rullianus in the following tale preserved by Livy. Many Romans that year became gravely ill. Soon it was determined that these sick citizens had been poisoned. A slave woman knew something about the matter and approached Rullianus with insider information. He promptly notified the consuls, and they, in turn, introduced the matter to the Senate. An investigation ensued. The slave brought some inquisitors along with her, and they caught in the act a number of Roman wives preparing poisonous draughts. When pressed, the wives denied any crime. Their potions were beneficial, they swore. The slave woman challenged the wives to back their claim by drinking their own concoctions. The wives drank and died – trapped in a lie or genuinely mistaken in their ministrations. Roman authorities then seized these women's attendants and learned that many women were involved in this dreadful business, some 170 in all. Unsurprisingly, this situation appeared to be a decidedly foul omen from the gods. Thus, the priestly annals were consulted for a ritual to restore peace with the gods. In the past, apparently, a dictator had hammered a nail into the temple of Jupiter on the Capitoline hill in response to some disaster. It was time to repeat the ritual. Gnaeus Quinctilius was appointed for the task. He drove the nail, no doubt with all the dictatorial authority he could muster, and relinquished his post.[15]

Judging from the year of his aedileship, Rullianus may have been old enough to serve against the Samnites in their first war with Rome. During the second, however, he was a commander. When war broke out in 326 BC, the Romans were in a stronger strategic position than before, now controlling Latium and its resources. That did not make the struggle any less difficult. Again, geopolitical conflicts in fertile Campania were a significant factor in sparking war. The Greek city of Palaeopolis – literally 'Old City' – which was combined with a city called Neapolis ('New City') encroached upon Roman farmland in the fertile Falernian district of Campania, so Livy patriotically asserts. Since Roman influence had been expanding in that region for decades, it is not too much of a stretch to suppose the Neapolitans saw the Romans as the provocateurs themselves. Either way, tensions flared, the Neapolitans refused to meet Roman demands – said Roman sources – and the consul of 327, Quintus Publilius Philo, led an army to besiege the city. When the siege lasted longer than Philo's term of office, the Senate initiated a new practice – prorogation. In the future when a consul or praetor needed more time in office to continue a task, the Senate could extend his command and name him a proconsul or propraetor to distinguish him from the regularly elected consuls and praetors for the year. This important innovation of prorogation provided more military flexibility to the Romans; so long as the Senate approved, commanders could have more time to conclude those military campaigns that often did not fit neatly into the confines of a consular year. Philo continued in command as proconsul and Neapolis fell in 326. Meanwhile, his colleague Lucius Cornelius Lentulus had journeyed in 327 to the Samnites, suspected of instigating Neapolis. With an army at his back, Lentulus issued demands. The Samnites objected, and the second war broke out.[16]

As is so often the case for this period of Roman history, Livy provides the main account. Occasionally there are briefer notices from the Sicilian Greek historian, Diodorus Siculus, who wrote a history of the Greek world – essentially the Mediterranean basin – in the mid-first century BC. The Second Samnite War has been aptly called 'the twilight of Roman history', because the first histories of Rome were written at the end of the third century.[17] It is not too much of a stretch to suppose the first Roman historian, Fabius Pictor, kin to Rullianus as it happened, could have heard stories, possibly about the Second and certainly about the Third Samnite War, from actual participants. The events of these wars entered the realm of living memory for historians like Pictor.[18] Our historical investigations rest on somewhat firmer ground; but only somewhat.

A Dangerous Disagreement: Papirius Cursor and Fabius Rullianus

It appears that the consuls of 326, Gaius Poetelius and Lucius Papirius Cursor, campaigned successfully against some Samnite towns during their term in office,[19] but reportedly concerns soon arose that the Vestini tribe to the north-east of Rome might join forces with Samnium. The Senate deemed the situation to be more than the consuls of 325, Junius Brutus Scaeva and Lucius Furius Camillus, could handle, particularly once Furius fell ill. Junius, presumably with senatorial instruction, appointed Papirius Cursor dictator – he had been consul the year before. Papirius in turn selected Quintus Fabius Rullianus to be his master of the horse. Why is not clear. Perhaps Rullianus had earned distinction as a soldier or a military tribune prior to this. Perhaps his role in investigating the poisoning incident left Papirius with a good impression of the younger man. Perhaps he was a logical choice as the ambitious son of the influential, three-time consul Marcus Fabius Ambustus. There is no evidence to guide us. Whatever good will Papirius and Rullianus may have had, however, seems to have been destroyed in the quarrel they would soon have in office.[20] For the moment, however, while the dictator and his master of horse focused on the Samnites, the consul Junius continued operations against the Vestini. Raiding their farmlands, he goaded them to battle. The Romans prevailed and the Vestini army was shattered, soldiers scattering to the various towns in the region. Fresh from victory, Brutus' troops stormed the Vestini towns of Cutina and Cingilia.[21]

Meanwhile, the army commanded by Papirius and his lieutenant Rullianus trekked to Samnite lands. The auspices under which they began the campaign, however, were of dubious portent. Auspices were the efforts at divination the Romans made to discern their gods' will before performing essentially any civil or military task. The most common signs by which the gods revealed their intents, so the Romans believed, were flight patterns of birds and the eating habits of consecrated chickens. Neither method was without its problems. Romulus, Remus and their followers supposedly brawled over conflicting interpretations of the birds in the air; Remus died, and Romulus was left to found Rome.[22] Gaius Hostilius Mancinus, according to another source, lost his supply of sacred chickens when they ran into a nearby wood, never to be found.[23] Despite the difficulties of interpretation, the Romans firmly believed that ignoring the omens was calamitous. In the First Punic War, the Roman fleet commander, Publius Claudius, took the measure of the chickens. They were not eating at all, a lieutenant observed. Claudius retorted if they would not eat they could drink and had them cast into the sea. This was the reason, the source pronounced, that the Roman fleet was lost at Drepana.[24] Auspices were a serious matter, and a commander could not afford to battle without the approval of the gods. Public opinion would not stand for it.

In this case, however, it was the entrails of the sacrificial animals that appeared troublesome, another commonly believed medium the gods used to communicate. So Papirius returned to Rome to repeat the necessary sacrifices with new victims. He ordered Rullianus to remain with the army and refuse any clash with the enemy while he was gone. It is a perplexing scenario. One wonders why the dictator would have marched all the way to Samnium if the omens were bad in the first place. Or if he had not taken the auspices until they reached Samnium, why did he need to return to Rome to retake them? No clear answer exists. In any event, once Papirius was gone, Roman scouts returned to camp and painted for Rullianus a picture of an unprepared enemy ripe for attack. That Rullianus thought this an opportune moment can be supposed from what he did: orders be damned, he and the army would attack the Samnites at a place called Imbrinum. His victory was complete. He made no mistakes, Livy loyally notes, perhaps drawing from a comment made by Fabius Pictor; there was nothing more that could have been achieved even if the dictator had been there. Details of the battle were sparse. Livy offers a single anecdote: the cavalry hurled themselves against the Samnite ranks unsuccessfully until a tribune, Lucius Cominius, instructed them to remove their bridles and leave the horses free to charge with all their spirit. The bridle-less Roman horse disrupted the enemy formations and the infantry mopped up.[25] It is not a particularly likely scenario. Roman cavalry, like essentially all ancient cavalry, could not hope to charge the front of unbroken heavy infantry unaided.[26] That course would only amount to a collision with a wall of shields, spears and men – resulting in chaos and vain self-sacrifice, not victory. Still, it appears the Romans won that day, though Livy notes some sources suggested Rullianus commanded the Romans to two victories, not just one. Others did not mention that he battled the Samnites at all. Yet a battle must have occurred; if not, the entire spectacle that happened next between Papirius and Rullianus makes little sense.

Livy reports that Rullianus gathered the weapons of the enemy and burned them, perhaps to keep Papirius from using them in a triumph for himself. Allegedly, Rullianus followed up with letters reporting his victory directly to the Senate, circumventing the dictator altogether.[27] If so, perhaps he really did battle the Samnites in a calculated plan to steal the dictator's honour and acted in a highly troublesome way for a subordinate.

Whether Rullianus plotted or not, Papirius was not happy, to say the least. He concluded business in the city and returned to Samnium. Word reached Rullianus that the dictator was on his way and in a vengeful mood. He availed himself of his soldiers in a lengthy speech Livy attributes to him, though it is unlikely anyone was taking notes that day. The troops were apparently willing enough to support their victorious commander, reasonably enough when they were fresh from victory. Papirius arrived, assembled the troops and publicly interrogated Rullianus about his disobedience. Livy heightens the drama in reporting what assuredly had been a tense situation: The dictator's lictors prepared their axes for an execution. They snatched at Rullianus, tearing at his clothing, but he broke free and fled to the *triarii*, the veteran soldiers, to protect him. The troops closest to Papirius pleaded with the dictator to relent. Indeed, Livy does his best to indicate that the whole camp wished the Master of the Horse pardoned for his impetuosity. Reportedly, night came before a resolution was reached, and Rullianus took advantage of the recess by fleeing to Rome to plead his case. This seems incredible. Perhaps the army was in a mutinous mood; otherwise, how did Rullianus make it out of the camp, given the dictator's prosecutorial position? His father, three-time consul Marcus Fabius Ambustus, urged him to summon the Senate, and Rullianus did so just as Papirius arrived, accompanied by his lictors. Just as the army had, the Senate also supported Rullianus. Still, there was no question Papirius had law on his side, and it seemed nothing would deter him from meting out justice with the executioner's axe.[28] These details add life to what would otherwise be a duller story, but the basic account may be sound. Rullianus' insubordination, despite his success, posed a threat to the chain of command so important for military success. He had also fought when the auspices were questionable and the dictator was still formally in command. Papirius had a legitimate point: his lieutenant had violated the religious and military laws that kept the Republic safe.

A final gambit remained for Rullianus, an appeal to the people (*provocatio ad populum*). The right of a citizen to appeal any magistrates' judgment to the citizens of Rome had long standing in Roman custom.[29] It was the last resort, and Marcus Fabius urged his son to present his case to the Roman people. An assembly of nearby citizens had gathered. Livy saw this moment as ripe for another speech, this one by Marcus Fabius on the topic of past dictators who had behaved less harshly than Papirius now. The historian makes sure the stakes are clear to readers:

> 'In Fabius' favour there was the prestige of the Senate, the support of the people, the help of the tribunes, and the memory of the absent army. On the other side the arguments put forward hinged on the invincible authority of the Roman people, military discipline, the dictator's edict (ever thought to have quasi-divine status), and the "Manlian orders", with love for a son subordinated to the interests of the state.'[30]

The last section with the reference to 'Manlian orders' needs some explanation. At one point during the Latin War, the dictator Titus Manlius Torquatus gave strict instructions to his soldiers not to engage in any fighting with the enemy under any circumstances. His son, also named Titus Manlius Torquatus, could not resist the jibes of a Latin cavalryman, however. He issued a challenge and killed the Latin in a duel. When the dictator heard the news, he executed his own son in front of the army for disobeying a direct order.[31] The tradition of the brutally lawful execution of military authority branded itself on the Roman psyche. If that event happened that way, it was a relatively fresh event for Marcus Fabius to reference and an indication that those Manlian orders were quite controversial.

Papirius would not relent in his anger. Still, he recognized the authority of the people to pardon his guilty subordinate: he would not die that day. Unsurprisingly, however, Papirius was through with the young Master of the Horse. He forbade Rullianus from exercising any of the powers of his office, left Lucius Papirius Crassus – a relative perhaps – in charge of the city and returned to camp in Samnium. Another battle against the Samnites followed. Papirius reportedly was a skilled tactician and ordered his troops well that day. Despite his able leadership, the soldiers simply refused to fight well, angered that Papirius did not honour their requests to save Rullianus but relented when the assembly demanded it. The battle was indecisive, but Papirius knew he had to win back the loyalty of his soldiers. He managed to do so in the camp, and the army soon recovered its morale and went on to defeat the Samnites soundly. A subsequent campaign through the Samnite countryside met no further resistance. The Samnites begged for peace, which was granted. Papirius capped the campaign by celebrating a triumph for his leadership.[32] Apparently, these operations took place over a couple of years, because Papirius' dictatorship seems to have extended until the consuls of 323 were elected and took office.[33]

Fabius Rullianus' First Consulship

Perhaps one might have thought Rullianus' reputation would suffer from his act of disobedience, but then again the Roman people had defended him against the irate Papirius. So it is not a complete surprise that they were willing to elect him consul for 322 BC alongside Lucius Fulvius. A dictator, Aulus Cornelius Arvina, was appointed, however, to conduct military affairs. He appointed Rullianus' father, Marcus Fabius Ambustus, as Master of the Horse. Livy details the campaign. Rumours of a Samnite offensive were in the air, reports that the Samnites had hired mercenaries fanning the flames. The dictator and his lieutenant marched to Samnium at the head of an army.

Livy's report of the campaign is rather odd. He suggests that the Romans did not pitch a proper camp but instead acted carelessly, as if the enemy was further away, a strange behaviour for an invading general. The Samnites arrived and pitched their own fortified camp close to the outer Roman sentries. Arvina opted to withdraw his troops and seek better ground for a battle. He tried to creep away at night, but his soldiers were detected and Samnite cavalry harried and hounded the army as it lumbered along. Samnite infantry followed along at daybreak and were able to catch the Roman army, beleaguered as it was by the enemy cavalry. Forced to engage, Arvina positioned the troops for battle.

The armies met and proved a match for each other for hours. They pushed and pulled, tore and hacked at each other, but no ground was given or taken. Realistically, the soldiers could not have fought without rest for hours but must have clashed and receded, flurries of sword and spear strokes punctuated by periods of rest, when the front lines were close, but not fighting, eyeing one another, sizing up foes and regaining strength for another confrontation.[34] Then the Samnite cavalry got it into their heads to attack the unprotected Roman baggage. This news reached Arvina, and he dispatched Fabius and the cavalry to maul the enemy while they were preoccupied with premature looting. They swarmed over the Samnite looters, cutting them down. Once the enemy cavalry was neutralized, Fabius led his riders around the Samnite infantry to attack the units from behind. When the infantry in front saw their cavalry comrades in the rear, they attacked with renewed vigour and pushed a final time. The Samnite infantry formations dissolved. Some fled, but others were trapped in the vice of Roman cavalry and infantry. The Romans then sought vengeance and demanded that the ringleader who had stirred the Samnites to break the truce, Brutulus Papius, be delivered to them. Papius saved himself, no doubt, from a worse fate in Roman hands by killing himself, and the Samnites delivered his corpse to Rome. The dictator Arvina earned a triumph.[35]

Was it really Marcus Fabius Ambustus, however, who led the cavalry on that day of battle? Livy wraps up this episode with this notice:

> 'According to some authors, this war was fought by the consuls, and they held the triumph over the Samnites. These also relate that Fabius [Rullianus] advanced into Apulia and took a great deal of plunder from there. There is no disagreement over whether Aulus Cornelius [Arvina] was dictator that year. What is disputed, however, is whether the purpose of his appointment was fighting the war or giving the starting signal to the four-horse chariots at the Roman Games (because the praetor Lucius Plautius happened to have been struck by a serious illness) and whether he resigned the dictatorship after discharging this not particularly noteworthy function of his office. It is not easy either to give preference to one version over another or to one author over another.'

Frustrated, Livy reveals an important insight into the problems of evidence he faced:

> 'I believe the historical record has been marred by funerary eulogies and false inscriptions on ancestral busts, with the various families all illegitimately appropriating to themselves military campaigns and public offices. This, at least, is the source of uncertainty with respect to the achievements of individuals and public records of events. And there is no

writer contemporaneous with those events whose account can be regarded as authoritative.'[36]

More often than not, the competing evidence Livy refers to has not survived, but this instance is an exception. The *Fasti Triumphales*, the inscription of magistrates who earned triumphs, carved at the very end of the first century BC, do not mark a triumph for the dictator Arvina at all, but do indicate that Fulvius triumphed over the Samnites, and Quintus Fabius Rullianus over both Samnites and Apulians. This would suggest that the other writers Livy notes were correct: Fulvius and Rullianus fought successfully against the Samnites. It is plausible enough. Rullianus' father, Fabius Ambustus, had held his first consulship in 360, making him likely in his seventies at this point, and quite probably too old to engage in the sort of active, vigorous cavalry command Livy describes.[37] Arguably, though, he could easily have been appointed to watch Arvina start the chariot races, appointed simply because every dictator had to have a Master of the Horse. Rullianus seems a much more likely candidate for the cavalry episode. Of course, much to modern readers' frustration, he could have conducted his army successfully against the Samnites and Apulians, and the cavalry episode could have been completely fabricated. Still, it is reasonable to suppose that the *fasti* were correct and that Rullianus made headway against Samnites and Apulians that year.

Disaster at the Caudine Forks

The year 321 marked the low point of Roman fortunes in the Samnite Wars. That year, the consuls joined forces and invaded Samnium. For various reasons they were lured into choosing a route that required passage through a rugged wooded canyon, part of what was called the Caudine Forks. Once in the defile, the Roman army was bottled up by the Samnites and trapped. Efforts to extricate themselves proved useless. Only the complete surrender of the Roman army and a forced truce with the Samnites saved the Roman soldiers. As a final act of humiliation, the Roman soldiers had to 'go under the yoke', marching underneath an arch made of spears to symbolize that they had been yoked into submission.[38] The peace would last for just five years.

Though the disaster at the Caudine Forks was humiliating enough, the Romans were far from defeated in any lasting sense and took advantage of the imposed peace with Samnium to secure their hold in Campania.[39] Rullianus only appears for a moment in this period, in largely administrative roles.[40] Meanwhile, operations in Apulia and Lucania resulted in new alliances for the Romans, each hemming in the Samnites more tightly. In response to all this Roman activity, the Samnites apparently stayed quiet and within their territory. Indeed, it was only when the Romans attacked the Samnite town of Saticula that they felt compelled to fight.[41]

The Middle Years of the Second Samnite War (317–311 BC)

War flared up again not too long after the Romans had accepted the Caudine Peace, and Rullianus played an important role in the Roman military effort. The exact events and chronology of the years 317–311 are probably impossible to establish with certainty. Essentially, our main sources for the period, Livy, Diodorus Siculus and the *Capitoline Fasti*, offer different versions of events and sometimes different actors. More often than not, the exact details are not critical for tracking Rullianus' exploits, however, and we can leave the tangled accounts for others to sort. The war against the Samnites had erupted again and Rome fielded consular armies, year after year, to meet its foes.

Rullianius next appears in the accounts for 315. Papirius Cursor, the dictator of 325, and Publilius Philo were the consuls. Rullianus, says Livy, was named dictator and given charge of military operations.[42] That alone is enough to spark curiosity. How was it that an able commander like Papirius was left in Rome while the younger man who had disobeyed his orders was in the supreme position of dictator and charged with prosecuting the war against the Samnites? And why indeed was he selected for this distinction over Papirius? The sources make no comment. Perhaps Rullianus had earned a reputation as the better commander? Perhaps, judging from the episode of 325, he had more senatorial support than Papirius? Perhaps the Romans simply did not generally allow the same individual to be dictator more than once – a trend generally supported by the *fasti*? Or perhaps this is just another instance where the Romans often did not select their commanders on an estimation of their strategic and tactical skill, at least not as far as we can see.

The exact events of Rullianus' dictatorship in 315 are something of a puzzle. In Livy's version, Rullianus marched to Samnite Saticula with reinforcements to take over Aemilius' army.[43] The Samnite army at Plistica struck camp, hoping to lure the Romans away from Saticula. Rullianus would not take the bait, even when Samnite sorties harassed the outposts of the Roman camp. His Master of the Horse, Quintus Aulius Cerretanus, found the Samnite cavalry feints too enticing, however, took a cavalry force and charged the Samnite riders. The Samnite general happened to command the harassing force, and Cerretanus met him with deadly impact, impaling the Samnite on the point of his spear. Then the commander's brother took vengeance, slaying Cerretanus in turn. The blow to Samnite morale, however, was too great, and the Samnite force withdrew from Saticula and resumed its siege of Plistica. Soon after, Saticula fell to the Romans. Yet the Samnites had their vengeance, storming Plistica.[44] After the fall of Saticula, still in 315 says Livy, the Roman armies shifted attention to Sora, a colony in south-east Latium that joined with the Samnites after they murdered the Roman colonists there. While on the march, the Romans encountered a Samnite army in Latium at Lautulae. Livy notes an indecisive battle was fought.

Then, according to Livy, the fallen Cerretanus was replaced by a new Master of Horse, Gaius Fabius, who levied a new army and left Rome to join the dictator. Sending note ahead to Rullianus, he received his orders to approach with his soldiers secretly. In the battle that followed, the Samnite army was caught between a Roman hammer and anvil and routed. Other sources disagreed that the battle was a victory. Livy conscientiously reports this: 'In some sources I find that the encounter [at Lautulae] went against the Romans, and that it was in this that the master of horse Quintus Aulius was killed.'[45]

Diodorus' account differs somewhat, particularly on Rullianus' role in 315. He agrees that Lucius Papirius Cursor and Quintus Publius Philo were the consuls for 315.[46] That year the Samnites overwhelmed the Roman garrison at Plistica and won over the Latin colony of Sora. Diodorus also places the Roman siege of Samnite Saticula that year. The siege spurred a Samnite army to gather and challenge the Roman forces. A battle erupted, but the Romans held firm at Saticula and eventually took the city. That Saticula fell this year is agreed on by both writers. Diodorus' account seems to suggest, unlike Livy's, that one or both consuls commanded at Saticula. More precisely, Diodorus does not suggest Rullianus had been named dictator yet. Diodorus also suggests that the army that took Saticula conducted operations against other forts and towns in the area. The Samnites yet again mustered an army to challenge the Roman forces. Only then did concerns about this army lead the Romans to appoint Rullianus, with Aulius as his second in command. They joined the army at Lautulae – Diodorus calls it Laustolae, but presumably he meant Lautulae. The armies clashed, the Romans suffered heavy casualties and their soldiers panicked. Aulius, however, stood his ground, desperately courageous as the ranks disintegrated about him. His courage won him certain death and certain glory. Rallying from the defeat, the Romans planted a new Latin colony at Luceria in the region and used it as a base of operations to continue their deadly struggle against the Samnites.[47]

Livy and Diodorus clearly agree that Saticula, Plistica and Sora were important towns where important military operations took place in the years, though they differ in details such as when the Samnites actually took Plistica. Diodorus, Livy and the *fasti* also agree that Rullianus held the dictatorship in 315, with Aulius Cerretanus as his second in command. Livy, however, draws from sources that assert Rullianus was in command from early in the year, commanded at Saticula and lost his second in command during a skirmish there. Diodorus disagreed, as did, as noted above, some of Livy's sources.[48] The *fasti* cannot rule out either possibility. They note simply that Aulius was killed in battle.[49] It would appear that the weight of the sources favour this second version, that Aulius fell at Lautulae.

However this may have been, it appears Rullianus led the Romans to a significant defeat at Lautulae in 315. Diodorus says so, while according to Livy, a number of his sources said so. Even Livy seems to hint at this. Livy calls the battle at Lautulae 'indecisive' and notes that the numbers lost on both sides made it difficult to ascertain whether the Romans had won or lost.[50] This hardly qualifies even as damning with faint praise; really just damning. What about the second battle? Livy occasionally mentions suspect second battles in his narrative to provide imaginary opportunities for defeated Roman commanders to redeem themselves. No other sources support this second battle. Several – Diodorus and the lost accounts Livy mentions – suggest there was no second battle. So it seems likely that Rullianus simply lost the battle and there was no rematch at that point.[51]

Rullianus stepped down for the consuls of 314 BC, Marcus Poetelius and Gaius Sulpicius. Again, the actual events of 314 are not entirely clear. According to Livy, the consuls recovered the colony of Sora with the help of one of its residents. Livy provides an elaborate story of subterfuge of uncertain value. The upshot, however, was that the Romans made their way past the walls and sacked the city. Several hundred of the survivors from Sora were branded as the rebels who had murdered the Roman colonists and surrendered the colony to the Samnites. They were led to Rome in chains, publicly scourged and beheaded in the Forum.[52] Meanwhile, Campania boiled with intrigue and Maenius was appointed dictator. His investigations in Capua quashed potential rebellion there.[53]

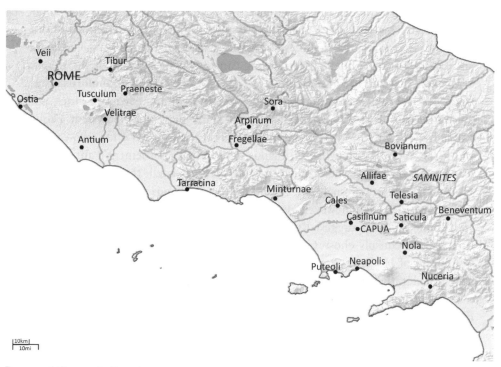

Rome and Campania-Samnium.

Also in 314, says Livy, Poetelius and Sulpicius campaigned against the Ausones (also known as Aurunci), another Italian people between Latium and Campania. Some disaffected youth from the region approached the Roman forces and agreed to betray the towns of Ausona, Minturnae and Vescia. The subterfuge worked and the Romans stormed the cities, massacring a great number of the Ausonians in the process.[54] During the same year, however, the town of Luceria surrendered itself and its Roman garrison to the Samnites. A Roman army took the city summarily and slaughtered Lucerians and Samnites without discretion, their rage fed by this second defection of the Lucerians. In the place of the massacred inhabitants, 2,500 colonists were sent to repopulate the town.[55]

Diodorus disagrees. He names one of the consuls Marcus Publius in his account for 314, though the testimony Livy and the *fasti* assert his name was Marcus Poetelius. Diodorus agrees that Gaius Sulpicius was the other.[56] This year a Samnite army returned to Campania. The consuls' combined armies checked the Samnite host near the town of Tarracina. The battle was evenly matched for a time. Slowly, though, the Roman legionaries prevailed and slaughtered a number of Samnites, 10,000 according to Diodorus. The Campanians in Capua, however, unaware of the Roman victory, rose against the Romans. To counter the threat, Gaius Manius was named dictator; he chose Manius Fulvius as his Master of Horse. The Capuans' desire to rebel quickly ebbed; the leaders of the rebellion killed themselves rather than be surrendered to the Romans, avoiding certain torture and a painful death.[57] Essentially, then, Diodorus agrees with Livy about Capua, adds a battle at Tarracina and omits any mention of the recapture of Sora.

The next year, 313, the sources essentially agree that Lucius Papirius Cursor and Gaius Junius Bubulcus Brutus were consuls.[58] The sources for the Roman campaigns that year are in something of a mess. Rather vaguely, Diodorus notes, 'there were repeated raids through the [Samnite] country, sieges of cities, and encampments of armies in the field.'[59] At some point, he notes that Fabius Rullianus was chosen to be dictator during the year and led a force to capture the rebel colony of Fregellae. Rullianus deported the settlement's anti-Roman leaders to Rome and ordered them flogged and beheaded, the brutal treatment typically meted to criminals and enemies. Then Rullianus took Calatia and Nola in Campania.[60] Livy, however, does not list Rullianus as a dictator that year. Indeed, he does not suggest Rullianus held any office at all. Instead, according to Livy, the consuls chose Gaius Poetelius as dictator, with Marcus Folius as his Master of Horse. These two recaptured Fregellae easily as the Samnites had abandoned it, then moved on to Nola.[61] Livy notes, however, that in some sources the consul Junius took Nola. The *fasti* support Livy that Gaius Poetelius was dictator but, unlike Livy, suggest that another Poetelius, Marcus, was the Master of the Horse.[62] Trusting Livy and the *fasti* over Diodorus makes sense, particularly when a second dictatorship appears to have been quite uncommon, though to be fair, Papirius Cursor, Rullianus' contemporary, was one of the exceptions.[63]

Ultimately, one can reasonably conclude that, regardless of who commanded in each case, 313 involved more Roman campaigns against the Samnites and victories at Fregellae and Nola.

The Censorship of Appius Claudius (313 BC)

So, by 313 our evidence suggests the Romans had reclaimed the colonies of Sora and Fregellae, and planted new colonies at Luceria, Suessa Aurunca and Saticula. This further closed their vice-grip on the Samnites and established beyond any shade of a doubt Roman control along the Liris River region of south-eastern Latium and the Volturnus River region of north-western Campania. That the Romans were there to stay was manifested when they began in 312 to build the Via Appia, the road from Rome to Capua. In 312, Marcus Valerius and Publius Decius were consul. Diodorus does not mention any initial campaigns against the Samnites for 312, instead noting that the Romans fought against the Marrucini and founded another colony.[64]

The year 312 was also notable for the censorship of Appius Claudius, who authorized the construction of two critical pieces of Roman infrastructure: the just-mentioned Appian Way and the Appian Aqueduct, a stable source of water for the growing city.[65] While Claudius secured fame with these public works, he added to this a fair amount of infamy for his other activities as censor. One episode in particular sheds some light on the censors and the mechanics of the ever-present political competition in the Republic. The censors of Rome were elected in pairs every five years and served for 18-month terms. Among other duties like auctioning public construction contracts, the censors had the prestigious power – as their name suggests – to maintain the census of Roman citizens. Reinforcing social hierarchy in writing, at the top of their lists were the senators. Unlike today, where senators are elected officials, those in the Republic were simply those recorded on the censors' lists as senators: it was a mark of distinction, a status granting honours and powers more than an office. Those Romans granted senatorial status had certain privileges. The right to wear special shoes and that most Roman of garments, the toga, specially emblazoned with a broad purple stripe, was one.[66] More substantial was the right to utter one's opinion in the meetings of the Senate, a body with substantial, though largely informal, political powers.[67] Somewhere about this time, presumably before Appius Claudius' censorship, the Ovinian law had been passed making senatorial status a fixed privilege, possessed for life so long as no censor struck the senator from the lists for displaying weak moral fibre. This in turn made senatorial status more desirable, for it placed its holder in a powerful and permanent role of political authority, one of the 300 who guided the magistrates and influenced all manner of political issues.

Apparently, the way Claudius and his colleague Gaius Plautius had revised the list of senators had provoked some serious upset. It appears some felt the censors had played favourites and made senators out of Romans with suspect credentials. Livy's narrative for 311 reports the problem. As soon as the consuls, Gaius Junius Bubulcus and Quintus Aemilius Barbula, entered office, they complained before a gathering of the people – seemingly an informal gathering rather than a voting assembly – that the senatorial order had been corrupted by the censors, who had put worse men before the better. They summarily announced that they would ignore the list and summon senators to meet according to the lists made in the censorship before Claudius and Plautius. The consuls must have had the necessary support. They did not have any particular right to challenge the prerogative of the censors, but in Roman politics it was often the case that the political right for many actions was granted after the fact by the tacit approval of the senatorial class and citizen assemblies. In other words, the consuls got away with it because enough Romans either wanted them to get away with it or did not care enough to stop them.

Roman Military Reforms c. 311 BC

Soon after this conflict over membership in the Senate, probably in 311, the Romans fundamentally transformed their military system. Traditionally, the military tribunes of the legions were selected at the discretion of the commanders. Up to this time, so far as we know, however, the Romans fielded two legions every year, one consul commanding each. From this year forward, the sixteen tribunes of the first four legions were elected by the Roman people. The creation of the new system for electing tribunes, however, presumes that the Romans now planned to field four legions yearly, and the normal size of a consular army became two legions plus allies. Clearly, Rome's military commitments were increasing, and the state accepted this as the new reality.[68]

Even more importantly, 311 is as compelling a place as any in the late fourth century for the Romans to have introduced manipular tactics to the Roman Army, a revolution in the way that their infantry fought that would define Roman warfare for the next two centuries. The trail of evidence is faint. There is a short Greek text known simply as the *Ineditum Vaticanum* – 'Unedited Vatican' text – that describes a discussion between a Roman and a Carthaginian just before the outbreak of the First Punic War (264–241 BC). The Carthaginian has asserted that the Romans will be bested by his people, because they know naval warfare, something the Romans merely played at. Kaeso, the Roman, rebukes the Carthaginian, noting that the Romans have a long tradition of learning military techniques and tactics from their rivals, then turning those techniques against them. He first notes that the Romans adopted the phalanx from the Etruscans. Then he says:

'The Samnite shield was not part of our national equipment, nor did we have javelins, but fought with round shields and spears; nor were we strong in cavalry, but all or nearly all of Rome's strength lay in infantry. But when we found ourselves at war with the Samnites, we armed ourselves with their oblong shields and javelins, and fought against them on horseback, and by copying foreign arms, we became masters of those who thought so highly of themselves.'[69]

The reference to *scutum* and *pilum* – 'oblong shields and javelins' – hints at a tactical overhaul of the Roman phalanx in the late fourth century. Added to this testimony is the speech the Roman historian Sallust attributes to Julius Caesar. Caesar asserts:

'Our ancestors, Fathers of the Senate, were never lacking either in wisdom or courage, and yet pride did not keep them from adopting foreign institutions, provided they were honourable. They took their offensive and defensive weapons from the Samnites.'[70]

Taken together, these fragments suggest that the Romans adopted military equipment from the Samnites, in particular the *pilum* (javelin) and *scutum* (oblong shield). The Samnite wars of the late fourth century are the logical time for this change. More precisely, since the Romans significantly increased the size of consular armies in 311, they may also have initiated manipular tactics then.

New weapons brought new tactics that helped Rome dominate the Mediterranean. This is a good point to stop and consider how this new Roman manipular army functioned. Instead of forming one massive and rather difficult-to-manoeuvre phalanx, as they had done prior to the reform, the Roman soldiers were now grouped into smaller and more flexible *maniples* – the word itself means 'handful'. Livy and Polybius provide the two systematic accounts of the manipular army. They do not agree on all points, and it may be that Livy describes the early system in the fourth century and Polybius reviews the refined system at the end of the third. Tracking any detailed evolution of the manipular army is difficult at best. Still, historians have spent considerable time poring over both accounts, and it is possible, with a critical eye, to construct a reasonable account of the Roman manipular army from both sources that will hold essentially true for the period.

The Roman Manipular Army

The core heavy infantry unit, the maniple, normally ranged from 60–120 soldiers, and the men in each maniple were collectively equipped according to their age and function. The youngest recruits served outside the maniples as velites. Polybius provides the most detailed description of them:

'The youngest soldiers or velites are ordered to carry a sword, javelins, and a *parma* [target/shield]. The target is strongly made and sufficiently large to afford protection, being circular and measuring three feet in diameter. They also wear a plain helmet, and sometimes cover it with a wolf's skin or something similar both to protect and to act as a distinguishing mark by which their officers can recognize them and judge if they fight pluckily or not. The wooden shaft of the javelin measures about two cubits in length and is about a finger's breadth in thickness; its head is a span long hammered out to such a fine edge that it is necessarily bent by the first impact, and the enemy is unable to return it. If this were not so, the missile would be available for both sides.'[71]

These troops served as the skirmishers supporting the maniples: they ran close to cast javelins, then retreated if the enemy pressed them. Not uncommonly they initiated battle, casting their missiles at enemy infantry to harass and demoralize them before the full clash of the heavy infantry.

The heavy infantry maniples were divided into three types of soldiers: *hastati*, *principes* and *triarii*. Polybius describes them as follows:

'The next in seniority called hastati are ordered to wear a complete panoply. The Roman panoply consists firstly of a shield, the convex surface of which measures two and a half feet in width and four feet in length, the thickness at the rim being a palm's breadth. It is made of two planks glued together, the outer surface being then covered first with canvas and then with calf-skin. Its upper and lower rims are strengthened by an iron edging which protects it from descending blows and from injury when rested on the ground. It also has an iron boss fixed to it which turns aside the most formidable blows of stones, pikes, and heavy missiles in general. Besides the shield they also carry a sword, hanging on the right thigh and called a Spanish sword. This is excellent for thrusting, and both of its edges cut effectually, as the blade is very strong and firm. In addition they have two pila, a brass helmet and greaves. The pila are of two sorts – stout and fine … Finally they wear as an ornament a circle of feathers with three upright purple or black feathers about a cubit in height, the addition of which on the head surmounting their other arms is to make every man look twice his real height, and to give him a fine appearance, such as will strike terror into the enemy. The common soldiers wear in addition a breastplate of brass a span square, which they place in front of the heart and call the pectorale [breastplate], this completing their accoutrements; but those who are rated above ten thousand drachmas wear instead of this a coat of chain-mail. The principes and triarii are armed in the same manner except that instead of the pila the triari carry long spears.'[72]

Two items of equipment made the Roman heavy infantry stand out from their rivals, and Polybius takes care when describing them. The first is the large, convex, oval shield, or *scutum*, reportedly adopted from the Samnites.[73] There are very few *scuta* that have survived the ravages of two millennia. Those specimens that exist support Polybius' description, while still illustrating that individual shields could vary greatly. One specimen from Egypt had no metal bindings and a wooden spine that ran vertically along the centre of the shield to reinforce it. Measuring 4ft by 2ft and weighing over 20lb, it was a large, heavy shield.[74] Other examples further attest to the variety. *Scuta* could weigh as little as 12lb, come equipped with wooden or metal bosses and be finished with or without metal bindings. Generally though, it appears that the *scutum* was intended to reach at least from shoulder to knee.[75] Quite possibly the *scutum* was meant to rest on the ground and extend to the neck of a soldier crouched in a fighting stance.

The *pilum* was another specialized piece of equipment that Polybius describes carefully to readers:

> 'Of the stout ones some are round and a palm's length in diameter and others are a palm square. Fine pila, which they carry in addition to the stout ones, are like moderate-sized hunting-spears, the length of the haft in all cases being about three cubits. Each is fitted with a barbed iron head of the same length as the haft. This they attach so securely to the haft, carrying the attachment halfway up the latter and fixing it with numerous rivets, that in action the iron will break sooner than become detached, although its thickness at the bottom where it comes in contact with the wood is a finger's breadth and a half; such great care do they take about attaching it firmly.'[76]

The grim function of the *pilum*'s design was to penetrate a shield and pass on into the body of the shield-bearer. Surviving examples commonly sport a pyramid-shaped point that facilitated armour penetration, with the weight of the device adding penetrating power. On top of this, the thin spit of metal joining head and shaft created very little friction and ensured that the *pilum* would continue its course after penetrating the shield. Modern tests with facsimile *pila* indicate that these weapons could readily pierce ¾in of plywood and still have the required punch to penetrate a human. The design had a coincidental benefit. The thin metal rod joining head and haft often bent upon impact with an enemy shield, hampering removal, weighing down the shield and making the spear useless for the enemy.[77]

Once a soldier's supply of *pila* was exhausted, he wielded the so-called 'Spanish' sword, *gladius Hispaniensis*. This short sword with a two–edged blade was, surviving examples suggest, 16–20in long with a sharp point.[78] Polybius emphasizes that the design of the blade afforded both stabs and cuts.[79]

In addition to the velites as skirmishers and the heavy infantry maniples in the battleline, Roman armies also fielded a contingent of citizen cavalry numbering, under normal circumstances, 300 per legion.[80] Polybius asserts the Roman cavalry were initially lightly armed, wearing no body armour to speak of. Over time they came to adopt what Polybius calls Greek-style arms and armour: an armoured corselet and sturdy shield, and a stronger spear with a butt-spike for use if the head snapped. When exactly this transition occurred is not clear. According to Polybius, 'Experience showed [the Romans] the deficiencies of their equipment, and they soon changed over to Greek methods of construction.'[81] He does not, however, provide any hint as to what those experiences were or when they occurred. A case can be made for the Second Punic War as the transitional point, but certainty is impossible.[82]

Forces of infantry and cavalry from the allies (*socii*) accompanied the Roman citizen infantry and cavalry into battle. The allies provided roughly the same amount of infantry as the Romans and about three times as much cavalry, says Polybius.[83] What little evidence we have about the allied infantry suggests that they too were armed with the panoply of *scutum* and *gladius*. Presumably they were also armed with *pila* and organized into a triple battle line of *hastati*, *principes* and *triarii*. Certainly Polybius says that the Italian allies used the same selection procedure for infantry that the Romans did. The Roman method, which Polybius outlined earlier, was to select men of the right age range and physique to make up 1,200 *hastati*, 1,200 *principes* and 600 velites. Given the same selection process, there is no good reason to suppose the allied soldiers were organized differently.[84] In fact when Livy refers to the allies, he consistently notes that they were organized into cohorts, a unit that in the middle Republic consisted of one maniple each of *hastati*, *principes* and *triarii* plus the associated velites.[85] Similarly, when battle accounts refer to cavalry, it is usually a combination of allied and Roman cavalry, and they make no distinction between these troops, suggesting the allied cavalry were armed and fought like their Roman counterparts.[86] Altogether, each consular army after the 311 BC reform totalled some 16,000–20,000 infantry and 1,600–2,400 cavalry: two Roman legions numbering some 8,000–10,000 infantry, an equivalent number of allied infantry, some 400–600 citizen cavalry and perhaps 1,200–1,800 allies.[87] These figures come from the late third century. Exact numbers are unobtainable for the fourth, but were perhaps in this range.

Though we know no absolute rules about deployment, it was common for the Roman Army to place allied infantry on the left and right wing, Roman infantry legions in the centre and cavalry on the extreme right and left. The three classes of heavy infantry – *hastati*, *principes* and *triarii* – were organized into three lines of maniples in a formation like the staggered pips on the 'five' side of a dice. Polybius says each class of troop in a legion filled ten maniples, the maniples of *hastati* and *principes* each held 120 soldiers, and the *triarii* maniples sixty men apiece. Livy puts the number at fifteen maniples each of *hastati*, *principes* and *triarii*, but his math is more than a little unclear and conflicts with other evidence about the numbers and disposition of maniples. It is possible that in the fourth century there were fifteen maniples for each class, a figure that by the end of the third century had become ten maniples. It is also possible that Livy or his source was simply mistaken, and the Roman manipular legion always consisted of ten maniples per class.[88]

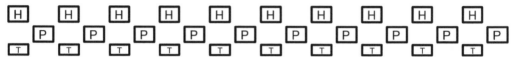

Maniples of a legion in a quincunx deployment

H = hastati maniple   P = principes maniple   T = triarii maniple

The operation of the manipular legion in battle was distinct from other large military formations of the day. In the following passage, Livy describes the mechanics of the maniples in action:

'The *hastati* were the first of all to engage. If the *hastati* were unable to defeat the enemy, they retreated slowly and were received into the intervals between the maniples of the *principes*. The *principes* then took up the fighting and the *hastati* followed them. The *triarii* knelt beneath their standards, with the left leg advanced, having their shields leaning against their shoulders and their spears thrust into the ground and pointing obliquely upwards, as if their battleline were fortified with a bristling palisade. If the *principes*, too, were unsuccessful in their fight, they fell back slowly from the battle-line to the *triarii*. (From this arose the adage, 'to have come to the *triarii*', when things are going badly.) The *triarii*, rising up after they had received the *principes* and *hastati* into the intervals between their maniples, would at once draw their maniples together and close the lanes, as it were; then, with no more reserves behind to count on, they would charge the enemy in one compact array. This was a thing exeedingly disheartening to the enemy, who, pursuing those whom they supposed they had conquered, all at once beheld a new line rising up, with augmented numbers.'[89]

Though Polybius, unfortunately, does not describe the normal operation of the maniples, his many references to battle corroborate that the normal practice was for the maniples to be deployed first *hastati*, then *principes* and finally *triarii*. He also notes that the second line was normally deployed behind the gaps of the first.[90] Presumably the front line used the gaps to withdraw as the second line used them to move forward and engage.

The actual mechanics of such a rotating force generate a host of questions. How large were the gaps between maniples? Presumably they would have had to be wide to allow for whole maniples of *hastati* to retreat through them in an orderly fashion. Did that mean the *principes*, and the *hastati* for that matter, fought the enemy with gaps in their own line, and would not these gaps have made the Roman line vulnerable to enemy infantry attacks? How exactly did the reserve lines relieve the front ranks in a way that would not devolve into chaos? These are problems that are likely never to be resolved by historians: the evidence is simply insufficient. Nevertheless, our ancient sources are clear that, however it may have worked, the Roman manipular system allowed fresh troops to replace exhausted ones, and this provided a significant advantage. Consequently, the Romans must have worked out a system of spacing and training for their troops to employ these relief lines, even though that method is unclear to us.[91]

With the Roman manipular army we find a sophisticated tactical system that, nevertheless, could operate with very little input from the commander. Though at first glance the claim seems wholly counterintuitive, extraordinary strategic and tactical skill was not exceptionally important to the consuls and, sometimes, praetors who commanded manipular armies. Certainly, spectacular military skill was not required for a Roman to command these armies successfully. In a very real sense, the commanders of Roman manipular armies were amateurs. They certainly would have experience of military life, serving their required stint as a soldier, usually in the cavalry. That experience for a consul would likely have been a decade or more in the past, however, and there is a great difference between following orders as a soldier and showing skill at commanding an entire army. But there was no formal training for commanders, no curriculum through which command skills were acquired and honed. Still, their armies, far more often than not, defeated their enemies, eventually enabling Rome to dominate the Mediterranean. This speaks to the power of the manipular system – not to mention the deep reserves of Roman manpower – that allowed even mediocre commanders a fair chance of success.

It is not that no difference existed between a brilliant commander and an incompetent one: the brilliant commander could draw every last bit of performance out of his troops, while the incompetent one could make strategic blunders that put the army in jeopardy. The Roman manipular army functioned so well in general, however, because it was a well-designed system that could operate with a minimal amount of input from the commander. In part this was because many other, often more experienced, Romans had input at different points in the system. It was generally up to the Senate, not the commander, where a commander and his army would be deployed for the year, and often whom the army would or would not fight. In short, the outlines of the commander's strategy for the year were often determined in part by the Senate, and often the Senate gave very specific instructions: cities to capture or garrison, regions to support or suppress, etc. Still, a general could choose to act independently in the field, and many did so.[92] The point, however, is that generals with less command skill could, if they chose, stick closely to the Senate's guidelines for the year and do quite well.

When it came to tactics, the manipular system's great strength was revealed. Refined over the years, the manipular army was a tactically sophisticated and effective system that operated largely independently of the commander. The division into maniples, the distribution of velites to support the maniples, the deployment into lines and the rotation of maniples were encoded into the system by veterans who passed on the knowledge to raw recruits. Military tribunes, the junior officers of the legion, were selected from two categories of men: those who had five years' experience and those who had ten.[93] Veterans of as many as sixteen years of campaigns also kept the new recruits in line, in addition to the centurions selected by the men, and standard bearers that communicated to the maniple where to go and when. The system worked more often than not, judging from the general success of Roman armies in battle. There was a great deal of collective experience in the ranks that more than compensated for a consul who had not been in the army for one or two decades. Truly, a general who was simply familiar with the manipular system could issue the orders necessary to put that system into action. The fact that all who entered public office had first to serve for ten campaigns ensured that commanders were at least familiar with how the maniples should operate.[94] And familiarity was all that was really needed to order the army into positions and set it into operation. At the risk of being too reductive, to be moderately competent, a general had to find some reasonably flat terrain, order the maniples to deploy into their normal positions and the cavalry to guard the flanks. So while the brilliant strategist could doubtless achieve great things with his army, all that was needed for success was an adequate commander who let the system operate as it was meant to.[95]

The Etruscan War of 311–309 BC

If the manipular reform began in 311, the Roman armies that year put it to good use. The consuls, Gaius Junius Bubulcus and Quintus Aemilius Barbula, certainly spent some of the year campaigning against the Samnites. Diodorus asserts the Romans invaded Samnium and twice defeated the Samnites near Talium. Following these victories, the Romans were able to operate freely against the towns and forts of Samnium and besieged some towns into submission.[96] Livy suggests that the consuls divided their forces, and Junius led the thrust into Samnite territory. The Samnites reportedly seized the town of Cluviae – the whereabouts of which is unknown – after starving the Roman guard into submission. Junius hankered to retake the town, and after his soldiers did so they followed up by seizing Bovianum, a Samnite capital.[97] The *fasti* confirm that,

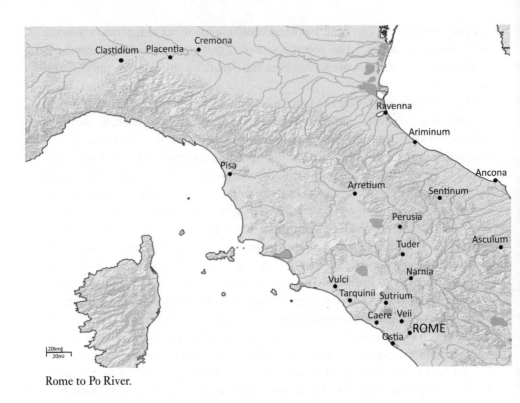

Rome to Po River.

whether one follows Livy, Diodorus or a combination, Junius earned a triumph over the Samnites that year, a likely indicator of a successful campaign.

Whilst war with the Samnites dragged on, a new threat rose in the north. After four decades of more-or-less peaceful relations, a group of inland Etruscan cities besieged the town of Sutrium, which Livy referred to as the gateway to Etruscan lands. While Junius had campaigned against the Samnites, it fell to his colleague, Quintus Aemilius Barbula, to deal with this Etruscan menace.[98] Leading an army north, he encountered an Etruscan army besieging Sutrium. Apparently they had not fully surrounded the city yet, for the Roman army camped 'before the city' in Livy's account.[99] The Etruscans opted for battle. A fierce enough one broke out, but dusk arrived without a clear victor. Etruscans and Romans alike had suffered severe casualties, though, and neither could stomach a second battle that season.[100]

This is how matters stood in late 311/early 310. The Romans and Samnites still warred. An Etrsucan force had been checked at Sutrium but remained camped in the field, still threatening the town. The Roman army that had checked those Etruscans also remained at Sutrium, burdened with too many casualties to take the initiatve.[101] With wars on two fronts and neither enemy quelled, the Romans elected Fabius Rullianus consul alongside Marcus Rutilius for 310. Rullianus was assigned Etruria and took along reinforcements. It may have been the first time he had commanded a manipular army. If so, it is an interesting but unanswerable question what adjustments he had to make as a commander. Though Diodorus would have it that Rutilius accompanied Rullianus and only later marched south to Samnium, we should probably accept Livy's account that Rullianus alone commanded in the north and Rutilius in the south. Diodorus tends to be confused when writing about consuls' provinces, and it would be quite odd if both consuls marched north to Etruria when the Romans were still at war with the Samnites in the south.[102]

When it comes to Rullianus' campaign against the Etruscans, confusions in the account gather like stormclouds.[103] Livy is the primary culprit here, cramming together more events in the Roman campaign against Etruria than can possibly have happened within the year 310. A reasonable solution is that some of the events he describes actually took place in 309, when Rullianus was proconsul in Etruria. Complicating matters further, Livy seems to repeat his description of Rullianus' campaign in his narrative, creating a doublet. In short, it appears Livy followed his account of Rullianus' campaign with a second, similar-sounding but fictional account of a campaign. Other difficulties arise from the frequent disagreements between sources, this time about the offices Rullianus held. Livy makes Fabius consul for two consecutive years, 310 and 309. The *fasti* disagree, however, and suggest that Fabius was consul in 310 and proconsul in 309. What's more, the *fasti* record a triumph for Rullianus as proconsul over the Etruscans in 309 but mention no particular military honours for 310, again suggesting that Rullianus' campaign in Etruria unfolded over the two years of 310 and 309.

While these problems provide grist for the specialists' mills, here we just need a reasonably plausible proposition for Rullianus' campaign in Etruria so that the story can continue. The basic details for the campaign seem to be these. Over the course of two campaign seasons, first as consul in 310 and then as proconsul in 309, Rullianus conducted operations against the Etruscans. Rullianus travelled through the foothills to reach Sutrium, but when he got to the plains around Sutrium, he spied a significantly larger Etruscan army, lines formed and ready for battle. Rather than handing the advantage to his more numerous foe, Rullianus formed his battle lines along the rocky foothills. The Etruscans, perhaps buoyed by their numbers, advanced fearlessly, eager to engage. The defending Roman battle line rained javelins and even stones from the high ground upon their approaching foes. The Etruscan lines wavered under the barrage. When the '*hastati* and *principes*' – a reference confirming that the Romans now used maniples – charged, the Etruscans broke and ran. Roman infantry followed close on their heels and the cavalry checked the fleeing Etruscans before they reached the safety of their camp. Those not killed or captured struggled their way into the murky Ciminian forest, heading for the haven of the mountains beyond. The Romans seized the Etruscan camp and its plunder, then Rullianus' council of officers considered their options.[104] Diodorus agrees with the outlines of this account, though in his reckoning both consuls commanded at Sutrium and defeated the Etruscans together. For him the Samnites seized the opportunity to attack some Roman allies with impunity, and when reports reached the consuls, Marcius took his part of the army down to Samnium to relieve the Roman allies there.[105] Of the two versions, we should again probably accept Livy's over Diodorus'.[106]

Pursuing the defeated army was risky, as the Ciminian forest was thickly wooded and virtually impassable for an army, and the Romans risked stumbling into an ambush. Marcus Fabius, Rullianus' brother – or perhaps, Livy's squabbling sources noted, it was Kaeso Fabius or even Rullianus' half-brother Gaius Claudius – offered to scout the woods ahead and take advantage, if needed, of his ability to speak Etruscan. Accompanied by a slave who also spoke Etruscan, Fabius – or Claudius – penetrated the woods and came upon an Umbrian town whose inhabitants were ready to side with the Romans, offering supplies and troops. Livy says Fabius found the 'Camertes', the inhabitants of Umbrian Camerinum, but this was very far indeed from Mount Cimino and the entry to Etruria, and it is difficult to see how they could have offered any practical aid in this campaign.[107] It has been suggested that perhaps Livy or one of his many copyists over the millennia meant to write Tudertes, the inhabitants of the much closer Tuder in Umbria.[108] Whatever the case, the matter is not mentioned again. Reportedly, though, once word of the successful scouting mission reached the consul Rullianus, he and his army began to negotiate the wilderness of the Ciminian forest. He headed with his army to the top of Mount Cimino and took advantage of the high ground to scout the land ahead. Seeing the rich farmlands of southern Etruria, the consul sent plundering parties. The raiders gathered loot and supplies, and though the Etruscan peasantry in the region tried to resist, they posed no problems for the raiders. About the time they returned, Rullianus received a deputation from Rome: legates, along with a couple of tribunes of the plebs for good measure. Their mission had been to order Rullianus not to risk crossing the dangerous Ciminian forest. They had arrived too late, however, to warn the consul, and fortunately so for the Romans, since Rullianus' trek had been successful. Accordingly, they returned to Rome with news of recent victories.[109]

Rullianus did not push deeper into Etruria, apparently, or if he did, no record of it remains. The Etrsucans of the south, eager to pay back the Roman raiding parties, mustered another army and passed through the woods back to Sutrium. They sighted the Roman army there and moved into the plains to do battle.[110] The Etruscans marched close to the ramparts of the Roman camp, hoping to provoke a battle, but Rullianus kept his troops within their fortifications. Evening came without serious conflict, and the consul ordered his soldiers to have supper and be ready for action at a moment's notice. Before dawn, he gave orders to wake the troops quietly. Their camp servants picked up the necessary tools, and on the side facing the Etruscans, quietly removed the camp earthworks and filled in the ditch. The work complete, the Romans charged into the sleeping

Etruscans, unleashing chaos. Some, the lucky ones, died in their sleep. Others
were slaughtered in the terror that ensued for those awakened by the noise. With
barely a chance to grab weapons, let alone to rally, the Etruscans scattered and
fled. Rullianus' troops had secured a significant victory.[111] The Etruscans scattered
in the woods, and the Romans again plundered their camp. Livy considerably
exaggerates the casualties: he says 60,000 Etruscans were captured or slain, more
than the size of two consular armies.[112] Capping the episode with a final note
of uncertainty, Livy adds, 'some authors have it that this battle, famous as it
was, took place on the other side of the Ciminian Wood, in the area of Perusia,'
but loyally averred, 'Wherever the battle was fought, however, it was Rome that
emerged as victor.' The main Etruscan cities of the region – Perusia, Cortona and
Arretium – sued for peace, and the Romans agreed to a thirty-year armistice.[113]
Rullianus celebrated a triumph for crushing the Etruscan threat and bringing the
war in the north to a swift close.

The Second Samnite War Continues

Meanwhile, in the same period in Samnium, 310–309 BC, Rullianus' colleague in
the consulship, Gaius Marcius Rutulus, reportedly stormed the town of Allifae
and captured a number of forts and villages for good measure.[114] The Samnites
mustered an army to counter Marcius in battle and defeated the Roman forces,
though Livy loyally – and probably without hard evidence to go on – notes that
the Samnites had lost as many troops as the Romans. Fear that Rullianus would
invite disaster in the forests of southern Etruria, building on the bitter defeat
in Samnium, led the Senate to decide upon a dictator. They set upon Papririus
Cursor as the best candidate, who, Livy says, 'was considered the leading military
man of the time', but of course Papirius came with a political price.[115] Though
they acted often from senatorial guidance in these matters, only an active consul
could appoint a dictator. The Senate was not even clear that Marcius was alive to
receive their instructions. Word would have to be sent to Fabius. What Roman
alive, however, would have been less willing to appoint Papirius dictator, the
man who had once worked for his very execution? The Senate was aware; the
rift was quite public. So they sent a delegation of men of consular rank – men
who had been elected and served as consuls in the past – to honour Rullianus
and sweeten the bitter medicine. Perhaps, but still Livy dramatizes: Rullianus
showed the disappointment openly, and left to seek his own counsel for a time,
but took the necessary steps and appointed Papirius. It is difficult to know what
to make of this report. As noted, the men had a public rift. Rullianus had been
dictator before when Papirius was consul, however, and there seemed to have
been no problem. The rhetorical effect of the account is also a bit suspicious.
Livy essentially has a dramatic episode that boils down to this: Rullianus put the
good of the Republic before his own personal feelings. This was a theme used

often in Roman rhetoric of the late Republic and early Empire, and an explicit value judgment that Livy often makes in his history: early Romans were better at putting their country before themselves.[116] Though Diodorus says nothing about Papirius' dictatorship, it seems reasonable to suppose the outline of Livy's account for Papirius is valid.[117] He, along with some newly recruited legions, travelled to Samnium, although where exactly is not clear from Livy's account. He relieved Marcius at Longula, a place in Samnium unknown to moderns, then he defeated the Samnite army.[118] This is certainly consistent with the *fasti*, which state that Papirius triumphed over the Samnites.

Though clearly his rival, Papirius enjoyed a prestigious reputation as a commander at Rome. But Rullianus had also clearly crafted a fine reputation of his own. His recent commands bore this out, and Livy explicitly makes the connection: consul in 310 and proconsul in 309, based on the strength of his campaign in Etruria, he was again elected consul for 308, alongside Publius Decius Mus.[119] His election conflicted directly with the Roman law passed some thirty years earlier that one could not hold the same magistracy twice within ten years.[120] It is a bit unsatisfying as an explanation but an important point, nonetheless, that political laws and rules at Rome were often suspended or just plain ignored when they proved inconvenient. Rullianus' consulship in 308 must count as one of these instances.

Casting lots for provinces returned Samnium for Rullianus and Etruria for Decius. Rullianus, as Livy reports, besieged Nuceria Alfaterna, refusing the city's overtures for peace. Then his troops drove home a solid victory against the Samnites, who were joined by the Marsi. For the finale to the campaign, his army defeated the Paeligni.[121] Diodorus, not for the first time, throws an evidentiary wrench in the works, stating that rather than fighting the Marsi, Rome had actually come to the Marsi's aid against the Samnites.[122] Possibly so. Fortunately, though this detail cannot be secured, the victory over the Samnites is credible.

Meanwhile Decius, says Livy, campaigned against the Etruscans of Tarquinii, those foes who had once sacrificed captured Roman soldiers to their gods. Then an Umbrian revolt, though its extent is not clear, ramped up the danger in the north.[123] Facing too many threats at once, Decius drafted a missive to Rullianus, urging his colleague to bring an army north if the war against the Samnites allowed it. Since Rullianus had quelled the Samnites for the moment, he marched north to support Decius' efforts. Allegedly a number of Umbrian tribes left for home when Fabius approached, and his soldiers easily defeated those who remained in the field. The Umbrians surrendered, and Livy notes that Rullianus had won the war that chance had assigned to another.

Perhaps. Certainly no decisive evidence rules out Rullianus' campaign in Umbria but, taken together, the narrative seems overly crammed for a consular year. Fabius' soldiers in Livy's version besieged Nuceria, fought and won a pitched battle against the Samnites – and possibly the Marsi – followed up with a battle against the Paeligni, then marched north to Umbria to fight another battle.[124] It is also difficult to ignore, however, that this story provides a great opportunity for a pro-Fabius writer to syphon a victory from Decius and accrete it to Fabius' string of victories. It would have been an extra advantage to a Fabian fan that the *fasti* offered no details to countermand his modification, such as a triumph for Decius. Scepticism is pardonable.

The Senate made Rullianus proconsul for 307 BC, and Livy drops a fascinating crumb: Appius Claudius, one of the two consuls for that year, strongly opposed a proconsulship for Fabius.[125] Why would that have been? The census of Claudius and Plautius in 312 had been highly controversial. Later, when Rullianus held the censorship alongside Decius Mus, he reversed some important decisions Claudius made. Since Claudius made those decisions back in 312, it is entirely reasonable to suppose the two had political differences of some sort that at least originated in Claudius' censorship. Perhaps this extended to a more general rivalry between the two. Such rivalries were not uncommon.

Reportedly, in 307, Claudius' consular colleague, Lucius Volumnius, campaigned against a new foe, the Sallentini, to the south-east in the arch of the Italian boot. Rullianus attacked the Samnites, while Claudius, says Livy, remained in the city 'to strengthen his power by civil arts'.[126] This seems highly unlikely. At this point in Roman history, to leave an elected consul without a military command and grant that command to a proconsul was not a normal procedure, and it is reasonable to suppose the Senate would not have done it.[127] This may be the result of the sources' not infrequent hostility to Appius Claudius and his alleged plebeian sympathies. In this case the result was the assertion that he remained at Rome, plotting. Unless, of course, he was truly blind – as his *cognomen* Caecus suggested. In this case he may very well have stayed at Rome, though how he would have won election to the consulship in 307 and yet again in 296 is very hard to explain.[128]

Either way, the war against the Samnites dragged on for a few more years. In 304, Samnite envoys came to Rome seeking peace. The Senate declared that one of the consuls, Publius Sempronius, would journey to Samnium with his army and investigate whether the Samnites truly wanted peace or were secretly preparing for another offensive. Sempronius investigated and declared that all appeared peaceful. A treaty was therefore forged between Rome and Samnium.[129]

Fabius Rullianus becomes the Greatest: The Censorship of 304 BC

The year 304 was also politically noteworthy for Rullianus, who won the censorship along with the not-to-be-excluded Publius Decius Mus. Though the consulship was the normal apex of an aristocratic political career, with its access to military commands and thus military glory, the censorship was an extremely prestigious feather for an older and very successful aristocrat. Few could hold the office, for the Romans elected but two censors every five years from among prior consuls. Their powers were extensive. As noted earlier, perhaps most importantly, they conducted the census and recorded the names of citizens and the military obligation each owed based on their wealth. They also created the Senate lists, recording who among Rome's social and economic elite had the privilege to attend and speak in the meetings of the Senate.

During his censorship Rullianus took steps to unravel the measures Appius Claudius had employed in his own censorship of 312, some of which must have been technically in effect for the past eight years. Livy asserts that a 'forum faction' had risen in strength after Claudius' censorship. It was apparently responsible for voting Gnaeus Flavius into office as curule aedile. Flavius' origin was obscure; his father was a freed slave. More problematically to the elite, the sources suggested, Flavius instituted some measures as aedile that ended certain elitist practices by the Roman aristocracy. He publicized the rules and procedures for civil law suits that used to be kept hidden and safe by the pontiffs. He also displayed the calendar around the Forum so that everyone, not just the priests, could know the dates on which it was permissible to hold trials. These steps meant that the aristocrats no longer had a lock on the scheduling and conduct of legal suits. Flavius even managed, through a vote of the assembly, to compel the chief priest to sanctify his dedication of a temple to Concord, though no aedile had ever been allowed to do so.[130] Livy hyperbolically asserted that the election of Flavius by this Forum faction effectively rent the Republic in two. Rullianus restored the balance:

> 'Fabius, for the sake of concord and at the same time to prevent elections remaining in the hands of the lowest-born, sifted out all the Forum crowd, throwing them into four tribes that he called "urban". This, they say, was so warmly welcomed that by such an organization of the orders he gained the cognomen "Maximus" which he had not gained by all his many victories.'[131]

The kernel of truth in this, if any, is hard to pin down, but perhaps Fabius Rullianus, now Fabius Maximus Rullianus, somehow returned the membership of the voting tribes to what it had been before Claudius' censorship. Hyperbole aside, since, from the aristocracy's point of view, Claudius and Plautius had toyed with the list of senators, perhaps they had also made some unpopular reassignments of low-born voters into different voting tribes in a way that, though impenetrable to us, upset the aristocracy. Fabius, then, in an equally murky procedure, restored the balance.

As censor, Fabius Maximus also reformed the ceremony of the *transvectio equitum*. Traditionally, this phrase has been translated as the parade of the knights, 'knights' being an older term English-speaking historians used to refer to the Roman cavalry. The word draws associations with medieval knights, however, and that is decidedly not what the *equites* were in the Roman Republic. 'Parade of the Cavalry' is a more precise term. At Rome, cavalry service was provided by the *equites*, the cavalry class, those men wealthy enough to provide themselves with the horses, equipment and training to serve in mounted combat. Among those liable to provide cavalry service, a select honoured group of 1,200 were supplied with horses at the public's expense – hence *equites equo publico*, 'cavalry with a public horse'. In addition to the state-subsidized horse, these *equites equo publico* had a privileged lead voting spot in the early centuriate assembly.

When it came to actual military use, the earliest cavalry at Rome may in fact have been nothing other than glorified infantry, wealthy Romans who could afford to ride to and from battle, unlike their pedestrian counterparts in the infantry. By the late fourth century, however, the Romans had developed a true cavalry arm, where riders manoeuvred and fought from horseback in coordination with the infantry – though it's worth noting that even then Roman cavalry were often willing to dismount to fight if they felt it was in their interests.[132] Infantry continued to be the decisive combat arm of Roman Republican armies, but in the late fourth century, cavalry became an even more prestigious form of service for the elite youth of Roman society. A parade of the cavalry in the heart of the city, the *Transvectio Equitum*, had existed essentially since the beginning of the Republic.[133] Some sources, Livy among them, attributed the creation of this parade to Maximus. A good case has been made, however, that Fabius did not institute the *Transvectio* but ramped it up into a full military spectacle where the cavalry troopers rode fully armed for battle while wearing any military decorations they had been awarded. This, the argument goes, coincided with a change in practice he instituted as censor where cavalry had to be physically fit to fight if they were to receive a public horse, not just of high birth and wealth. With these changes, the Fabii Maximi became associated with the prestigious cavalry, a connection that would be remembered each year during the parade, as Livy's reference suggests.[134]

Quintus Fabius Rullianus, now called, if he had not been before, Quintus Fabius Maximus Rullianus, had a pretty spectacular career when he retired from the censorship at the end of his term. He cut his teeth in the wars against the hardy Samnites. As Master of the Horse in an important, not to mention tumultuous, campaign, he earned a reputation as a commander. Consul three times, in 322, 310 and 308, he conducted important campaigns against Samnites and Etruscans. Benefiting from family pedigree, senatorial connections and, no doubt, a reputation as a commander of character, he was made proconsul by the Senate in 309 and 307, a recent political and military innovation that allowed Rullianus to continue his grim work against the Samnites and Etruscans. Ultimately, he played a significant role in the campaigns that would lead Rome to dominate Italy. His exploits as a commander had perhaps warranted him an epithet like Maximus. Yet it was reportedly his efforts as censor to restore the balance of power after the upheavals initiated by Appius Claudius that earned him the name. By the time he had ended his censorship, Fabius Maximus was an older man, certainly in his 50s, perhaps in his 60s. Yet his star had not yet dimmed. The battle to come, near the town of Sentinum, would seal his epithet of 'The Greatest'.

Chapter 4

The Battle of Sentinum

Fabius Maximus Rullianus between the Samnite Wars

When Fabius Maximus Rullianus (referred to simply as Fabius in this chapter) held the censorship in 304 and acquired the *cognomen* Maximus, he had a largely unparalleled record in a highly competitive aristocratic arena. The consulship was the pinnacle of an aristocratic career, giving the office-holder a singular opportunity to earn *gloria* as a commander – the military praise that served as social and political currency. As such, the political elite coveted the office and, consequently, took steps to ensure it was not dominated by too small a clique. The most obvious step was the law requiring ten years to pass before a former consul could hold the office again.[1] This law was ignored or overridden at various times in Roman history, but still serves to illustrate the desirability of the consulship. By 304 BC, Fabius had held the consulship three times, twice in the years 310–308. In 304, the three-time consul began his term as censor and made some striking changes to the cavalry and perhaps to the registration of the voting tribes. He cannot have been a young man. If he fulfilled the obligatory ten years of military service before holding his first office, he would have been in his late 20s at least when he held his curule aedileship in 331 – older if he had held the lower post of quaestor first. He was, therefore, at least in his mid-50s, fast approaching, if not at, a venerable age for a Roman, and could be counted as one of the most successful military and political men the Republic had ever seen.

Troubles again with Etruria (302 BC)

A rumbling in the sources about a position for Fabius in 302 can probably be discarded. Some suggested Fabius served as a master of horse in 302, but Livy did not believe them. In their version, when danger flared up among the Etruscans and elsewhere, Marcus Valerius Maximus was appointed dictator. The dictator reportedly went with his subordinate to Etruria, but then travelled back to Rome to retake the auspices. While he was absent, the Master of Horse dispatched foragers whom the enemy ambushed. Readers may rightly be wary that Fabius allegedly again engaged in action without his commander, and the account that the dictator needed to retake the auspices seems to be a poor copy of the incident between Papirius and Fabius a quarter of a century earlier. This episode seems contrived; perhaps the shared *cognomen* of Maximus confused the Roman annalists.

Overall, the handful of years between Fabius' censorship and his next call to command (303–297) were relatively peaceful. War with the Samnites had paused; the two peoples would be at peace for a little while longer. Meanwhile, the plebeians of the Republic gained some important steps in their quest for parity with the patricians. A tribune named Ogulnius passed a law that broke the patrician lock on two critical priesthoods, the pontificate and the augurate, and opened them to plebeians.[2] The pontiffs were the board of priests responsible for overseeing that proper rituals, temples, laws and practices were maintained to please the gods and keep the Republic healthy. The augurs, on the other hand, were responsible for interpreting the will of the gods through divination, especially through observing the flights of birds. Since the gods were believed to be so important to the success and survival of the Republic, these religious positions had great importance to the senatorial aristocracy, and holding one or more positions was an important element in an aristocratic career. That same year, reportedly, the consul Marcus Valerius passed a law through the assembly formalizing every citizen's right to appeal any punishment to the people, as Fabius had done more than two decades past. Overall, though, Livy appears bored with the year: he notes that Valerius conducted an 'insignificant' campaign against rebellious Aequi. Apuleius apparently besieged the Umbrian town of Nequinum, in Livy's day Narnia, but had not wrapped up the action before his year in office ended.

Fabius' name surfaces again in 299. Marcus Fulvius Paetus and Titus Manlius Torquatus were elected consuls, but the election itself was not without an interesting twist. According to Livy's sources, historians Licinius Macer and Aelius Tubero, Fabius Maximus was elected consul by all of the voting centuries of the assembly even though he had not submitted his candidacy.[3] The old warhorse reportedly demurred, suggesting the voters should elect him consul in a year when there was more fighting to be done. At that moment, he could be of service in a more administrative position. Accordingly, these two writers related, Fabius was elected curule aedile alongside Lucius Papirius Cursor (son of the dictator from 325). This is more than a bit odd. The curule aedileship was an important step in an aristocratic career, but a low-ranked one that was not usually repeated. It would be strange for Fabius to hold an essentially non-military post, a low-ranked one at that, and one that gave him the same powers as the son of his rival, particularly if he did tell the assembly not to vote for him until a proper military challenge arose. As it happened, grain supplies were scarce in the city that year, and if it were not for Fabius' steady hand guiding the marketplace, the sources suggested, many Romans would have starved. As aedile, he supposedly authorized an import of grain to counter the drop in supplies. But Livy was uncertain about this account, and the first-century historian Piso had named different aediles for the year. It does seem rather odd for such a distinguished aristocrat to hold such a minor position, but that is not enough to rule out the possibility.[4] That the famous Fabius would become an aedile in the very year when grain supplies ran short, and save the citizenry, seems a bit too good to be true. As we have seen, a great deal of fabricated embellishment was attached to Fabius' name, and this may have been an example.[5]

The Third Samnite War begins (298 BC)

In 298, the short peace with the Samnites ended. Events took a turn that would lead to the last great war with the Samnites and bring Fabius Maximus to centre stage one final glorious time. The Lucanians of southern Italy had refused to ally with the Samnites, who accordingly attacked them. The Lucanians begged the Senate for protection from the Samnites. The Senate hardly had to debate the matter. They eagerly forged a treaty. The fetial priests – charged with ritually declaring war – consequently trekked to Lucania to deliver an ultimatum to the Samnites: leave Lucania or suffer the consequences. Samnite messengers intercepted them on their way and sent them packing with a scarcely veiled threat: the fetial priests had best not deliver the ultimatum to the Samnites, or they would certainly come to some harm. Then, as now, attacking messengers was considered very poor form, though perhaps later Roman historians added this detail of barbarism to make the Roman cause seem more just. Regardless of whether the fetials did receive such a threat, the Senate pushed for war, and the centuriate assembly voted its agreement. War it would be.[6]

The grim realities of a third war against this hardy foe made the citizenry clamour for Fabius, when his name was not among the candidates for 297, or so Livy has it. Fabius, however, refused to stand. He was old and of an age when his physical labours should be at an end. Holding yet another consulship, he predicted, would tempt divine fate itself to strike him down for his hubris. There were more than enough courageous souls from the younger generation to fill all of Rome's needed offices.

Were these sincere claims made by Fabius, political theatre on his part or a rhetorical addition by the sources? It is difficult to know. Livy's sources are closer to the events they described and, presumably, more likely to capture authentic bits of information like Fabius' protest. Is it possible that Fabius engaged in this exchange with the Roman citizenry to gauge his political support? Certainly, but such a manoeuvre – remaining aloof from the election and hoping to get elected anyway – was risky if he truly wanted the position. Still, Fabius may have felt confident enough of his support to take the chance. Effectively being begged to take command again would burnish his reputation brightly. There was no greater foundation for a Roman's political prestige than the claim that he served the Republic when it was in need. On the other hand, he was getting old for a Roman, and he may well have wished to be spared the rigours of command. Judging from his continued commands over the next few years, however, he must have had good health. Whatever his motives may have been, any efforts to dissuade the voters, however, merely fanned their desire to have him lead.

The play was not complete. Fabius demanded that someone publicly read the law that prohibited anyone to be re-elected consul within ten years of having held the office. The assembled citizenry shouted they did not care. Those tribunes of the plebs present insisted they could suspend this law and free Fabius from this limitation. Even if Fabius were angling for the glory of reluctantly accepting a consulship forced on him by the Republic in need, this matter of reading the law on multiple consulships probably should be dismissed as an embellishment fabricated by the sources. Not only had he been elected consul twice in 310–308 without protest in violation of the law, but a careful counting of the years shows that in fact it had been ten years since Fabius last held the office and so he was, in fact, eligible.[7] This is a slip that he presumably would not have made, but certainly the sources for this event could have. In the end it is reasonable to suppose Fabius managed to manipulate events to make his consulship appear a godsend, and then the sources embellished the event further. The centuriate assembly gathered despite his admonishments and named him consul. Before the vote for his colleague began, Fabius, Livy says, essentially told the assembly that if they were going to force him to be consul, they should select his friend Publius Decius Mus to be his colleague. That was good enough for the assembly, which voted accordingly.[8] Taken together, these elements illustrate what Fabius' record suggests; he was a most influential aristocrat with a record of success in elections and general success in commands. He was at the top of his game.

The Fourth Consulship of Fabius Maximus Rullianus and Battle against the Samnites

Fabius' fourth consulship raised him to a level of political success enjoyed by only a few Romans in history. Though he was getting on in years, he clearly was vigorous enough in his command. The consuls planned a two-pronged invasion for 297 BC, with Fabius driving into Samnium to its north-west along a route that passed the colony of Sora. Decius, meanwhile, penetrated Samnite territory further to the south by way of the Sidicinii's territory. When they entered Samnite territory, the Romans started pillaging, systematically cutting a swathe of destruction across the land. Cautious scouting kept the pillagers safe from harm. Unable to ambush the Roman forces, a Samnite army, exceedingly large says Livy, opted to challenge them in the open plains and deployed near Fabius' position.[9] He accepted the challenge, and a battle commenced.

Livy gives some details about this battle and, with some speculation, some missing details can be supplied.[10] The front lines of infantry engaged and neither gained the upper hand. As noted before, one should imagine alternating melees and small withdrawals as the *hastati* or *principes* clashed with their Samnite foes. Not only for use in the initial impact of the battlelines, Roman soldiers would launch *pila* at the foe as available, adding to the damage and disruption their enemies suffered.[11] The conflict must have continued for quite some time with no clear winner; both battlelines remained intact on the field despite what must have been a gruelling struggle. Hoping to tip the balance, Fabius ordered two tribunes to act: his son (also a Quintus Fabius Maximus) and Marcus Valerius. Seek the Roman cavalry forces first, he ordered, rouse them with a speech about their glorious position as cavalry and tell them that, since the infantry could not decide the battle, it fell upon them to charge the enemy formations and scatter their foes. As a clever tactical stroke should the cavalry fail in their task, Fabius ordered a subordinate named Scipio to withdraw with the *hastati* of the first legion, make his way secretly around the enemy forces to high ground and threaten the rear of the Samnite army. That this was possible suggests either that Fabius had not committed all the *hastati* of his legions to battle, or the *hastati* of the first legion had rotated back from the enemy and allowed the *principes* to move forward. Otherwise the *hastati* would have withdrawn while in contact with the Samnite front lines, and that hardly seems like a surprise manoeuvre. Also, Fabius later ordered the *principes* to enter the fray, suggesting that, at this point along the line, the *hastati* were still largely engaged.

The cavalry, Livy reports, charged in front of the army's standards but were unable to disrupt the enemy, who stood firm. If this is indeed what happened, there must have been considerable space between the battlelines at rest, space enough for the cavalry to insert themselves. And if they did attack the heavy infantry from the front, small wonder that they were repulsed. Cavalry, despite fantastical images that persist of horsemen colliding with their pedestrian foes, would have great difficulty assaulting a line of unbroken infantry; the horses would resist mightily any effort to collide with an effective wall of men and shields.[12] So the Samnites must have held firm in the face of the charge, causing the cavalry to veer off, or worse, collide in a tangle of men, arms and horses. Livy preserves a hint of detail: the cavalry 'generated little more panic in the enemy than they did in their own side'.[13] In other words, they were the first to blink in this high-stakes chicken match. Defeated and demoralized, the Roman troopers fled behind the front lines.[14]

Encouraged by the failed attack, the Samnites in the front pushed more vigorously against their Roman foes. Fabius ordered the *principes* into the battle, and they relieved the *hastati* and checked the Samnite rally. At this point Scipio had finished his circuitous trek with the *hastati* maniples, which must have taken some time, and his force revealed their position to the rear of the Samnites with a shout. The Samnites, understandably, were shaken by the threat to their rear. Reportedly, Fabius and his soldiers added fuel to the fire by shouting that Decius' army had arrived and would soon join the fray. The spectre of another army – one that was nowhere near as it happened – tipped the Samnites over the edge. They fled the battlefield, pursued by Roman soldiers eager to slay them. The Romans seized a number of enemy standards and claimed a resounding victory.[15] Meanwhile, Decius claimed his share of success to the south, and the two consular armies continued to pillage the Samnite countryside.

Livy offers a puzzling anecdote for the end of the year. Fabius set out for Rome to hold the elections for the next consuls. The first centuries to vote all wished to make Fabius consul. Somehow, however, Appius Claudius persuaded the voters to name him as the second consul. If the election results stood, both consulships would go to patricians, a direct violation of the Genucian Law of 342 BC. Fabius would not accept his own election, however, insisting he could not hold two consecutive consulships. The nobles – presumably here Livy meant patricians – persisted, begging Fabius to serve and restore the consulships to the patricians. Fabius was firm: he would not be elected by the very assembly he had summoned. The centuries voted again, ultimately, and Lucius Volumnius was elected as Appius Claudius' plebeian colleague.[16] It's an odd story. It gratuitously reintroduces the Struggle of the Orders, and seems to duplicate Fabius' initial refusal to be consul in the elections from the year before. This may well be a spurious story that stuck to the already famous Fabius. It certainly served to illustrate his loyalty to the Republic and its conventions over his own ambitions or those of the patricians. In any case, Fabius and Decius continued their commands for 296 as proconsuls. Decius, in fact, had continued raiding Samnium during the elections, pillaging farmlands and hoping to provoke another Samnite army to battle. None took the bait, however, and Decius escalated operations, shifting from pillaging to an attack on Murgantia, an important fortified Samnite town. The Romans eagerly attacked Murgantia and stormed it swiftly. Several other strongholds followed, including Ferentinum. The sources did not agree which combination of commanders, Fabius, Decius and Volumnius, led these later assaults.[17]

Still more Etruscan troubles and Fabius Maximus' fifth Consulship

Meanwhile, trouble brewed in Etruria where a menacing coalition of Samnites, Etruscans, Umbrians and Gauls began to coalesce. While the other commanders were in the south, Appius Claudius travelled north to meet this threat. He may have engaged in some skirmishes, but seemingly nothing that effectively checked the growing threat to Rome. Subsequently, Volumnius eventually made his way to Etruria with his own forces, leaving the proconsuls in the south. Volumnius joined forces with Appius Claudius, and the two consuls won a victory over the coalition in Etruria, though apparently not a decisive one.[18] Meanwhile, the proconsuls continued their operations in the south. Fabius quelled a rebellion of sorts in Lucania, south of Samnite territory, as Decius continued his operations in Samnium. A Samnite force, however, managed to bypass Decius and invade Campania, wreaking some havoc in the Falernian district. Volumnius, however, had completed his objectives in Etruria, fortunately for the Romans, and arrived in Campania to check the Samnite invaders.[19] But the enemy coalition in Etruria was not pacified, and, with the departure of one of the consuls from the region, troubles continued. Between the fighting in the north and the raid into Campania, Rome was on edge. The law courts were closed for business, a sure sign of emergency. Then the magistrates scraped the barrel with an emergency levy of older men and freed slaves. News of Volumnius' success against the Samnite marauders in Campania, however, calmed the Senate considerably. To lock down control of Campania, the Senate decided to plant two new Latin colonies on its north-west border, Minturnae and Sinuessa.[20]

But the threat in Etruria remained. The consul Claudius apparently wrote a report to the Senate painting a grim picture.[21] A confederation of Rome's enemies – Etruscans and Samnites, Umbrians and Gauls – had joined forces to crush the Romans. Volumnius, presently at Rome, concurred as he addressed assembled citizens about the threat. Something had to be done. Who would command the Roman invasion of Etruria?[22] The centuries reportedly chose Fabius and Volumnius as their consuls. Yet again Fabius, the sources say, resisted the appointment; this was the third time in three years, just in case the reader has lost count, and it shakes credulity to believe he complained this much in any sincere sense. Unable to shake the will of the centuries, he asked for Decius to be selected as his co-consul so that a truly collegial colleague would support him, one who knew his mind and his habits. Volumnius reportedly agreed and the centuries voted their support. Fabius had been elected to his fifth consulship, a record matched only twice in the centuries of the early and middle Republic, once by his grandson.[23]

Despite the supposed harmony between the consuls, trouble bubbled quickly. The patricians manoeuvred to have Fabius assigned the command in Etruria without the customary drawing of lots. Decius, after conferring with some unnamed plebeians, challenged the manoeuvre in the Senate. The matter remained unresolved and was put before an assembly. The consuls pleaded their cases. Fabius' argument was succinct: why had the citizens elected him consul at all, old as he was, if not to fight the foe in Etruria? Decius, too, stayed on point: consuls always drew lots, letting the gods dictate where their provinces would be. However formidable a statesman and general Fabius was, assigning provinces without lots ran counter to cherished custom and personally slighted Decius for good measure. The assembly took Fabius' side; the elder statesman would command in Etruria.[24] The assembly had voted to ignore constitutional custom, another example that the constitution, unwritten and conventional as it was, was often flexibly interpreted when the need arose.

When citizens flocked to serve under him in Etruria, Fabius declared he would levy only a single legion and a large contingent of cavalry, because he was not worried about the enemy's numbers and wanted to make sure there would be plenty of loot to go around for his soldiers. Fabius reportedly moved with this small force to Etruria and relieved Appius Claudius of his command in the winter. Claudius promptly returned to Rome and insisted in the Senate that Fabius needed a colleague and additional forces to handle the dangers in Etruria. Was Claudius playing a game? Judging from their earlier disagreements over the census, the two very well may have been rivals; at least they were likely not on the best of terms. Perhaps Claudius hoped to diminish Fabius' scope for personal glory by insisting he needed Decius' support. If the forces gathering in Etruria were as great as those reported by Livy, however, Claudius probably had a good point. If Fabius had only levied a legion initially, that brashness certainly did not put him in the best light. Fabius supposedly returned, either of his own volition for some business or other, or because the Senate summoned him.[25] He readily agreed to have a colleague accompany him and asked that Decius join him. Did he really have a choice? Given the earlier discord, Fabius seems to have made a virtue out of a necessity. Still, Decius and he had worked together well in the past, so while it may have been a bit embarrassing for Fabius, it was hardly a significant political dent in his reputation. All agreed that Fabius and Decius should unite forces, and the two consuls set off for Etruria.[26]

That the two consuls ultimately prosecuted the war in Etruria together is fairly certain. They commanded perhaps the largest army the Romans had ever fielded. Four legions of citizens and an even greater force of Latin and allied soldiers made up the infantry, so somewhere in the neighbourhood of 40,000 men. A great force of Roman cavalry accompanied the infantry, though whether Livy means their numbers were inflated or they were simply veteran troops is not clear, and that cavalry was bolstered by the addition of 1,000 Campanian cavalry. Nor were these forces Rome's only commitment to the war in Etruria. The propraetors, Gnaeus Fulvius and Lucius Postumius Megellus, commanded smaller armies in the region.[27]

The Battle of Sentinum (295 BC)

In central Umbria, not too far from the Adriatic coast, the consular army met its foe at Sentinum. The enemy formed two armies; one of Samnites and Gauls, the other of Etruscans and Umbrians. Before they could engage the Roman army in a proper battle, Fabius and Decius sent word to the propraetors to ravage the Etruscan frontier and, hopefully, divert some of the enemy forces. The distraction worked, and the Etruscans and Umbrians abandoned their allies to protect their frontiers. A window of opportunity opened for the Romans to attack while the Etruscan and Umbrian contingents were away. After an initial few days of skirmishing, the Samnites and Gauls proved game enough to fight a pitched battle. The armies clashed.[28]

The armies formed for battle, but before the carnage, what seemed to be an omen manifested itself. A wolf on the hunt chased a deer into the space between the armies. The deer broke for the Gallic lines and was slain by a Gallic warrior. The wolf, however, veered to the Romans and passed through the ranks unscathed. Some Romans took it as a good sign, since the wolf represented the Roman patron Mars and had survived, unlike the deer. The story is elaborate and may be an embellishment. Still, the Romans were serious enough about reading divine portents, and in this respect the story has a ring of authenticity that should perhaps be accepted.

Livy's details for the Battle of Sentinum are quite elaborate. He likely had sources with access to valid testimony, since the great battle took place during the lives of the grandfathers of the first historians, Fabius Pictor and Cincius Alimentus. There is every reason to suppose a significant event like this was well reported by those who were present, though likely in a pro-Roman fashion. Indeed, many references to this battle as a turning point exist,[29] but Livy offers the only detailed account of the battle itself. In such circumstances it is perhaps best to consider not whether Livy's battle account was completely accurate, something that cannot really be known, but whether it is a plausible description of a battle that can be supplemented using what we know about ancient battles. In this way, the battle at Sentinum provides a good opportunity to glimpse the Roman Army of the time in action.

The armies formed battlelines, no doubt slowly as thousands of men on both sides moved to their assigned positions. The Samnites deployed on the Roman right against Fabius and two legions. Though they are not mentioned in the deployment, a portion of the allies must have been with them. Decius and the other legions and allies held the Roman left opposite the Gauls. Thanks to the diversion of the Etruscans and Umbrians, the two armies were comparable in size.[30]

The battle likely began, as many did, with skirmishers facing off, duelling, casting javelins at each other and the main battlelines. Then the heavy infantry lumbered forward and the front lines clashed. Livy contrasts the troops under Fabius' and Decius' commands. Fabius' troops fought conservatively, defending more than attacking as the consul instructed. They aimed to prolong the battle and exhaust their foes, likely by defending against a series of clashes initiated by the enemy. Decius, on the other hand, eagerly spurred his troops to advance. They failed to break the Gallic line initially, but must have held their own against the enemy. Eager to break the deadlock, Decius joined his cavalry squads and charged the Gallic cavalry. Presumably he hoped to remove them from the equation. If the enemy cavalry stayed in play, they could not only check the Roman cavalry but threaten the Roman infantry flank. Once they had routed the Gallic horsemen, the Roman cavalry could attack the enemy infantry with impunity. So far, so good; Livy's narrative reasonably captures cavalry's role in battles of the Republic.[31]

The Roman troopers drove back their mounted foes and proceeded to threaten the enemy infantry lines. Ideally, but probably unlikely, the cavalry charge would simply scare off the Gallic infantry. If they remained in place, as these soldiers seem to have done, the Roman cavalry began the grim business of fighting their way into the Gallic flank. This likely involved a slow but steady penetration of the infantry formations, using horse and rider to muscle into the ranks as the horsemen attempted to intimidate and slaughter their pedestrian foes. The Gallic infantry at the extreme right of the battleline must have found themselves in an uncomfortable position, to say the very least, having enemies now to their front and side. Such stressors could only have increased their disruption. Relief soon came in the form of Gallic war wagons, from where it is not entirely clear. Livy asserts that these were unknown to the Romans, and the new noises of the war wagons rolling across the field panicked the Roman horses. A nice detail, but it is unlikely the Romans, who had been fighting Gauls for at least a century, had never encountered such a thing before. Still, the psychological, not to mention physical, impact of these wagons must have been considerable. Whether startled by surprise or simply overcome, the Romans were not able to withstand the wagon charge and fled.[32] At this point some of the Roman horses, with the wagons in pursuit, crashed through the front lines of their own infantry, spreading panic in the ranks. How exactly this should be visualized is not quite clear. It may have been the case that the front lines were in one of their pauses, and this left space for the cavalry to collide with their own infantry. Or perhaps this is simply a dramatic detail that needs to be excised from the account.

The *Devotio* of Decius

Ultimately, Livy's picture of the battle is generally plausible. On the Roman left, the Gauls fended off the initially successful cavalry strike. The cavalry may or may not have disrupted their own infantry, but either way the Gallic infantry rallied and the Romans found themselves hard-pressed. At this point, Livy says, something rather remarkable happened. The consul Decius formally devoted himself and his enemies to the gods of the earth and the ancestors. Essentially, he offered himself as a sacrifice to the gods so that they would destroy Rome's enemies that day. He summoned the pontifex, Marcus Livius, who was serving in the army, and intoned the necessary formulas. The pontifex added to the prayer:

'In addition to the customary formulae, Livius also added that he was driving before him terror and defeat, slaughter and bloodshed, and the wrath of the gods above and below; that he would "smite with deadly curses the standards, spears, and weapons of the enemy"; and that the place of his own destruction would also be that of the Gauls and the Samnites.'[33]

The prayers complete, the bargain made, Decius charged into a thick knot of Gallic infantry, flung himself into their midst and died. Later they would find his body covered by Gallic corpses.

This is not the first time that Livy describes the ritual of devotion. The first time, perhaps suspiciously coincidentally, concerned the consul's father, also P. Decius Mus, and then Livy suggests that there was a recognized procedure to the proceedings.[34] Yet despite the claim of a standard procedure, only the three related men called Decius Mus survive in the sources as Roman commanders who devoted themselves and their enemies to divine destruction. The act itself of willfully seeking death in battle to gain divine sanction for one's comrades was not uncommon in the ancient world. It appears in Roman legends too, like that of Horatius Cocles, a soldier who sacrificed himself to check an army at a bridge along the Tiber and saved Rome.[35] At Rome the practice of devotion developed, perhaps from instances of heroism like this, where a commander could sacrifice himself and his enemies to the gods of the underworld.[36]

Livy describes the ritual in full in his tale of Decius' father, who sacrificed himself in battle against the Latins in 340 BC:

'In the confusion of this movement Decius the consul called out to Marcus Valerius in a loud voice: "we have need of Heaven's help, Marcus Valerius. Come therefore, state pontiff of the Roman People, dictate the words, that I may devote myself to save the legions." The pontiff bade him don the purple-bordered toga, and with veiled head and one hand thrust out from the toga and touching his chin, stand upon a spear that was laid under his feet, and say as follows: "Janus, Jupiter, Father Mars, Quirinus, Bellona, Lares, divine Novensiles, divine Indigites, ye gods in whose power are both we and our enemies, and you, divine Manes, I invoke and worship you, I beseech and crave your favour, that you prosper the might and the victory of the Roman People of the Quirites, and visit the foes of the Roman People of the Quirites with fear, shuddering, and death. As I have pronounced the words, even so in behalf of the republic of the Roman People of the Quirites, and of the army, the legions, the auxiliaries of the Roman People of the Quirites, do I devote the legions and auxiliaries of the enemy, together with myself, to the divine Manes and to Earth." Having uttered this prayer he bade the lictors go to Titus Manlius and lose no time in announcing to his colleague that he had devoted himself for the good of the army. He then girded himself with the Gabinian cincture and vaulting, armed, upon his horse, plunged into the thick of the enemy.'[37]

Decius' grand self-sacrifice at Sentinum galvanized the Roman left. The pontifex, Livius, delegated by Decius, now commanded this wing. He bellowed the news of Rome's divinely sanctioned victory: Decius had given himself as an offering to the gods, and they would destroy his enemies. The Romans fought on.

Meanwhile, Fabius had dispatched *triarii* under Cornelius Scipio and Gaius Marcius to support the left. This is plausible enough. The *triarii* were the final line of heavy infantry, and ordinarily would not engage unless the other lines had failed completely.[38] It should have been simple enough to order the *triarii* on the right to shift left behind the main battleline. At about the point that Decius had sacrificed himself, the *triarii* on the Roman right had traversed to the left. The Gallic infantry in the front lines had apparently been fighting in a looser formation, but at this point decided to close ranks and lock shields. Doing so would protect them more from Roman attacks and make them that much harder to drive back. Scipio and Marcius rallied the Romans in the front, ordering them to grab whatever spears and javelins were at hand in the space between the armies and hurl them at the Gallic shield wall.[39]

While the Roman left ebbed and flowed against the Gauls, the legions under Fabius stood, letting the Samnites tire themselves in attacking. When Fabius judged that their foes' energy had flagged, he dispatched the cavalry to outflank and attack the left of the Samnite infantry. The cavalry harried the Samnite flank, and Roman infantry surged forward from the front. The stress of attack on two sides and the strength of the Roman push caused the Samnite formations to disintegrate under the strain. Livy understates: the Samnites 'failed to stem the assault'. Effectively, they had devolved into a mob of individuals, each frantic to save his own skin. They fled from their positions to their camp, leaving the Gallic infantry vulnerable and alone. Victory was all but secure on the Roman right when Fabius received the news of Decius' sacrifice. He had no time to grieve his friend and took the necessary steps to win the battle. He ordered the elite Campanian cavalry to circle to the Gallic rear and strike the enemy from behind. The *principes* of the third legion would circle too, follow up the cavalry strike and assault the Gallic rear at the point where the cavalry had caused disorder.[40] Again Livy's description points to the importance of morale and orderly formations to the infantry's success. The cavalry used their greater height and mass to work into the less well defended Gallic rear and the *principes* explicitly aimed for the areas of disruption caused by the cavalry, expanding upon the chaos and further demoralizing and disrupting the Gallic soldiers. Worst of all for the Gauls, they would be trapped between Roman forces.

The orders given and the cavalry and *principes* off on their mission, Fabius now moved to obliterate the fleeing Samnite force. He vowed to build a temple to Jupiter Victor, 'Jupiter the Victorious', and to dedicate enemy spoils to the god, the sort of bargain with the gods that Romans not infrequently made to seal their battlefield victories. Then he pursued the Samnites with his infantry. They surged back to their fortified camp, but many remained trapped outside the palisades as those fleeing choked the gates. Here the Samnite general, Gellius Ignatius, fell, valiantly and vainly attempting to rally his forces outside the gates. Soon enough the Romans took the camp itself.

Meanwhile, the Campanian cavalry and *principes* caught the Gallic infantry in the rear, and those enemy formations dissolved in fear. Reports claimed that the Romans felled 25,000 of the enemy that day while losing about 9,000 of their own soldiers.[41] Though ancient casualty figures, really all ancient figures involving the manpower of armies, tend to be inflated, these numbers seem reasonable insofar as the great enemy losses reflect the wholescale slaughter of Samnites and Gauls that day. The estimate for Roman losses is also substantial and likely not understated. Presumably, if the sources lied to exaggerate the Roman victory, they would play down the number of casualties, not inflate them. When the battle finished, Fabius had enemy spoils gathered and burned for Jupiter while Roman scouts searched for Decius' corpse. Once found, under corpses of his enemies, Decius had a proper Roman funeral in the field, and Fabius paid tribute to the heroic commander.[42]

Elsewhere, Roman forces also met with success. The propraetor Fulvius ravaged Etruscan lands and managed to win a solid victory against the Etruscan army that came to check him. The Romans had scored some stunning victories. After the battle, Fabius left Decius' legions to guard Etruria and returned to Rome, where he was granted a triumph against the Gauls, Samnites and Etruscans, a point confirmed by the *Fasti Capitolini*. That is a little troubling, since Livy asserts the Etruscans were not at the Battle of Sentinum. If they were, then Fabius' glory for the victory would only have been greater. However it truly was, Fabius processed with his victorious soldiers through the streets of Rome in a triumph. Livy supposes they followed the normal custom for soldiers to compose and sing crude songs about their general to ward off any divine punishment for hubris. He reports that each soldier received eighty-two bronze coins plus a cloak and a tunic, rewards that, Livy moralizes, 'in those days were not to be looked down upon'.[43]

The Roman victory at Sentinum was clearly significant, a severe blow against the manpower of Rome's enemies. In hindsight, it seems to have been a watershed victory. The Etruscans, Gauls, Samnites and to a lesser extent Umbrians were powerful opponents of Roman expansion. United, they might have checked the Roman domination of Italy in the third century BC. After Sentinum, however, they never united against Rome again.[44] Though the Samnites would thrash against Roman domination once or twice more, history had favoured the Romans in this.

Here at this moment of triumph, Fabius Maximums Rullianus was also at the apex of his career. He was arguably one of the most famous of the Fabii, eclipsed only by his great grandson, Fabius Cunctator, who rescued Rome from catastrophe in the early years of the war against Hannibal. Few contemporaries could match his record of offices and battlefield victories. His legend was preserved and embellished in the later centuries of the Republic as Romans grew eager to maintain the history of their people.

Quintus Fabius Maximus Gurges and the end of the Samnites Wars

Fabius Maximus Rullianus' son, Quintus Fabius Maximus Gurges, by contrast, had the far from enviable position of establishing a name for himself in the shadow of his illustrious father. He may not have been wholly successful. Certainly, it did not help that his detractors labelled him Gurges, 'greedy', after he squandered his inheritance from his father.[45] His career began, typically enough, as a lower official in the *cursus honorum*, probably an aedile, though his official capacity is not recorded. What Livy does record is that Fabius Maximus Gurges fined a bloc of married women for committing adultery. Though it seems a bit like his father's arrest of the poisoners at the beginning of his own career, the reference appears authentic enough. However, the lack of details raises questions. Was there a trial? Presumably. What passed as evidence against the women? Nothing is known. The only additional detail is that Gurges apparently used the fines he levied to build a temple to Venus that still stood in Livy's day, more than two centuries later, an occasional practice of aediles who levied fines, judging from references in Livy.[46]

Q. Fabius Maximus Rullianus
(cos. 322, 310, 308, 297, 295;
dict. 315; cens. 304)

|

Q. Fabius Maximus Gurges
(cos. 292, 276, 265?)

| *son or grandson*

Q. Fabius Maximus Verrucosus
(cos. 233, 228, 215, 214, 209;
dict. 217; cens. 230)

Fabius Gurges, unsurprisingly as the son of perhaps one of the most distinguished Romans of the day, eventually made his way to the coveted office of consul. Livy notes Gurges' election at the end of 293, only a few lines before his monumental history breaks off. Books 11 through to 20 of Livy's history have not survived, either due to the lack of interest among the medieval monks who copied such things, or some series of chance accidents such as fires, floods or any other disasters that consume paper and parchment. Thus an assuredly important source of evidence about Fabius Maximus Gurges' career is lost. Fortunately, there are other sources. During the Roman Empire, a fan of Livy's great work wrote an epitome, a summary of the contents of each of his books. The epitome for Book 11, the one that recorded Fabius Gurges' career, offers a somewhat damning summary:

> 'When the consul Fabius Gurges had fought unsuccessfully against the Samnites and the Senate was deliberating about removing him from the army, his father Fabius Maximus pleaded that this disgrace should not be inflicted on his son; and he swayed the Senate particularly because he promised that he himself would go as a lieutenant to his son, and he carried through on his promise. Aided by his advice and efforts, his son the consul defeated the Samnites and celebrated a triumph; Fabius led the Samnites' commander Gaius Pontius in the triumphal procession and then had him beheaded.'[47]

To summarize a little flippantly what may have been the contemporary Roman perspective, essentially Fabius Gurges required his daddy's help to succeed against the Samnites as they made what would be their final push against Roman domination. The Senate concurred and Rullianus became his son's legate. Apparently Gurges' command was extended and he continued as a proconsul against the Samnites in 291, it seems with his father still serving as legate.[48]

Fragments from some other historians corroborate this basic narrative, but disagree on some of the details. Cassius Dio suggests that Gurges was formally charged in front of an assembly, not the Senate, for his defeat by the Samnites. His father Rullianus spoke for him, however, and rather than defending his son's conduct as such, he listed his own significant services to the state and those of his ancestors, the sort of tack one could well expect from a Roman aristocrat for whom a record of service was political and social currency. Then 'the Romans' decided Rullianus should continue as his son's legate, and, with this assistance, the younger Fabius should be proconsul. The eleventh-century Byzantine chronicler Zonaras, who used Cassius Dio as a direct source, provides a slightly different take. War with the Samnites broke out only after the consuls had been elected, and the Senate decided that more experienced generals should accompany both into battle, Rullianus accompanying his son Gurges. Somehow Gurges took the field before his father had arrived and was defeated by the Samnites. Then he was put on trial and Rullianus promised to chaperone him, however much that phrasing was probably avoided at the time to preserve Fabian dignity.[49] The precise details are unrecoverable from these accounts. The Senate normally determined who the promagistrates of the year were, so perhaps it makes more sense that they debated whether Gurges should continue in command, but we know of several occasions where unsuccessful commanders were charged in front of a citizen assembly. Clearly though, Gurges ran into trouble, experienced a level of public criticism and was required to depend on his father's assistance in the future. One can only imagine the dissatisfaction Gurges must have had being bailed out and monitored by his father. Cassius Dio certainly thought about this, for he reported that Rullianus made sure at all opportunities to let the army know that it was the consul Gurges in command, not he. No doubt, however, Gurges' detractors loved the ammunition, regardless of whether they had the opportunity to use it.

That year (291 BC) there was an interrex. A bit of a problem arose. Lucius Postumius Megellus was interrex but also elected consul by the assembly he presided over for voting, a clear conflict of interest.[50] The matter apparently did not stop the political machinery, and Postumius was duly inaugurated with his colleague Gaius Junius Bubulcus. For the year 291, the Senate had authorized Fabius Gurges as a proconsul, assisted by his legate-father, to continue campaigning in Samnium. A fragment from Dionysius of Halicarnassus' incomplete books 17 and 18 suggests Postumius wrote a letter to Fabius commanding him to evacuate Samnium so that he could rightfully command there as consul. The Senate received word of this and sent a rebuke to Postumius. Postumius reportedly responded curtly. The Senate did not control the consul; rather the consul dictated to the Senate. He entered Samnium with his army and met Fabius as the proconsul was besieging the Samnite town of Cominium. Then he reportedly drove Fabius away, and Fabius, Dionysius notes, 'yielded to [Postumius'] madness'.[51] We hear no more of this unusual and arguably rebellious act on the part of Postumius, nor does he appear as an officeholder again in the sources. One more tantalizing detail: Postumius was formally condemned by the Senate for using his soldiers to work his own farmlands, apparently clearing some sort of grove.[52] Clearly Postumius had some friction with the Senate and with Fabius, but it is not clear how much should be made of this testimony. Still, whatever Postumius did in Samnium, Fabius still managed to campaign successfully. Livy's epitomator notes that Gurges earned a triumph from his victory against the Samnites, and the Samnite general processed as part of the parade and was executed.[53] The *fasti* are damaged at this point, but part of the name 'Maximus' is visible, suggesting support for the version in the summary of Livy. The *fasti* offer no hint that Postumius Megellus earned a triumph, unsurprisingly given his rocky relationship with the Senate.[54]

These were the last throes of the Samnite resistance in the third war. In 290, during the consulship of Publius Cornelius Rufinus and Manius Curius Dentatus, the Samnites met with a final defeat. They surrendered, and the great Samnite wars were over.[55]

Gurges managed to win election to the consulship on two more occasions. This may surprise those unfamiliar with Roman consular elections. As counterintuitive as it may seem, a reputation for tactical and strategic skills was not always considered an essential part of a consular candidate's desirability. This is suggested by the fact that consuls who had been defeated in battle were not demonstrably less likely to win election to a rarer-still second consulship than those who had not lost a battle.[56] Further, Gurges could point to a successful command as proconsul and to his highly impressive lineage, things that would also appeal to the voters. During his consulship of 276, Fabius Gurges apparently campaigned in the south against the never-say-die Samnites, Lucanians and Bruttians, and successfully, judging by the triumph the *fasti* states he earned against the three. This was during the period when the Hellenistic King Pyrrhus of Epirus from the western Balkan peninsula had joined forces with the major Greek city of Tarentum in the arch of the Italian boot. Pyrrhus had stirred up dreams of Italian resistance to Roman hegemony in the south, but not for too long. Bloody and costly victories over the Romans in 280 at Heraclea and 279 at Asculum – from which the phrase 'a pyrrhic victory' was born – were countered by a decisive Roman victory at Beneventum in 275, the year after Fabius' consulship. Gurges' campaigns were planned to pacify southern peoples who hoped to profit from Pyrrhus' early victories.[57]

Fabius Gurges may have held his final consulship in 265, perhaps most important for being the final year before the great wars with Carthage that would occupy the rest of the third century and provide the theatre of glory for Gurges' grandson, Fabius Maximus Cunctator. Gurges' campaign that year, though no doubt important to maintaining Roman influence over Italy, seems far from glorious. It centred around the Etruscan Volsinii. Apparently the lords of Volsinii were embroiled in some manner of serf or slave revolt. They sought Rome's help to quell the uprising – how different from three decades before, when Etruscans clashed with Romans in battle. The Senate dispatched Fabius Gurges with an army to pacify the rebellious rabble. Gurges' army shattered the serfs in battle, and they holed up within the city's defences. Gurges ordered an assault, but while storming the city he died in action, and it was left to his colleague, Lucius Mamilius, to destroy the resistance of the serfs. The Romans starved the serfs into submission, then in a brutal reinforcement of social hierarchy, the consul scourged the rebels to death and razed the city.[58]

Quite some time ago it was suggested that perhaps this Fabius, consul in 265, was not the Gurges who was consul in 292 and 276, but really his son of the same name. This is certainly possible. The consul of 292 would have been at least in his 60s, perhaps too old to campaign. As far as the evidence shows, no Fabius Maximus held office between the consul of 265 and the consulship of Fabius Maximus Cunctator in 233. If the consul of 265 was not Gurges' son, a whole generation passed with no Fabius in the consulship, which is a bit odd for such an influential family. It appears more likely that Gurges' son, father of Quintus Fabius Maximus Cunctator, who was born around 268, was the consul who died in the assault against the serfs of Volsinii.[59] If so, Cunctator really never knew his father, but he assuredly learned of the Fabian legacy.

The Great Delayer: Fabius Maximus Cunctator

From Gurges (consul of 292) or Gurges' son (possibly consul of 265) descended that Fabius who alone could vie with Rullianus as the most famous, the most honoured of the Fabii: Quintus Fabius Maximus Ovicula Verrucosus Cunctator, to list all the *cognomena* he held at one time or another. The age in which he lived was witnessed by many from the senatorial class who left records and wrote histories, though the works of most of them have not survived. Fabius Pictor, Cincius Alimentus and even Cato the Elder were acquainted contemporaries with Cunctator and later generations of Fabii Maximi. And so, hopefully, when the much later first-century AD biographer Plutarch offers a fragment or two about Fabius' youth, it is credible. As his biographer has it, Fabius had a tiny wart above his lip that earned him the *cognomen* Verrucosus, or 'warty'. As a child he was reportedly slow to respond and act, but gentle and kind, earning another *cognomen*, Ovicula, or 'little lamb'. Plutarch makes sure to point out that Fabius was not slow-witted by any means, but simply controlled and stoic – though Plutarch may have just been trying to foreshadow Fabius' famous strategy of delay against the great Carthaginian foe, Hannibal. The suggestion that Fabius trained his body for war and his voice for public speaking, if true, could readily be said of many of his aristocratic contemporaries, a reputation for *virtus* and skill at oratory being critical resources for those seeking pre-eminence in Roman politics.[60] The college of augurs co-opted him into their ranks as a youth. Beyond this and Plutarch's general assertions about his childhood, Fabius Maximus Cunctator remains hidden until his consulship of 233.

The years between 265 and 233 had been momentous for the development of Roman power. Perhaps most importantly, Rome clashed with the powerful maritime empire ruled by the city-state Carthage for control of the strategic island of Sicily. Sicily was centrally located in the Mediterranean, straddling the lucrative trade routes from the eastern shores to the western. It also straddled the middle ground between the regions of North Africa dominated by Carthage and those of Italy dominated by the Romans. In 264, war erupted between the two powers and lasted for more than twenty years. In the process the Romans learned how to use a navy effectively against a maritime power, though horrifically, tens of thousands of fledgling Roman sailors drowned in the process of trial-and-error. When the war ended in 241, the Republic had acquired its first province outside Italy and rolled back Carthaginian influence to the western edge of the island. Frictions between the two hegemonies did not end with the war, however.

In the years between 241 and 218, the start of the second great war against the Carthaginians, the Republic took advantage of Carthaginian weakness in the face of a mercenary revolt to seize control of the islands of Corsica and Sardinia. In 227, two new praetors were added to the existing two and assigned to administer the provinces of Sicily and Sardinia, clear enough sign, if any had doubted it, that the Romans intended to keep their maritime gains.

The year Fabius first held the consulship, 233, he commanded against the Ligurians of north-western Italy. The Ligurians had raided Italy south of the Apennines for some time, until Fabius' army drove them back to their own lands.[61] It is worth noting that for the Romans to send a consul this far north reflected the extent to which they were the leading power in Italy by 233, some sixty years after Sentinum. Fabius celebrated a triumph. Plutarch asserts, rightly as far as can be checked, that this was the only occasion Fabius defeated an enemy in a pitched battle during his lengthy political and military career.[62] During this campaign Fabius dedicated a temple to Honos. Arguably, he hoped to strengthen even further the connection between the Fabii and the Roman cavalry reaffirmed by his ancestor Rullianus' reform of the Parade of Cavalry.[63] Three years later, Fabius won election to the censorship. The office is recorded in the *fasti*, but beyond that nothing is known.[64] In short, Fabius Maximus had reached the pinnacle of success in regular fashion, holding consulship and the rarer censorship. No doubt he enjoyed prestige and position in the senatorial aristocracy, where offices held were a source of rank and influence. Years would pass, however, before the Republic would be forced to fight for its life against a massive Carthaginian invasion, and Fabius Maximus would be called upon in a time of need. Then, his deeds would live on for centuries and earn a lasting place in Roman history.

Chapter 5

Fabius Maximus Cunctator and the War against Hannibal

Fifteen years after Fabius Maximus Verrucosus triumphed over the Ligurian raiders of the Alpine foothills, the Roman Republic would face its greatest challenge yet. Hannibal Barca, son of the Carthaginian general Hamilcar, who had been forced to surrender at the end of the first great war against Rome, would take his revenge. Marching an army from Carthage's Spanish holdings across the Alps and into northern Italy, he plunged into Rome's sphere of influence in early 218 BC. Rome and Carthage were at war again, and the victor of this contest would win the western Mediterranean. The Republic would call upon Fabius Maximus Verrucosus in this time of need, and his service ensured Rome's survival.

Hannibal's Invasion (218 BC)

To understand Fabius' role in the early years of the Second Punic War requires understanding the nature and strength of Hannibal's invasion.[1] After crossing the Alps and entering Italy, Hannibal's forces first clashed with Romans on the banks of the Ticinus River, a tributary extending north from the mighty Po River that drained northern Italy. The Roman army sent to intercept him had not yet made contact. But as scouts from both armies went about their business, the commanders learned how close their enemies were. Both Hannibal and the Roman consul in command, Publius Cornelius Scipio, opted to reconnoitre with their cavalry; Cornelius took the additional step of bringing light infantry along,[2] a reasonable enough precaution. Roman cavalry and light infantry often coordinated their tactics, the infantry providing a flexible defensive line and the cavalry a swift striking arm.[3]

Dust clouds betrayed the approach of both expeditionary forces, and the two commanders marshalled their troops for action. Cornelius deployed the light infantry and Gallic cavalry in the front, followed by the Roman and Italian cavalry. Hannibal led with what Polybius refers to as his 'bridled cavalry'. The distinction here is between the cavalry who rode with typical tack and the light Numidian cavalry who famously manoeuvred their horses with no need for reins or bridle.[4] According to Polybius, the enemy cavalry 'met front to front and for some time maintained an evenly balanced contest'.[5] The Romans engaged in their not uncommon tactic where some cavalry dismounted to fight on foot. Polybius seems to suggest that some of the Carthaginian troopers did the same, with the result that both a cavalry and an infantry battle took place. Livy includes this detail but suggests that the normal tactic of cavalry, dismounted cavalry and infantry fighting together was somehow a mistake that confused and hampered the Romans.[6] Despite his misunderstanding, the sources are clear that while the main forces engaged, the Numidians flanked the Romans and assaulted the rear of their formation. The Roman and Italian cavalry crumpled under the additional vector of attack and scattered across the plain in defeat.[7] Cornelius himself was seriously wounded. Most writers, Livy mused, suggested that his own adolescent son – the future Cornelius Scipio Africanus, nemesis of both Hannibal and, in a different way, Fabius Maximus Verrucosus – rescued him from certain death, though one Roman historian attributed the rescue to a slave.[8] With a cluster of survivors, Cornelius escaped back to camp. Presumably other survivors also made their way back. Though the encounter was minor by Roman and Carthaginian standards, the loss made the Roman commander pause. He withdrew his army to the south side of the Po, tearing up the planking of the bridge as he went to deny the Carthaginians an easy crossing. Hannibal took the opportunity to treat with various Gallic tribes, seeking their assistance in throwing off the shackles of Roman control.

The river forded, Cornelius' army marched to the colony at Placentia and stopped to lick their wounds. Hannibal was not far behind and hoped to push the Roman army into a full-scale battle. Denied that satisfaction, the Carthaginians camped some 4 or 5 miles away.[9] There, Hannibal treated with various Gallic envoys.[10] Though the initial clash with Hannibal had been disheartening, Polybius probably rightly noted that the Romans, upon hearing the news, were still largely confident. They had defeated Carthaginian armies in the past, well within the lifetime of many, and indeed had subjugated most of the Italian peninsula by one way or another. Their armies were essentially intact, so there seemed no reason to fear. Cornelius, wounded and in no condition to launch a second battle, awaited the support of his co-consul, Tiberius Sempronius Longus. Sempronius marched confidently north through Rome, gathered additional levies at Ariminum and joined Cornelius. Rome awaited news of a decisive victory.[11]

Hannibal did not idle away the time. He acquired the nearby Gallic town of Clastidium, surrendered by the Rome-appointed garrison commander. Livy supplies the name and the price: Dasius from the southern Italian city of Brundisium, for 400 gold coins. It was a bargain at any price, for Clastidium stored Roman grain, supplies that the Carthaginians could put to good use fuelling their invasion. Never one to miss a political opportunity, Hannibal rewarded the turncoat commandant and allowed the garrison to leave safely. With any luck, more Italians would follow Dasius' lead and join the Carthaginian cause.[12] Then Hannibal pressed the point for Rome's regional allies: the Romans could not protect them. Detachments of infantry and cavalry scoured the countryside, raiding and pillaging.

The Battle of the Trebia River (218 BC)

Those Gauls still allied with Rome flooded to the Roman encampment, where Sempronius and Cornelius' armies had united, seeking aid from the consuls. Sempronius readily obliged. He dispatched most of his cavalry and 1,000 light infantry to check the Carthaginian raiders. Crossing the Trebia, they clashed with the Carthaginians. The Romans got the better of their enemy until Carthaginian reinforcements from camp entered the mix. Sempronius, monitoring the skirmish from camp, sent the rest of his cavalry and light infantry into the melee. They tipped the balance. Hannibal checked his troops – the time was not right for a general battle – and the Romans won the skirmish.[13]

This soon led to the first pitched battle of the war. Sempronius needed little prompting to seek a decisive engagement, and this trifling victory served. Though eager to fight, Polybius says that Sempronius gave his colleague the courtesy of a consult. Cornelius, still out of action from his wound, urged caution. Sempronius, says Polybius, craved the credit for a major victory while Cornelius was still recovering and the newly elected consuls had not yet entered office.[14] Believing this, however, does not require supposing Polybius could read the minds of the dead. It is plausible enough. Roman aristocrats measured the success of their careers, their lives, using qualities like *gloria*, the praise that accompanied victories, especially battlefield victories. If Sempronius was to monopolize the *gloria* of a decisive victory against Hannibal, he had only a small window within which to act. Hannibal was game enough. Crushing Roman armies in pitched battles was core to his initial strategy. Keeping the Romans on the defensive would encourage his newly won allies and, he likely calculated, win more to the Carthaginian fold. Hannibal chose the terrain, never a good sign for his enemies. On his side of the Trebia lay a plain described by Polybius as 'flat indeed and treeless, but well adapted for an ambuscade, as it was traversed by a water-course with steep banks densely overgrown with brambles and other thorny plants, and here he proposed to lay a stratagem to surprise the enemy'.[15] The stream bed would cloak soldiers-in-hiding, and Hannibal sent his brother Mago with a detachment of 1,000 cavalry and another 1,000 infantry to lurk in the depression. He ordered the remainder of the army to break their fast and prepare for battle. Meanwhile, the Numidian cavalry issued forth to goad the Romans to battle, crossing the river and flinging missiles at the Roman camp. Already spoiling for a fight, Sempronius countered, first with his cavalry, followed soon by 6,000 velites and then the whole of his army. In his haste he sent the troops out before they had eaten their morning meal. To make matters worse, the cold winter snows were falling. The previous night's rains had fed the frigid Trebia too. When the Roman forces forded the river, pursuing the Numidians, the water was chest high on the infantry. When it came time for battle, Polybius pointed out that the cold and hungry Romans stood in stark contrast to their warm and well-fed Carthaginian enemies, and he was probably right to do so.[16]

The Roman forces waded through the frigid river. Hannibal deployed a screening force of some 8,000 spearmen and slingers to occupy them while forming his main battleline. This line, 20,000 strong, consisted of his Spanish, Gallic and African infantry. On each flank he deployed his cavalry, some 10,000 in all and more than double the Roman cavalry forces. He made the additional touch of positioning his remaining elephants on the flanks. Polybius, in his typically terse way, says Sempronius 'drew up his infantry in the usual Roman order'. Presumably he meant the manipular army with its three lines, and an arrangement with the four Roman legions in the centre, the allied infantry on each side and cavalry on the wings.[17]

Sempronius had seriously underestimated the Carthaginian commander and his troops when he allowed his own to wade a wintry river and fight while hungry. Perhaps against a lesser enemy the formidable manipular army would still have won the day. Hannibal, however, had selected the terrain and the time, planted the trap and lured the Romans in. To the extent that any commander can control a battle, he controlled it. Sempronius had two full consular armies under his command, with 16,000 Roman infantry, 20,000 allied infantry and 4,000 cavalry that he distributed on the wings. They approached the Carthaginian forces with measured steps. When they drew close, the light infantry surged forth to begin the struggle. The Roman velites got the worst of it; they laboured in cold, wet clothing and had flung most of their javelins at Numidian cavalry earlier in the day. The preliminary skirmishing done, the light troops retreated through the ranks of the heavy infantry in the main battle line. Then the infantry clashed.[18]

The Carthaginians mauled the Romans that day. Their more numerous, better-rested and fed cavalry drove the hungry and wet Roman cavalry back and exposed the flanks of the Roman infantry. Numidian cavalry and Carthaginian spearmen assailed those vulnerable infantry flanks, making it extremely difficult for them to resist the main attack of the Carthaginian battleline. This was enough to make a grim situation for the Romans. Then the Carthaginian forces lying in ambush stirred into action and sealed the Romans' fate. The Roman army disintegrated, and thousands died. By some miracle, a force of 10,000 Roman infantry in the centre carved their way through the enemy and managed to retreat to Placentia. The rest were slaughtered, captured or lost. It was a striking defeat.[19]

In the aftermath of the bloody battle, Hannibal continued his diplomatic efforts. Roman prisoners were held captive for ransom. Hannibal freed the Italian allies in the Roman army, however, and instructed them to tell their home towns that the Carthaginian general came as a liberator, there to end Roman domination of the peninsula. As winter approached, he encamped his army at Clastidium, where he had seized the Roman supply depot. In the spring of 217, when the bitter winter ebbed, Hannibal's army continued its journey south and entered Etruria.

Disaster at Lake Trasimene (217 BC)

At Rome, Gaius Flaminius and Gnaeus Servilius Geminus won the consulship for 217 and were dispatched with full armies to check the invasion. Calamity followed upon calamity. Flaminius and Servilius occupied Arretium and Ariminum respectively. They seem to have hoped to catch Hannibal between them and crush his army. When Hannibal entered Etruria and his troops began pillaging farmland, Flaminius seems to have believed he could tail Hannibal from behind and herd him toward Servilius. And so Flaminius' army marched. While shadowing Hannibal, Flaminius mistakenly believed the enemy was safely far ahead of him, and deployed no scouts that could have told him otherwise. Thus, the Romans were completely surprised when the Carthaginian army ambushed them along the shores of Lake Trasimene. The Romans journeyed along a narrow route beside the lake. Surprised on the march, many were not even wearing their armour. Some did manage to equip themselves, and a defence was hastily mustered, but the cause was lost. Ten thousand soldiers died on the shores or drowned in the waters; 15,000 were captured. Flaminius died in action, skewered by a Gaul. For good measure, Hannibal overwhelmed the cavalry contingent that the other consul, Servilius, had dispatched to screen his own march westward: 2,000 died and another 2,000 were captured.[20]

Clearly, Hannibal's invasion posed a threat that the Romans were not fully prepared to meet. Generally speaking, the Romans met force with force in their rise to dominate Italy. Their manipular army must have offered some tactical advantages over many of their enemies; Polybius judged it was superior to the phalanx on anything but mostly flat and empty ground.[21] It likely allowed soldiers to be employed more efficiently than less structured warbands of Gauls and Germans. Over the long haul, however, the success of the manipular army was fuelled by the deep reserves of manpower the Romans could summon. This was a product of the extension of the Roman franchise and the development of alliances throughout Italy that brought with them troops. Unsurprisingly, given these advantages after the Latin settlement of 338, the Romans relied on direct confrontation and pitched battles to decide their conflicts with enemy states, not unlike their Greek and Italian rivals. And while the Romans certainly did not win every fight, they won enough that their proclivity for head-on battles was rewarded. The disasters at the Trebia and Lake Trasimene, however, suggested their offensive approach was not working. They had lost two battles. Some 55,000 Roman and allied soldiers were either dead or captured, more than those in the standard consular armies of the year.[22] Hannibal and his army had not been checked or even slowed, and now marauded through areas of Italy that only a generation or two ago had been free from Roman control. What could be done?

The Dictatorship of Fabius Maximus (217 BC)

The grim news of Trasimene, Polybius reports, dismayed the Romans.[23] Rightly so after two major defeats. Polybius continues:

> 'Abandoning therefore the system of government by magistrates elected annually they decided to deal with the present situation more radically, thinking that the state of affairs and the impending peril demanded the appointment of a single general with full powers.'[24]

It's helpful to remember that Polybius' readers were literate Greeks interested in learning more about the Romans. Consequently, he was laying it on a bit thick for an unfamiliar audience. The appointment of dictators had been a regular practice in the past centuries. It is worth noting, however, that while dictators had been chosen often to hold elections and hammer the occasional sacred nail, it had been a little more than thirty years, a generation, since a dictator had been appointed for military purposes.[25] This likely reflected an understanding among aristocrats that the well-established supply of offices, honours and opportunities for *gloria* should not be disrupted, if possible, by giving supreme authority to an individual.

Now Polybius' introduces Fabius Verrucosus to his narrative:

> 'The Romans had appointed as dictator Quintus Fabius [Verrucosus], a man of admirable judgement and great natural gifts, so much so that still in my own day the members of this family bear the name of Maximus, "Greatest", owing to the achievements and success of this man.'[26]

Polybius seems to be mistaken on the point of the *cognomen* Maximus, since, as we have seen, Fabius Rullianus first earned the epithet in 304, and the *fasti* confirm it was held by Verrucosus' ancestors. To be fair, however, Fabius Verrucosus would certainly contribute as much as any in clan Fabius to the *cognomen* Maximus.

Polybius fails to clarify exactly how the Romans came to appoint Fabius, but Livy supplies the missing details. The consuls alone could, in ordinary circumstances, appoint a dictator. These were anything but ordinary circumstances. One of the consuls was dead. The Carthaginian army lay between the second consul and the city, making communication difficult, if not impossible. Rather than standing on ceremony, the practical – and perhaps panicked – Romans summoned an assembly to name a dictator.[27] The assembly chose Fabius to deliver them from the current emergency, and assigned to him M. Minucius Felix as his Master of Horse. That Fabius did not select his own lieutenant would prove eventful, but there likely was no reason to suspect that at the time: the state was in crisis, the people responded and the dictator grasped the reins of power.[28]

Polybius rushes through the next steps, noting only that Fabius sacrificed to the gods and then led a relief force out of the city.[29] Polybius' disinterest in Roman religious scruples did not reflect the Romans' attitudes. Livy supplies plausible enough details.[30] Fabius immediately convened the Senate and persuaded that venerable body that the Romans were in arrears to their gods and payment was due. It probably took little to sell in the present crisis. Accordingly, the Senate ordered the proper officials to dust off and consult the famous Sibylline Books to determine the gods' will. These books came into the Romans' possession some centuries before. As the story went, a mysterious woman offered nine books of prophecy to King Tarquin. Finding the price too steep, Tarquin rejected her offer, whereupon the woman promptly torched three. She then offered the remaining six books for the same price as the original nine. Tarquin had not yet learned his lesson and rejected the second offer. She destroyed an additional three tomes and made a final offer: three books for the original price. Shaken by these events, Tarquin consulted his priests, and they confirmed the books were divine. Tarquin closed the deal and the woman vanished, never to be seen again.[31] Romans consulted these oracular texts when concerned that their relationships with the gods had gone awry. So it was on this occasion. The priests who tended the books reported many debts were owed to the gods. The list shines light on some of the details of Roman religion. Mars was owed a sacred spring; Jupiter demanded games in his honour; and both Mens, the goddess of right thinking, and Venus Erycina required temples. Finally, the Romans owed the gods a *lectisternium*.[32] Livy describes this last ceremony elsewhere in his history:

['F]or eight days [the Romans] appeased Apollo and Latona and Diana, Hercules, Mercury and Neptune, with three couches spread as magnificently as it was then possible to furnish. The rite was also celebrated in private houses. Throughout the whole city doors stood ajar, everything was left out in the open to be shared by anyone who wished, and they say that all visitors – whether known or unknown – were welcomed hospitably, while people exchanged friendly and courteous words with their enemies, setting aside their quarrels and disputes. Prisoners too were freed from their chains for those days; and afterwards they felt [it was wrong to imprison again] those whom the gods had helped in this way.'[33]

In these ways the Romans hoped to placate their angry gods. Among this list of obligations, the temple to Venus Erycina stands out. Her cult was established when the Romans took the Sicilian town of Eryx from the Carthaginians in the First Punic War. It recalled the stalwart defence of the citadel from Hamilcar's attempts to storm it. The symbolism was clear; Rome would again withstand the assault of a Barca, this time Hamilcar's son, Hannibal.[34]

Fabius' Master of Horse, Minucius, did not rest either, but dedicated an altar to Hercules. The choice begs for a moment's consideration. Ostensibly this dedication linked Minucius to a legendary hero, a good way to boost his image and stir Roman confidence. The Fabii, however, had claimed their descent from the demigod Hercules for some time, and it is hard not to see Minucius' choice, in light of the future discord the two soon had, as a jab at his superior, Fabius.[35] Overall though, the religious devotions supervised by Fabius indicated he had a strong grasp on the importance of religious scruples to the Romans. Disasters of the sort they had recently experienced surely meant that the crucial *pax deorum*, the 'peace of the gods', had been disrupted and needed to be set right.

Next came the matter of replacing those soldiers who had fallen at Trasimene. The Senate authorized Fabius to levy fresh troops as he saw fit and add them to the consul Servilius' army. Accordingly, Fabius recruited two new legions and ordered them to muster in Tibur to the north-east of Rome. His next move reveals that he already had at least the kernel of a strategy in mind. He decreed that all those in the path of Hannibal's raids should destroy their farms, especially the crops, and flee, leaving nothing for the marauders.[36]

Or so Livy would have it. There are good grounds, however, for doubting that Fabius made such a decree, or at least whether inhabitants of the Italian countryside effectively followed it. Not only does Polybius fail to mention any decree; quite simply, Hannibal seems to have had no difficulty obtaining food for his army.[37] He ransacked the countryside, drawing food and plunder from the essentially defenceless local populations as his army worked its way south through Umbria and Picenum to the shores of Apulia in south-east Italy, pitching camp near the blue waters of the Adriatic. There his army rested and recovered, fully supplied by its depredations of the countryside.[38] It was during this respite that Hannibal's African infantry equipped themselves in Roman armour and weapons looted from thousands of corpses.

Decree or no decree, Fabius left the city to attend to religious matters while he tended to the military. Livy preserves an anecdote. Fabius left the city along the Flaminian Way to the north-east. He spied in the distance the consul Servilius closing with a cavalry squad. Fabius sent a messenger to remind the consul of ancient protocol: the consul must approach the dictator without his lictors, the attendants who marked the offices of consuls, praetors and dictators. Servilius complied and bystanders realized they had witnessed the authority of the dictator.[39] It's a good story, custom tailored to emphasize Fabius' gravitas, but does it run afoul of other evidence? Livy says that dictatorship had been so little used that it had been blotted from the memory of Fabius' contemporaries. Solid evidence suggested, however, that Fabius himself had been dictator just a few years prior. Indeed, Livy apparently forgot his own reference several chapters earlier, that Fabius had been named dictator for the second time.[40]

Political theatre this may have been, but Fabius may also have been testing the waters. It had been over thirty years since a dictator had been appointed to command the armies. The moment of crisis had arrived in the war against Hannibal, and Fabius was about to initiate a strategy that would be controversial and allow for no division among those in control of the legions. He had to assert his supreme control as dictator. He may well have exerted his authority over Servilius as an object lesson. In any event, he assumed control of the consul's army, reinforced with the newly raised legions. Presumably informed of the Carthaginians' movements, Fabius led the reinforced army to Apulia and encamped near the city of Aecae, several miles from Hannibal's force.[41] Hannibal, game to school the Romans yet again, drew out his forces in battle order and hoped Fabius would commit. He waited, then waited some more, but Fabius refused to play the Carthaginian's game.

At this point in his narrative, Polybius sketches Fabius' plan. It is lengthy but worth quoting in full:

'For the enemy's forces had been trained in actual warfare constantly from their earliest youth, they had a general who had been brought up together with them and was accustomed from childhood to operations in the field, they had won many battles in Spain and had twice in succession beaten the Romans and their allies, and what was most important, they had cast to the winds everything else, and their only hope of safety lay in victory. The circumstances of the Roman army were the exact opposite, and therefore Fabius was not able to meet the enemy in a general battle, as it would evidently result in a reverse, but on due consideration he fell back on those means in which the Romans had the advantage, confined himself to these, and regulated his conduct of the war thereby. These advantages of the Romans lay in inexhaustible supplies of provisions and men. He, therefore, during the period which followed continued to move parallel to the enemy, always occupying in advance the positions which his knowledge of the country told him were the most advantageous. Having always a plentiful store of provisions in his rear he never allowed his soldiers to forage or to straggle from the camp on any pretext, but keeping them continually massed together watched for such opportunities as time and place afforded. In this manner he continued to take or kill numbers of the enemy, who despising him had strayed far from their own camp in foraging. He acted so in order, on the one hand, to keep on reducing the strictly limited numbers of the enemy, and, on the other, with the view of gradually strengthening and restoring by partial successes the spirits of his own troops, broken as they were by the general reverses. He was, however, not at all disposed to respond to the enemy's challenge and meet him in a set battle.'[42]

Here we have the basics of Fabius' strategy, and Livy offers essentially the same summary.[43] Keep this new Roman army safe in camp. Take advantage of abundant supplies and forbid any foraging by Roman soldiers, for journeying away from the safety of camp would only invite disaster. Avoid pitched battles. Snare and slaughter Carthaginian soldiers foolish enough to forage too far from camp. Above all, play for time. The Romans could draw from deep wells of manpower and food; they could afford to wait. Time would increase their soldiers' confidence as they whittled away the enemy by killing those who strayed too far from the Carthaginian pickets. Eventually, Fortune would offer a suitable chance to check Hannibal.[44] For the Romans, used to head-on confrontations, however, this would not be a popular strategy.

Unable to compel Fabius to battle, Hannibal marched his army westwards. The Carthaginians entered Samnium, ravaging the fields of the Roman colony Beneventum. Subsequently, they seized the unfortified town of Telesia. Hannibal planned, it seems, to provoke the Romans to battle by attacking their allies. Fabius proved imperturbable. His army trailed Hannibal's along the high ground, hounding the Carthaginians but refusing to engage.[45] Fabius crossed lands that his father – or grandfather – Fabius Maximus Gurges had stood and fought on, something he was no doubt aware of, but he remained firm in purpose. From Samnium, the Carthaginian army and its Roman shadow trekked west to the fertile plains of Campania. Hannibal camped in the Falernum district on the northern end of Campania and let slip his marauders to plunder the countryside. He had the advantage: either he would compel the Romans to do battle or their timidity would alienate their allies as the Carthaginians despoiled the plains. Indeed, Fabius did follow the Carthaginians to Campania, perhaps at the instigation of Minucius. The dictator's iron resolve, however, kept the Romans camped on the heights of Monte Massico north of Falernum, waiting, watching.[46] Consequently, the Carthaginians plundered freely, amassing supplies as the Romans watched.[47] Their far greater numbers of cavalry largely guaranteed their foragers' safety.

The more historically minded of the Romans might have noted the strategy of this Fabius Maximus was a far cry from the exploits of the great Fabius Rullianus at Sentinum. Even those less aware of the Fabian pedigree knew that avoiding decisive battles, even if a sound strategy at the moment, was not a particularly Roman custom. This policy of waiting could not have sat well with many Romans at home and in the army. Minucius and some officers chafed to engage Hannibal. Perhaps they communicated their distress with Fabius. Certainly Polybius says Minucius took every opportunity to criticize Fabius. Perhaps those disagreements reared up in the council of officers. Plutarch suggests the very army preferred Minucius over Fabius.[48] Livy imagines a rant Minucius hurled at his general.[49] It is more than a little puzzling, however, to figure out how Minucius could engage in that level of insubordination without earning severe penalties from the dictator. Perhaps here Livy, or his sources, simply supposed Minucius' later disagreement must have been vented early on. There is another possibility. Since Minucius had been selected by the people, not appointed by Fabius, the dictator technically was not able to curb his Master of Horse. Ultimately, Fabius must have been well aware of the criticisms of his strategy in the camp and in the city.

Late in the summer, Hannibal determined to find suitable winter quarters outside Campania. Polybius simply notes that Hannibal wished to relocate, but gives no reason other than that he wanted a place where he could collect his army's loot for the winter.[50] Livy states that the Carthaginians would soon exhaust the food supply of the region, but Campania was one of the most fertile regions of Italy and Livy had a habit of inventing hardship for the Carthaginian army where none probably existed.[51] Hannibal must have had other reasons for wishing to leave Campania. Perhaps the fact that just a few mountain passes controlled access to and from it, and he did not want to be bottled up in the region. Perhaps he desired access to the sea at this early stage, but dared not besiege Neapolis with Fabius' army lurking behind him.

Regardless of his reasoning, an opportunity had materialized to snare the Carthaginian, and Fabius acted. He anticipated Hannibal's exit route and prepared a counter. A large detachment, some 4,000 Romans, occupied the obvious pass Hannibal would need to take while the rest of the army occupied a nearby hill in plain sight of the pass.[52] The Romans had the high ground and the advantage. Hannibal clearly understood this, for he tried once again to coax the Romans into the plain and a set battle, but in vain. Fabius would neither descend to do battle nor concede the pass. The Carthaginians could certainly attack the Roman positions, but they would fight at a substantial disadvantage. Hannibal, however, had a plan, unorthodox but very clever. It went like this. His troops corralled 2,000 cattle and lashed dry wood to their horns. When night fell and obscured their activities, he ordered servants in the Carthaginian camp to ignite the wood and led the bovine torches to a high point near the pass, followed by Carthaginian spearmen. The Romans occupying the pass mistook the many fires for the torches of the enemy and left their position to challenge these decoys. This gave Hannibal time to escape with his army through the now unguarded pass. Adding insult to injury, in the morning Hannibal sent a unit to retrieve the spearmen who had goaded the cattle, and they did so successfully, killing 1,000 Romans in the process. Throughout all of this, the main army under Fabius' command remained in camp, the dictator refusing to be drawn into what he suspected was a trap.[53]

This appeared, by most standards, a serious blunder. Fabius had let an entire army escape when his forces occupied the high ground exiting the plain. Was not the point of Fabius' strategy to prey on foragers and stragglers, and wait to force a battle on advantageous terms? If the dictator would not fight under such favourable circumstances, what good was he? Such apparently was the logic of many Romans, for once word of this missed opportunity reached Rome, public opinion soured against his strategy.[54] It was at this time that Fabius was summoned to Rome to address religious matters, a point upon which Polybius and Livy agreed.[55] Some modern historians argue that this was merely a cover for the real issue: Fabius' policy had quickly grown unpopular and he was summoned to answer for his decisions.[56] Perhaps. Still, we have seen several occasions where Roman commanders had to pay extra attention to religious obligations. The two motives are not mutually exclusive, and the Romans were willing enough to recall even successful commanders to supervise the necessary rituals. Wartime was no time to neglect the gods. Certainly once Fabius returned to the city, he could easily be called upon to answer for his conduct.

Fabius had to leave the army to Minucius' care. According to Livy, Fabius all but begged Minucius to continue his strategy: dog the Carthaginians but avoid pitched battles. Perhaps, as Livy suggests, Fabius pointed out the advantages of the strategy and the critical respite the Romans had gained simply by avoiding any more disastrous battles with Hannibal.[57] The Roman army initially kept to the plan. As Hannibal's forces trudged eastward, working their way back to Apulia, the Romans followed behind.

At Rome, political pressure had been building against Fabius, and the fiasco in Falernum cannot have helped the dictator's image. Livy says two additional factors further damaged Fabius' standing. The first was that Fabius' farm, which lay within the area despoiled by the Carthaginians that summer, had been left untouched by Hannibal. The Carthaginian hoped thereby that the Romans would suspect Fabius of colluding with the enemy. Second, Fabius had apparently exchanged prisoners with Hannibal, following a protocol that had been established in the first great war against the Carthaginians. He did not consult the Senate in this, however, and accordingly the Senate was slow to grant funds for the trade. Fabius managed to solve both these problems in a stroke. He tasked his son with selling the unspoiled estate and used the proceeds for the ransom.[58]

Meanwhile, Hannibal's scouts reported Apulia had an ample food supply, and the army worked its way there. A town in the region called Gereonium seemed to be an ideal spot for a supply depot. The town rebuffed Hannibal's overtures, however, so he quickly captured the city. Slaughtering the inhabitants, Hannibal used the now-empty buildings as grain magazines. Then he established a fortified camp outside the town, complete with a trench and palisade. From this position, Hannibal dispatched foraging parties throughout the region. Despite his alleged eagerness to engage Hannibal, Minucius cannot have shadowed the Carthaginians too closely, for he only received word of Gereonium's fate after the fact.[59]

Once he arrived in Apulia, the new Roman commander forsook the protection of the hills and marched his army down onto the plain. Now the two camps were separated by a single hill that offered a tactical advantage to the occupier. Hannibal sent troops to take the position by night: Polybius says they were spearmen, but Livy asserts they were Numidian cavalry; perhaps they were both.[60] Minucius dispatched a force to scatter the troops, and the Romans moved their camp to the hill. The two armies were very close now. When Minucius formed his battleline, it occupied all the space between the camps. Now it was Minucius who hoped to goad his opponent into battle. Hannibal had been compelled to send many of his soldiers out in foraging parties, however, and now he refused to engage. While the Roman force lay deployed outside Hannibal's camp, Minucius also dispatched cavalry and light infantry to harass the Carthaginian foragers, apparently with some success. The Roman army was eager to act and began to assault the palisade walls of Hannibal's camp – whether on Minucius' orders is not clear – when Hasdrubal arrived with some 4,000 foragers to relieve the Carthaginian camp. Bolstered by these reinforcements, Hannibal's forces issued forth from their own camp. Somehow a pitched battle seems to have been avoided, but the sources say that the Romans got the better of the Carthaginians that day, killing a number of foragers and troops at the camp. Certainly, Hannibal found his current position untenable, and withdrew the short distance back to the stronger camp at Gereonium.[61] Minucius judged this a victory, and apparently it was received as one back in Rome.

In the city, rumour of Minucius' success kindled animosity against Fabius and his strategy. Fabius' prudence smacked too much of cowardice. Polybius is terse on the form opposition to Fabius' strategy took, and we must turn to Livy and Plutarch to tease out the details. Apparently a tribune of the plebs, Marcus Metilius, spoke at the *rostra*, the platform crafted from the bronze rams of enemy warships. He excoriated Fabius for his timid treatment of Hannibal, and extolled Minucius. It was not uncommon in the Republic, not even during the war against Hannibal, for a tribune to challenge publicly a more established aristocrat in the hopes of acquiring fame. In this particular case, however, what the tribune proposed was remarkable: the Roman assembly should grant Minucius dictatorial powers, effectively making his authority equal to that of Fabius.[62]

Livy implies that this challenge to Fabius developed over a few days. Metilius first proposed the change in Minucius' official status. Fabius, in turn, refused to address the people directly, but spoke in the Senate several times and, as part of his duties, held elections for a replacement consul.[63] Indeed, in Livy's version Fabius left in the night to return to his army before the assembly voted on Minucius.[64] Livy also identifies another player, Gaius Terentius Varro. This rising politician, whom we will encounter again later, had held the praetorship in 218. He, like Metilius, reportedly aspired to exploit the dictator's stumbles, gaining political favour by attacking the unpopular politician. Livy asserts he was the only one who had the courage to urge the proposal forward.

Plutarch – who ultimately, it should be noted, may have relied on Livy's account – compresses events. In his version, Metilius delivered a diatribe against Fabius, who countered with his own speech to the assembly. He made a simple point. He must finish the necessary sacrifices and return to the army so that he could punish his Master of Horse for expressly disobeying his orders.[65] This threat prompted Metilius to propose the assembly bestow dictatorial powers on Minucius.[66] According to Plutarch's reckoning, the whole matter could have taken as little as a day. More likely, as Livy seems to imply, the whole process took at least a few days to allow for sacrifices, assemblies, proposals and votes. It is also more likely to suppose that Metilius made the proposal. Varro, currently a senator but not holding public office, may have spoken in favour of the motion to raise Minucius, perhaps even worked with Metilius, but Metilius was tribune and had the legal power to summon the popular assembly to a vote.

Either before he left the city or on his way back to the army, Fabius learned of the assembly's decision to raise Minucius to equal status. What happened next varies slightly from source to source. All agreed that Fabius was unruffled, publicly at least, about the change. All agreed Minucius crowed about his unexpected rise. These characterizations, however, smack of a morality tale designed to contrast Fabius' measured patience with Minucius' brashness. The dramatic effect suffered if Fabius bemoaned his fate while Minucius humbly assumed his new command. Still, it is difficult to imagine that these men had no rancour for each other, regardless of how they chose to bear it. But what did it mean for practical purposes to have two equally ranked supreme commanders? There were two options, essentially those employed by consuls in joint command: divide the army or alternate command of the whole army daily. One can only imagine whether this meeting between the two commanders was clipped and cold or hyperbolic and heated. Regardless of who suggested it, the commanders opted to split the army.[67]

When Hannibal heard the news, he crafted a plan to crush Minucius. As so often seemed the case, yet another hill between enemy camps served as the point of contention. The crest brought with it command of the surrounding plain. That plain had many hollows in which soldiers could readily hide. It was perfect terrain for an ambush, and ambushes were this Carthaginian's trade. Hannibal, accordingly, dispatched 500 cavalry and 5,000 infantry to lurk in the depressions and await the opportunity to ambush the Roman forces. He assigned a small force to take the hill, wagering this would eventually draw Minucius' legions into a full battle. Never slow to be provoked, Minucius sent light infantry with cavalry support to claim the hilltop. Hannibal's plan worked. Minucius ordered the legions into action, and the Roman heavy infantry followed its vanguard, ready for a fight. The expeditionary forces clashed on the hilltop, light infantry tailed by cavalry on both sides. The Punic cavalry enjoyed their usual superiority in numbers and dominated the encounter, repelling the Roman light infantry and, presumably, the cavalry. Rebounding velites collided with their own heavy infantry, causing some disruption among the more orderly soldiers. Then the trap was sprung. Minucius' legions faced an enemy on higher ground to the front, which was bad enough. Worse still, Carthaginian troops streamed from the hollows and hammered the Roman flanks and rear. Under this pressure, the orderly Roman formations dissolved, and the soldiers clumped together around the legions' standards. Many lay dead and dying. Minucius' command – and his life it seemed – would not last much longer.[68]

Encamped nearby, Fabius watched Minucius' position deteriorate. Livy and Plutarch seize this moment in their accounts to bludgeon readers with yet another example of Fabius' superior character. 'There it is,' Livy had Fabius declare once the plight of Minucius' army was clear,

> 'Misfortune has not overtaken rashness more quickly than I feared. Though made equal to Fabius in authority, [Minucius] finds Hannibal his superior, both in courage and in fortune. But another time will do for upbraiding and resentment; for the present, march out from your trenches, and let us wrest from the enemy his victory and from our fellow citizens a confession of their blunder.'[69]

Plutarch attributes similar words to the dictator. Neither was in a position to know what was said. Still, they surely could read the situation as easily as we. Minucius had blundered, and Hannibal exploited the opportunity. But the image passed down over the centuries of Fabius Maximus Cunctator, 'the delayer', would not allow for a moment of sour grapes. Still, whether he raged or remained a paragon of placidity, there was nothing practical for Fabius' force to do but try to rescue the trapped legions. Fabius' army reached the legions just in time, coming up from the rear and drawing their defeated comrades through their ranks to safety.[70] Now faced with an organized force of fresh troops, Hannibal declined further engagement. He kept a garrison force on the hill just won and withdrew most of his troops to their camp by Gereonium.

Meanwhile, the Roman forces and commanders reconciled. There were likely harsh sentiments harboured by both commanders, and certainly the ancients recognized this as well. Polybius noted, 'To those who were actually present at the action, it was evident that all was lost by the rashness of Minucius, and that now, as on previous occasions, all had been saved by the caution of Fabius.' Livy develops this moral into an entire scene. First Minucius gulped down some crow, telling his army:

> 'Soldiers, I have often heard that the best man is he who can himself advise us what is profitable; the next best he who listens to good advice; but that he who can neither counsel well nor obey another has the meanest capacity of

all. Since to us the first rank of intelligence and capacity has been denied, let us hold fast to the second or middle state, and while we are learning to command, make up our minds to obey a man of wisdom. Let us join our camp to that of Fabius; and when we have brought our standards to his tent, and I have given him the name of "Father" – as befits his goodness to us and his great position – you, soldiers, will salute as "patrons" those whose hands and swords just now protected you; and, if nothing else, this day shall at least have conferred on us the glory of possessing thankful hearts.'[71]

Fabius, says Livy, received Minucius and his apology with a simple handclasp of forgiveness. He had a magnificent opportunity to say, 'I told you so.' Whether he took that opportunity remains an open question.

With Hannibal retired to winter camp and the Roman army largely intact, the conflict subsided somewhat. The dictator and his lieutenant laid down their offices, new magistrates were elected for the coming year and Romans waited to see what spring would bring.

This is as good a time as any to consider for a moment what exactly Fabius had accomplished during his term as dictator. Perhaps most importantly, after two horrific defeats in as many years, Fabius prevented Hannibal from destroying another Roman army. Critically, the Roman alliance system still held firm for the most part. So, really, Fabius gained the Romans a respite, and quite likely that lull allowed the Romans to regain some confidence. More importantly, arguably, his time as dictator illustrated that something different than an unimaginitive aggressive strategy was called for. The Romans needed to consider quite carefully how and when they would encounter Hannibal.

Turmoil in the Consular Elections for 216

Lest we forget how problematic the evidence for third-century Romans often is, even in the well-documented Second Punic War, Livy follows up his account of Fabius' dictatorship with this seemingly hair-pulling nugget:

'Nearly all the annalists state that Fabius was dictator in his campaign against Hannibal; [The Roman historian] Coelius even writes that he was the first to be created dictator by the people. But Coelius and the rest forget that only the consul Gnaeus Servilius, who was then far away in his province of Gaul, had the right of naming a dictator. It was because the nation, appalled by their great disaster, could not put up with so long a delay that resort was had to the popular election of an acting dictator. Thereafter the general's successes and his great renown, and the additions which his descendant made to the inscription which accompanies his portrait, led easily to the belief that one who had been made acting dictator had been dictator.'[72]

One modern historian supposed, based on the original Latin, that not all sources agreed Fabius indeed commanded against Hannibal at all.[73] An easier reading, given the context, supported by the various translators, is that Livy's sources agreed Fabius was in command, but simply disagreed what office he held and what the constitutional basis of that office was.[74]

The exact order of events surrounding the end of the dictatorship and the resumption of normal elected magistracies is murky to be sure. At the end of his term, Livy recounts, 'The dictator had sent for Servilius and for Marcus Atilius his colleague, to take over his armies, for his six-months tenure of authority was drawing to a close.' When Fabius and Minucius relinquished their offices, military command returned to the consuls of 217. They continued in their posts through the autumn and winter. According to Livy,

> ['The consuls] constructed winter quarters early and, in complete harmony, spent the rest of the autumn prosecuting the war with Fabius' tactics. When Hannibal went out to forage, they would appear at the appropriate moment at various points, hounding his column and waylaying stragglers. They would not risk an all-out battle, which the enemy was doing all he could to bring on, and Hannibal was reduced to such a state of deprivation that he would have headed back to Gaul had he not feared that his leaving would be necessarily seen as flight. For he was left with no hope of provisioning his army in those parts, if the incoming consuls followed the same tactics for the war.'[75]

Polybius, however, states that the dictators Fabius and Minucius did not retire from office until the new consuls for 216 assumed office. At this point, the commands of the two consuls of 217 were extended, both now serving as proconsuls.[76] The new consul, Aemilius Paullus, commanded the proconsuls to avoid pitched battle and instead skirmish regularly with the enemy to train and instill confidence in the legionaries. Servilius, Polybius notes, followed these orders to the letter and limited his army to small operations. In these small clashes, the proconsuls' actions were 'both skillful and courageous'.[77]

The discrepancies about the transfer of power are problematic, but not worth getting bogged down in. Both sources agree there was a period between Fabius' retirement and assumption of command by the newly elected consuls for 216. In that period, the consuls of 217, at least Servilius, commanded the Roman troops in Apulia. More important is the seeming difference in Polybius and Livy's analysis of the period under Servilius. Livy clearly states that the Romans, by adopting Fabius' strategy, were successfully starving the Carthaginian forces. Polybius offers no such judgment. As we have seen, it is something of an open question exactly how much Fabius' strategy for 217 caused actual hardship for the Carthaginian army.[78] It is a good time to remember, however, Polybius' ultimate assessment. Fabius' strategy was not to starve the Carthaginians but to take advantage of their need to forage by attacking straggling foragers, while building Roman confidence and waiting for opportune moments to attack.[79]

Still, this is not the only place where the two historians differ. Polybius spares few words for the consular elections for 216, simply noting that Lucius Aemilius Paullus and Gaius Terentius Varro were selected.[80] Livy, in contrast, reports a heated political contest.[81] At the centre of the storm was the successful plebeian candidate of the year, Gaius Terentius Varro. The ancient sources have little good to say about Varro. In Livy's estimation he was no more than a demagogue who attacked Fabius during the latter's dictatorship to win influence with the crowds and, ultimately, political support for his own ambitions.[82] In this section, Livy's wording is ambiguous. He asserts that Varro was opposed by the '*patres*'. The word literally translates as 'fathers', which can mean two things in this context. Either Livy is referring to the senatorial group as a whole, or he is referring specifically to the patricians, that small pedigreed group of Romans.[83]

We have seen the Conflict of the Orders rear its head in all manner of accounts about the Fabii. In this case it is less plausible to suppose that the largely resolved struggles between patrician and plebeian were the main issue. Rather, in the more than a century old patrician-plebeian aristocracy where ancestors' offices were a most important source of entitlement, the conflict was more likely about the feared demagoguery of a *novus homo*, a 'new man', whose ancestors had not held the consulship. Or perhaps the conflict was over, in fact, the approach to the war, since Varro seemed to oppose Fabius' policies.[84]

Despite any opposition, Varro won his consulship. It remained for the assembly to choose his patrician colleague. Livy suggests the rival patrician candidates withdrew their names at this point, and Lucius Aemilius Paullus ran unopposed. This was, suggested Livy, part of a senatorial plot to find a colleague who could check Varro's power. Perhaps: not all senators, after all, opposed him. The support of the tribune Baebius demonstrates this. But it may be that the highest pedigreed senators, those with ancestors that had held the consulship, resisted Varro. Ultimately, the true nature of the electoral politics for that year are lost in the shadow. The result, however, is clear: Terentius Varro and Aemilius Paullus took the consulship.[85]

The winter slipped away and the spring brought ripened crops that could supply the Carthaginian host. Accordingly, Hannibal shifted his troops out of Gereonium, marched to the south-east and seized the citadel of Cannae. It was a choice that underscored the critical importance of supplies in the war. The city itself was in ruins, but the citadel had served as a Roman supply depot. Hannibal seized the supplies and the strategic position, no doubt dismaying the Romans mightily in the process.[86] The proconsul, Servilius, had done nothing to check Hannibal here, perhaps unable to do so without violating his orders and engaging in a full battle with the Carthaginian. Once Cannae was lost, Servilius peppered the Senate with missives seeking further instructions. Closing with the Carthaginian force at Cannae would spark a pitched battle, the proconsul noted in these letters. He also noted the painfully obvious: Hannibal was again devastating the countryside of Rome's allies while the Romans appeared to do little more than watch. Polybius asserts that the Senate at this point determined to engage Hannibal in a set battle, but ordered Servilius to wait for the new consuls to arrive.[87]

Then the Senate augmented the field armies of the year. Polybius says that the Romans opted to field eight legions this year and levied four new ones to complement the existing field army. Here Polybius reminds readers that each legion numbered 5,000 in times of emergency like these. He also notes that the Romans' Italian allies regularly provided infantry equal to the number of Roman infantry and about three times as many cavalry troopers. By his reckoning, then, the new Roman army would number some 80,000 infantry, with eight legions of Roman legionaries and an equivalent number of allied foot.[88] Livy, however, shares a discrepancy between his sources. Some suggested 10,000 recruits were levied, others that the state levied four entirely new legions, bringing the total to eight, and still others that it increased the size of the four existing legions.[89] It is difficult to say what the real numbers were at that point. What can be noted, however, is that Romans fielded a very large army, by most accounts larger than the normal maximum of two consular armies, each with two legions and a comparable number of allies.

But the fresh recruits could not depart to the Apulian front just yet. Livy reports the omens of the year that the Senate felt compelled to address:

'A shower of stones had been reported as having fallen at Rome on the Aventine, and about the same time at Aricia; in the Sabine country the images of the gods, and at Caere the waters that flowed from the hot spring had been drenched with blood, a prodigy all the more alarming from its having occurred so often; and in the arched way which used to lead to the Campus Martius some men had been struck by lightning and killed.'[90]

These portents revealed the gods' displeasure and the Senate instructed the priests in charge of the Sibylline Books to consult them again and take the necessary steps to make amends for whatever the Romans had done to offend the gods.

Neither Livy nor his sources, it appears, could resist the chance to chop away a little more at Varro's reputation. Accordingly, he tells us that the new consul ranted further: generals like Fabius could only prolong the war, but he would end the struggle as soon as he met the enemy. His colleague, Paullus, in turn noted that it was premature to predict a glorious victory when the consuls had not even set foot outside the city. At this point, Fabius approached Paullus with words of advice. Livy attributes a full speech to the cautious former dictator.

Hannibal was a mighty foe, indeed, but Varro would also prove a foe to Paullus, Fabius warned. Varro would seek battle at once, and if he closed with Hannibal, more Roman troops would be slaughtered. Better, Fabius advised, that Hannibal be starved through the steady pressure of the Fabian strategy, wasting away slowly in a foreign land. So, Fabius charged, it fell to Paullus to check the rash impulses of his colleague and the troops. Move cautiously; act prudently; avoid battle.[91] Livy constructed a particularly clear piece of reasoning from hindsight in this segment of his work. For Livy, Fabius should have delivered exactly this kind of speech. Whether he did is not at all clear. Recall that Polybius asserted the Senate had decided to fight and demonstrated its will by levying so many additional troops. In this light, Fabius' sermon seems particularly out of place. These discrepancies between Polybius and Livy fit into the general structure of events in this period.[92] Livy provides a complete narrative of conflicts that took place before the armies gathered at Cannae, both between the enemy forces and within the Roman command structure itself. Paullus and Varro strained against one another, the one moving cautiously, the other urging haste and a decisive engagement against the Carthaginians. Hannibal, meanwhile, did his best to ambush the Romans here and there, or otherwise get them to commit to battle for – and Livy is particular about this point – his army was close to imploding from lack of supplies.[93] Polybius has no such narrative. Recall in his version of events it was the consul of 217, Servilius, who had followed the Carthaginians to the Cannae district and waited there, under senatorial orders, for Paullus, Varro and the new recruits to rendezvous.[94]

Where Livy constructs a speech for Fabius to deliver to Paullus, Polybius assigns a speech to Paullus, delivered to the whole army once the forces had joined. He assured the troops that, this time, they would thrash the enemy, since they now had strength in numbers far beyond the forces gathered at Trebia and Trasimene. He noted that in the previous battles the Roman soldiers had been mere tyros, unused to the hardships of battle. These legionaries were recruits no more after fighting against the Carthaginians for two years. They were tried and tempered, ready for the decisive blow.[95]

Polybius' speech is no more likely to harbour any of Paullus' actual words, than Livy's did for Fabius. But even the basic tenor of each one's narrative is strikingly different here. Livy's Paullus cleaves to the Fabian strategy, cautious and slow-moving in the face of Varro's impetuosity. Polybius' Paullus eagerly readies for an engagement, no less willing than Varro himself to commit to a pitched battle.

Several factors suggest that even if Paullus was the more cautious of the consuls, the Senate was largely determined to engage Hannibal under conditions favourable to the Romans, and it is not at all clear Paullus truly opposed that. First, we have Polybius' testimony, and it is worth noting that Polybius was the closest in time to the events described, writing less than a century after the battle and, he claimed, able to speak to eyewitnesses from as far back as the events of

220.[96] Perhaps more telling is the testimony the numbers of levied soldiers gives. If indeed there were any plans to continue skirmishing in the Fabian manner, it is very difficult to explain why the Romans then levied so many troops. Skirmishing and shadowing operations did not require so many men as were recruited for 216. Indeed, such a large army would be very difficult to manage and supply. The leaders of the Senate were intent on battle, and the evidence is not strong enough to suppose Paullus seriously opposed the rest of the Senate on this.[97]

This is not to say that the commanders saw eye-to-eye. Polybius notes that the veteran Paullus and the novitiate Varro wrangled over the proper terrain on which to engage the enemy. The consuls led the army until they sighted the Carthaginians, and camped four or five miles away. The armies rested in perfect cavalry country: treeless plains. Hannibal enjoyed considerably more cavalry than his Roman opponents. Accordingly, when it was his day to command, Paullus kept the Romans out of battle, though the untested Varro argued the point with him. He would not have long to wait, however, before it would be his day of command, his decision.[98]

The next day Varro was in command, and he moved to engage the Carthaginians. Hannibal dispatched cavalry and light troops to strike as the enemy marched, causing difficulty for the Romans' light infantry and cavalry. Though initially in difficult straits, some of their own heavy infantry arrived to buttress the Roman forces. Fighting together, the force of infantry and cavalry got the better of the Carthaginians until darkness crept in, forcing the armies to part. This engagement left Paullus with a strategic dilemma the next day. The terrain still greatly favoured the superior numbers of Carthaginian cavalry. Withdrawing this close to the enemy, however, was not safe; it would be too easy for Hannibal to harry the Romans as they marched away. Paullus delayed, placing two-thirds of the army on one bank of the River Aufidus (usually identified by historians as the left bank) and the rest across the river to harass Carthaginian foragers.[99]

Polybius asserts that word reached Rome of the dispositions of the forces, but it seems unlikely. Any truly up-to-date information probably could not travel quickly enough. The distance from Rome to Cannae as the crow flies is about 200 miles, a distance that would probably take several days to ride, even before factoring in the mountains and limited road networks that a terrestrial messenger would have to travel.

The following day, Varro's day of command, Hannibal gave his soldiers a respite, and consequently the Romans too. The commander reportedly spoke to his troops, then dispatched them to take care of themselves and their gear, to ready for a fight.[100] Command shifted back to Paullus the following day, however, and Hannibal's efforts to draw the Romans into pitched battle failed. Paullus reportedly still hoped for more advantageous ground. As usual, Hannibal tried to force the issue, and his Numidian cavalry stung the Roman foragers, attempting to goad the whole army to fight.[101]

The Battle of Cannae (216 BC)

Then, Varro's day of command arrived again. Ready to take on the Carthaginians, he gave the orders to form the army into battle order, and the Roman leviathan – perhaps the largest army the Romans had ever fielded – rolled into action. Deploying a Roman army from camp into its ultimate battle formations had to have been a slow process, perhaps doubly so due to the twice-as-large army. Some 80,000 soldiers had to move from their camp to their positions in the battleline under the careful guidance of officers. The process had to be done in some orderly fashion for the safety and effectiveness of the army, though any standard plans or procedures for deployment are lost to us. Ultimately, the army must have required several hours to deploy.[102]

Varro, however, tampered with the normal deployment of the manipular army. He crossed to the right bank and anchored the left of the battleline to the river with the Roman citizen cavalry. Next to the cavalry he stationed the main battleline, the heavy infantry. Polybius notes here, however, that the consul 'reduced the gaps between the maniples more than usual, and increased the number of ranks within the maniples until their depth was several times greater than their length'.[103] The allied cavalry anchored the left wing and the velites, as often happened, deployed in front of the main battleline.[104] The veterans and centurions in the Roman infantry surely noticed their cramped deployment; it is hard to imagine none were seriously concerned by the breach in protocol.

Hannibal deployed his own troops in a somewhat unorthodox position. Left, next to the river bank and opposite the Roman cavalry, stood his Spanish and Gallic cavalry. Next to them he deployed half of his African heavy infantry. Spanish and Gallic infantry occupied the centre, followed by the other half of his African infantry and the Numidian cavalry on the far flank.[105] Nothing particularly novel about that. But then Hannibal drew forward the Spanish and Gallic infantry so that they were farther ahead than the Africans on the wings, and the infantry line bulged out in a crescent.[106]

If Polybius is correct, Hannibal's forces numbered only half those the Romans fielded. Yet his clever tactical deployment, combined with Varro's misguided deployment, resulted in disaster for the Roman legions. At best, Varro planned for his deeper maniples to punch through the Carthaginian centre; at worst, he simply wanted to cram as many men in the limited deployment space as possible.

So the battle began.[107] After the initial skirmishing, the Spanish and Gallic cavalry on Hannibal's left clashed with the far smaller force of Roman cavalry anchoring the Roman right to the river. Polybius notes that the common wheeling and manoeuvring of cavalry forces did not occur. Instead, the two forces, locked in a death match over the protection of the Roman flank, dismounted and fought on foot. The outnumbered Roman cavalry fought determinedly, so most of them died holding their positions. Then the main battlelines clashed. Just as Hannibal seemed to have predicted, the tightly packed and deeper maniples drove in the Carthaginian battleline. As the Spanish and Gallic infantry were driven back and the bulged crescent formation inverted, the horrific brilliance of Hannibal's plan became clear to any who might have had a distant view of the battlefield that day. Hannibal's heavy African infantry on the wings had not yet engaged. When the maniples drove in the Carthaginian centre, they effectively pushed forward until they were outflanked by that African infantry. The Africans turned about, left and right respectively, and hammered the Roman maniples on their exposed flanks. The Roman infantry were enveloped. Meanwhile, the Numidian cavalry on Hannibal's right engaged the Italian cavalry on the Roman left. Neither side gained the advantage for a time. Then the Spanish and Gallic cavalry on the left, their destruction of the Roman cavalry complete, rode around the back of the Roman army to catch the Italian cavalry in the rear. As the final stroke to close the circle, the Spanish and Gallic cavalry wheeled one more time and struck the Roman battleline in the rear. The horrific butchery of that day, when the Carthaginians slaughtered some 50,000–70,000 Roman legionaries with sword and spear, is chillingly understated by Polybius: 'The Roman legions held on as long as they could turn and present a front to the enemy who now surrounded them. But the constant attrition of the outer ranks meant that the survivors gradually closed in on one another, and in the end they all died where they stood.'[108] Hannibal's victory was colossal. Compared to the many tens of thousands of Roman dead, the Carthaginians lost only some 5,500 infantry and 200 cavalry.[109]

Rome in Crisis

Once word of the disaster reached Rome, the praetors convened the Senate to take emergency measures. Livy paints a picture, reasonably enough, of grief, fear and uncertainty. Fabius, one of the highest-ranking senators alive, had a steady hand and proposed a plan. Information was critical. By sending scouts on horseback along the main roads, the Appian and Latin Way, they could gather news and perhaps meet with survivors. It was crucial to determine where Hannibal was and what, if any, remained of the Roman forces at Cannae. Keeping calm and maintaining order in the city were equally critical, so the Senate limited families' rights to mourn, at least publicly, and restricted those openly grieving to their homes. Quiet also had to be imposed on the city so that vital news could reach the senators and they could respond accordingly. Finally, guards should bar the city gates to contain any who might flee and stiffen the resolve of the people to defend the city if need be. There was no debate, reports Livy, and the Senate and praetors put Fabius' plan in motion. In the days that followed, news began to stream into the city confirming the magnitude of the disaster. Varro reported the defeat and death of the consul Paullus, and noted some 10,000 soldiers survived and had regathered under his banner. The Carthaginians remained at Cannae sorting through their plunder.[110]

At Rome, the Senate and magistrates continued to manage the crisis: gathering intelligence, notifying the relatives of those slain at Cannae and limiting public mourning. Religious rites were performed, emergency financial measures ordered for a depleted treasury and other steps were taken. The methods of reconciling with the gods at that time were marked for their brutality. Following the oracles of the Sibylline Books, a Gallic man and woman and a Greek man and woman were buried alive in the Forum Boarium in a spot marked by stones that Livy reprovingly notes, 'even before this time had been defiled with human victims, a sacrifice wholly alien to the Roman spirit'.[111] Fabius had taken the lead in managing the crisis from the start and likely played an important role in these decisions the Senate made after Cannae.

The Senate appointed a dictator for the crisis, Marcus Junius Pera, who chose Tiberius Sempronius Gracchus for his master of horse. They took emergency measures to muster and equip forces. Younger and older males than usual – under 17 and over 45 – were recruited. The allies were called upon to supply troops. A more horrific measure no doubt for the hierarchical Romans was that 8,000 volunteer slaves were enrolled into two special legions. New weapons and armour began to be manufactured, and the battle spoils from slain enemies were taken down from their monumental positions on the temples and put to more practical use.[112]

Meanwhile, the focus of the war shifted from Apulia to Campania. The Senate had ordered Marcus Claudius Marcellus, one of the praetors in 216, to gather the remnants of Varro's army and join it with other forces to deploy a Roman army in Campania, no doubt to check any attempt Hannibal might make on the region and Rome itself. Hannibal, meanwhile, marched his army to Samnium and fortified the town of Compsa, a hefty day's march from the Appian Way, that road of Appius Claudius that stretched from Rome to Campania and beyond. Leaving a force here under a subordinate, Mago, with instructions to win over the Samnites, Hannibal continued with his main force into Campania.[113]

When the worst had been weathered – at least the Romans hoped – the Senate turned to the matter of refilling its ranks. Many senators had died in the two years since Hannibal plunged into Italy, and no newcomers had been co-opted to take their place. Now the institution was short of some 177 members. It was not exactly clear who should make up the new senators; many senatorial sons, who might have replenished the ranks, had also died in the fight against Hannibal. Spurius Carvilius proposed granting Roman citizenship to two leading Latins from each Latin state, and that the new Roman senators be drawn from their ranks. Livy reports that this proposal was ill-received, with Titus Manlius noting that he was the descendant of the consul Manlius who once threatened to kill any Latin in the Senate house with his bare hands. At this point, reportedly, Fabius offered a negative, but far less dramatic rejection of the proposal. Rome was at the tipping point, and the allies' loyalty was both uncertain and critical to any recovery: raising their hopes and expectations through even the hint of such a proposal was just foolish. Carvilius' proposal, even the barest whisper of it, must be suppressed. And so it was. Here Livy presents us with a seeming paradox: how could the later historian know about a proposal that was stifled that day in the Senate? Presumably he did not make it up; it is a very particular episode and not likely to have been totally invented. The most plausible guess is that the historian Fabius Pictor, a contemporary senator, preserved it in his account of Rome.[114]

At some point during all this, Hannibal arrived in Campania, presumably to try again to gain control of the strategic port of Neapolis. Concerns about the region spiked dramatically with the news that Capua, the chief city of Campania, had defected to Hannibal. Attempting to stop the important Campanian town of Nola from also defecting, the praetor, Marcus Claudius Marcellus, occupied the town with a sizeable force. Reportedly, Marcellus and Hannibal met in a minor battle outside Nola, one that sounded chimes of hope. Here, Marcellus repelled the Carthaginian, who went off to seek easier targets in Campania for defection.[115] At the end of the year, the Carthaginian army wintered in Capua.[116] By the end of 216, Hannibal still held the advantage, and defections of Italian cities would continue until, by 212, half of Italy no longer sided with Rome.[117] Still, in late 216 the Romans did not surrender in the face of the disaster at Cannae and were prepared to contest Hannibal's foothold in Campania.

Back in Rome, sometime after the emergency measures the Senate had taken, the Senate adjusted Roman convention and appointed a second dictator to fill its ranks. Marcus Fabius Buteo, the dictator, acted as a censor and enrolled new senators. Livy reports:

'After reading out the names of the members of the old Senate, Fabius [Buteo] began by replacing deceased members with men who had held curule offices after the censorship of Lucius Paullus and Gaius Flaminius, but who had not yet been selected for the Senate; and he prioritized them on the basis of who had been elected first. He then chose former aediles, plebeian tribunes, or quaestors and, after these, men who had not gained magistracies but who had spoils from the enemy affixed to their houses, or who had been awarded the civic crown. In this way 177 members were added.'[118]

Marcus Fabius Buteo resigned his office as soon as the task was complete. Following the rejuvenation of the Senate, the first dictator Junius, his master of horse, Sempronius, and the praetor Marcellus were summoned from their forces in Campania to provide a status report. The three commanders did so, then Junius held the consular elections for 215.

Those elections came to include a rather curious incident involving Fabius, and are worth investigation. The centuriate assembly selected Lucius Postumius, currently off fighting Gauls, as their patrician consul, and Tiberius Sempronius Gracchus, who had served with distinction under the dictator Junius in 216, as the plebeian one. Livy records, perhaps from official records, that Fabius Verrucosus now sought to dedicate a temple to Venus Eryx that he had vowed while dictator. The Senate approved, and when the new year came (215), consul Sempronius appointed Fabius to the position of *duumvir* for dedicating the temple. Late in 216 or early in 215, however, consul-designate Postumius met a rather grisly end. He led his legion into a forest ambush and, it is said, died fighting. Once the Gauls mopped up the shattered Roman forces, they took Postumius' head, scraped it clean and covered it in gold. It became the wine cup for the high priest of the tribe.[119]

Marcellus, Fabius and the Consulship for 215 BC

So Rome was already short of one consul when 215 began, and the plebeian Sempronius held an election to pick his colleague. The centuries named Marcellus, the fiery warhorse who had tangled with Hannibal in Campania after Cannae. On inauguration day, Marcellus entered office as thunder rippled in the skies. Livy says:

> 'The augurs were summoned and gave it as their opinion that there had been something amiss with his election; and the Senate followed by spreading the rumour that the gods were displeased at the election of two plebeians to the consulship – a thing which had never happened before. Marcellus resigned and Fabius Maximus was chosen in his place. It was Fabius's third consulship.'[120]

Many have noted the curiosity of this incident. Fabius was an augur; Fabius replaced Marcellus. Surely Fabius had manipulated the state religion to procure his own election?

That the two were rivals is likely, but then any fellow senator who was not a close friend and who could compete for prestige could be a rival. Still, on at least one occasion, Marcellus seems to have made a particular play for honours that the Fabius family had claimed for generations, the connection to the cavalry and to the god Honos. Back in 222 at Clastidium in northern Italy, during a significant cavalry engagement against the Gauls, Marcellus dedicated a single temple to two gods, Honos and Virtus. His purpose in dedicating a temple to Virtus was clear and uncomplicated. Virtus was the divinification of that Roman quality of martial manliness, a perfect choice for a Roman who took great steps to demonstrate his martial qualities. The dedication to Honos was more politically complicated. The god had strong associations with the cavalry. Granted, Marcellus was about to engage in a massive cavalry battle when he made the pledge. But the cavalry and the god Honos had strong connections to the Fabii, at least since the censorship of Fabius Rullianus back in 304. That connection had been reasserted by Fabius Verrucosus when he dedicated a temple to Honos in 233. In the competitive system of the Roman aristocracy, it strains belief to the breaking point to think that Marcellus innocently encroached on Fabius Verrucosus' family honours. It is no more credible to suppose that Fabius did not notice the ploy. The two were thus almost certainly rivals.[121]

It is difficult to extricate Fabius from the heart of these electoral affairs. As a leading senator and patrician, he may well have been one of those implying the gods were angry with two plebeian consuls. Indeed, he could have initiated the charge himself. And it may well be that this implication influenced the priests in their deliberations. Going deeper, Fabius had been an augur for some time and just that year was made a pontiff.[122] He had a great deal of religious authority and, in fact, must have been with the college of augurs when they ruled on the thunder. The matter is more complex and intriguing than even that. Marcellus, too, was an augur. How should we imagine this episode to have played out? Did thunder rumble? Was Marcellus recused from the augurs' discussions because he was the candidate? If he was not excused, did he and Fabius lead the debate in the significance of the thunderous omen? And could Marcellus, who did a great deal to promote his own piety, his connection to the gods, really disbelieve an omen that his colleagues accepted? The possibilities excite the imagination.

But a critical question, noted by many along the way, is whether reducing the religious beliefs of the Roman political class to a binary scale of piety or manipulation ignores that the two were not mutually exclusive. Patricians, of course, and Fabius in particular it turned out, were served by asserting that the gods wanted a patrician consul. We assume, with modern prejudice, that the Roman gods do not exist and therefore assume that claims about the gods' wishes that had political impact must have been manipulative, self-serving. But the Roman gods, as the Roman state religion held it, were concerned with maintaining a politically and militarily strong and healthy state. Why could the patricians not have believed that the gods believed part of this required the alliance of one plebeian and one patrician consul? Thunder was a recognized omen from the gods. If it did rattle the heavens at the moment of Marcellus' inauguration, why could it not be a message from the gods? Of course there is the real possibility that thunder was not widely heard that day. It would seem, however, that Marcellus and his supporters should then have made a strong challenge to the entire objection, but no trace of one remains in the sources. Though our sources are always problematic and certainty is unobtainable, what evidence we have points to a general acceptance that thunder had been heard. In such circumstances it would have been most difficult for Marcellus, who tended to his image as a pious Roman at least as much as any other senator, to challenge if the bulk of the augurs went against him.

The Campaigns of 215 BC

Whatever intrigue lurks under the sources' reports, the consuls for 215 were Fabius and Tiberius Sempronius Gracchus. Early in this, his third consulship, Fabius reportedly issued another order to Rome and its allies. All grain should be gathered from farms and collected in fortified towns to prevent their seizure by Hannibal. Along with the edict came Fabius' threat that he would despoil the farms of violators and seize their slaves for the auction block.[123] Then the primary commanders for the year assumed their posts. Marcellus returned to the army he had commanded and focused on keeping Nola safe. The consul Sempronius assumed command of the legions of volunteer slaves at Rome. Fabius assumed command of the rest of Junius' army at Teanum. With marches and countermarches, sieges and rescues, the Roman armies and Hannibal's force carried out a complex dance through the region that year, each trying to gain or regain control of the cities and towns of Campania. Capua remained in the Carthaginian sphere. Casilinum, an important town near the Appian Way along the Volturnus River at the northern end of Campania, had been under Carthaginian control in 216, but shed that garrison sometime late in the year before coming back under Carthaginian control again in the winter/spring of 215. Nola and Neapolis stayed with the Romans. There seem to have been no major engagements in the region, though Livy mentions a second battle at Nola between Marcellus and Hannibal that may well have been imaginary.[124] In any event, Fabius, according to Livy, did little in the way of active campaigning in 215. While at Cales with his army, he spent most of his time dealing with auspices and with all manner of omens, reports of which assailed him almost nonstop. Fabius conducted many sacrifices on behalf of Rome to atone for past wrongs. All was not easily resolved, however, for it appears his soothsayers continued to report that the entrails of the sacrificial victims did not indicate success. Was this the reason Fabius remained at Cales, or was the report of unfavourable omens a later apologetic effort to explain his military inactivity that year?[125] It is not clear. The next time Fabius appears in the accounts of 215, however, Hannibal had departed for a winter camp in Apulia, and Fabius took the opportunity to gather grain from Nola and Neapolis to stock the magazines at the Claudian camp above Suessula. He left a force to hold the camp through the winter and deployed the rest of his men to build a new camp closer to Capua. From here his troops devastated the Capuan countryside. The Capuans, though they lacked the infantry forces to seriously endanger the Romans, built a camp outside their city and relied on their strength in cavalry to challenge Fabius' forces.[126] After a while, however, Fabius surrendered control of the farmlands around Capua to lure the Campanians into planting their crops. Then when the grain was high, he returned and seized it for fodder, hauling the stalks to the Claudian camp for winter supplies. Then he fortified the burgeoning market town of Puteoli and left a garrison there.[127]

* * *

Hannibal's invasion of Italy posed an existential crisis like none the Republic had seen. Historians can and will continue to speculate on the impact Fabius' dictatorship had on the Roman war effort. Still, it is clear the Romans suffered great defeats before Fabius took the helm. Then they returned to their normal strategy of decisive battle in 216 with Cannae and the slaughter of at least 50,000 Roman and allied soldiers resulted. Fabius played an important role in the Senate's response to Cannae and went on to serve as consul in 215. More cautious tactics corresponded with his period of leadership. It is certainly a stretch to say that Fabius was solely responsible for the strategy and tactics that would reverse the pattern of Roman defeat. Equally certain, however, his penchant for cautious engagement was significant in the ultimate reversal of Roman fortunes.

Chapter 6

The Fabian Strategy and the End of the War

y the end of 215, the crisis of Cannae had passed. The Romans, guided by Fabius' examples and leadership in the Senate and as consul in 215, developed a more measured strategy, targeting towns and focusing on supply chains rather than the headlong pursuit of a decisive battle against Hannibal. And so the war gridlocked by the end of 215. Armies moved like chess pieces from town to town and region to region. Hannibal and the Romans simultaneously strove to protect their allies and punish their enemies in Italy. Some battles punctuated the process, but sieges, counter-sieges and raids were the primary military activities in the middle years of the war.[1]

Consular Elections for 214 BC

We left Fabius in late 215 at Puteoli in Campania. After he fortified the town and stationed a garrison there, he headed for Rome to hold the consular elections. Determined to avoid distraction and hold the elections as swiftly as possible, he bypassed the city entirely and made his way straight to the outlying Campus Martius, the 'field of Mars', where the centuriate assembly gathered for elections.[2] By the late third century, the centuriate assembly had adopted a procedure whereby one century, one voting block of citizens, received by lot the right to vote first. The vote of this 'prerogative century' was announced publicly before the rest of the centuries voted and, accordingly, could have an important effect on later voters. On the day Fabius held the consular elections, the junior century – 'junior' meaning men under the age of 45 – of the Aniensis tribe voted first. It named Titus Otacilius and Marcus Aemilius Regillus to hold the consulship for 214. Ordinarily, voting would then proceed century by century, the centuries of wealthier citizens voting first, until two candidates received a simple majority of the 193 centuries. But this was no ordinary election. Fabius, the presiding magistrate, halted the assembly and rebuked the Aniensis juniors. Livy constructs a reasonably lengthy speech for Fabius; the introduction sets the tone:

'If we now had peace in Italy, or a war and an enemy that would grant us some latitude for sloppiness, then anyone attempting to curb the enthusiasm you bring to the Campus to bestow office upon men of your choosing – I would think such a man had too little consideration for your liberties. But, in the case of this war and this enemy, no mistake made by any commander has yet failed to precipitate disaster on a massive scale. You must therefore proceed to the vote for electing your consuls with the same caution that you exercise when you go in armour to the battlefield, and every man should say to himself: "I propose a consul who can match Hannibal as a commander."'[3]

From here, Fabius explained exactly why Otacilius and Aemilius did not fit the bill. Aemilius was already the flamen Quirinus, the chief priest of Jupiter, and his religious obligations could not be neglected because of military duties – a good argument for the punctiliously religious Fabius to have made. Otacilius, on the other hand, had failed miserably as a praetor commanding the fleet the previous year. The centuries should entrust neither to command Rome's cherished youth, its soldiers, and pit them against Hannibal. Diatribe completed, Fabius ordered the junior century to vote again.[4]

What can one say about this irregularity? It is not likely the sort of episode to have been completely fabricated. Here Fabius exerted powerful, some no doubt would also say illegal, pressure upon the voting assembly. He was not done, however. Otacilius furiously challenged Fabius' harangue; he meant to be consul, and Fabius was patently trying to hold the consulship again. Fabius stood firm. He sent his lictors to quell the unruly Otacilius and warned the praetor that, because he had not entered the city from the battlefields, his lictors still had the axes in their fasces. The threat was crystal clear and brutally blunt to a Roman, though for us the idiom requires some unpacking. Consuls, praetors and dictators were all accompanied by lictors, attendants who, among other things, aided the magistrate in the execution of his orders. Each lictor carried the fasces, a collection of wooden rods tied together into a cylinder. An axe could be inserted in the centre of the bundle when the consul was outside the city. The lictors used the rods to compel and the axes to execute, should the need arise. When inside the city, a magistrate's lictors had to remove the axes from the bundles because the magistrates held no imperium – right of command and execution – within the city of Rome and citizens had the right of appeal.[5] In short, Fabius' lictors reminded Otacilius that the consul had not entered the city, his consular imperium was still intact and Otacilius had best watch himself … or else.

The threat deflated Otacilius. Regillus, meanwhile, seems not have made a peep throughout the spectacle. The century re-voted, chose Marcellus and Fabius himself, and the rest of the centuries, says Livy, followed suit. Later writers would refer to this formidable pair of consuls as the sword and shield of Rome. Otacilius, however, did not suffer a complete reversal of fortune. He was elected praetor again, one of four that year that included Fabius' own son, Quintus Fabius Maximus. Livy's pronouncement on Fabius' electoral rigging is worth repeating:

'In view of the critical situation and the pressing needs of the war nobody felt bound to seek a precedent for his re-election or suspected him of a dangerous lust for power; on the contrary, people praised the greatness of spirit which allowed him, knowing as he did that the country needed a supreme soldier and that he himself was undoubtedly the man, to rate his own unpopularity, if there were any, as of less importance than the public advantage.'[6]

Certainly, this reasoning made sense to later historians. Did it at the time? Judging simply by the fact that Fabius pulled it off, there must have been enough support for his actions. It is just another reminder that where moderns try to split political and religious reasoning from each other and from personal ambition, the three were intertwined for the Romans, and arguments like those Fabius employed could be very persuasive to voters.

War in Campania

The consuls for 214 BC, Marcellus and Fabius, assumed their office and held the initial meeting of the Senate for the year. As usual, a series of omens indicated the Romans needed to atone to their gods. These were the reports:

'At Lanuvium ravens had made a nest inside the temple of Juno Sospita; that in Apulia a green palm took fire; that at Mantua a lake, the overflow of the river Mincius, appeared bloody; and at Cales it rained chalk, and at Rome in the Cattle Market blood; and that on the Vicus Insteius an underground spring flowed with such a volume of water that the force of a torrent, as it were, overturned the jars, great and small, that were there and carried them along; that the Atrium Publicum on the Capitol, the temple of Vulcan in the Campus, that of Vacuna and a public street in the Sabine country, the wall and a gate at Gabii were struck by lightning. Moreover other marvels were widely circulated: that the spear of Mars at Praeneste moved by itself; that an ox in Sicily spoke; that among the Marrucini an infant in its mother's womb shouted "Hail, triumph!"; that at Spoletium a woman was changed into a man; that at Hadria an altar was seen in the sky, and about it the forms of men in white garments. In fact at Rome also, actually in the city, directly after the appearance of a swarm of bees in the Forum – a wonder because it is rare – certain men, asserting that they saw armed legions on the Janiculum, aroused the city to arms, whereas those who were on the Janiculum denied that anyone had been seen there except the usual dwellers on that hill. Atonement was made for these omens with full-grown victims on the advice of the priests, and a season of prayer to all the gods who had festal couches at Rome was proclaimed.'[7]

Once the consuls arranged the necessary rituals and sacrifices, discussion shifted to the conscription and assignment of armies. In the midst of these preparations, rumours flew about that the war had spread to Sicily. Otacilius commanded the navy and would investigate, but the Republic was in financial straits due to the tremendous military burdens of the past few years, and now the fleet lacked sufficient sailors. To remedy this, the consuls declared that citizens, based on their wealth, would supply sailors and money to pay the sailors.[8]

Meanwhile, the Carthaginian army stirred from its winter quarters in Apulia and returned to Campania. Hannibal reoccupied his camp on Mount Tifata. There he stationed Spanish and Numidian troops to hamper any Roman effort to besiege Capua. Then he journeyed with the rest of his army to Puteoli, the market town Fabius had recently garrisoned. Along the way, five young aristocrats from the southern Greek city of Tarentum approached Hannibal. All had fought for the Romans, and all the Carthaginians had captured. Hannibal had treated them well as prisoners of war, according to his plan to win over Rome's allies. These youths took Hannibal's good treatment well and campaigned for other young Tarentines to abandon Rome and shift their loyalties to Hannibal. Now, the cabal calculated, if the general brought his army to Tarentum, they could engineer a revolt and secure the city for him. Hannibal assuredly was intrigued: Tarentum was a major prize. The port could import supplies and reinforcements from Carthage and its new ally, Philip V, King of Macedonia. Hannibal pledged he would come. Not immediately, as it happened, for there was still much to be done in Campania.[9]

When the Carthaginian forces arrived at Puteoli, they probed the Roman defences, but without success. The town was well fortified and the garrison, perhaps 6,000 Roman troops, held firm. Thwarted, the Carthaginians vented their frustrations on the surrounding countryside.[10] At some point during these springtime raids, word reached Rome about Hannibal's movements. Fabius rejoined his army, then ordered a quick march to Campania.[11] Marcellus, meanwhile, returned to the strategic Campanian town of Nola, and Fabius took a position outside Casilinum, currently in the hands of the Carthaginians.[12] They did not have to wait long. After ransacking the farmland around Puteoli and Naples, Hannibal marched to Nola. Marcellus' troops clung to the city, repelling the Carthaginians. Perhaps, as Livy says, the Romans suffered only 400 casualties to the Carthaginians' 2,000. Indeed, Livy judges the defence of Nola as just short of a major victory, but he may well have done so to justify the title posterity had given Marcellus: the sword of Rome. Marcellus had dispatched a lieutenant, Gaius Claudius Nero, with the bulk of the cavalry. His assignment: circle the Carthaginian army and, once it had assaulted Nola, attack the enemy rear. It was a tactic worthy of Hannibal, but Nero bungled the plan – at least Livy's sources blame him. Marcellus tongue-lashed Nero because Hannibal had faced certain destruction, Livy hyperbolically reports. Perhaps this could have been the case, though an ultimate victory over Hannibal does sound a little too grand. More likely the Romans simply held the city. Still, that was sufficient to frustrate Hannibal, who reckoned it was time to test Tarentum and marched his army out of Campania.[13]

At some point in 214, presumably after Hannibal's failed attack on Nola, Fabius set his sights upon Casilinum, which guarded the Appian Way to Rome. Currently Carthaginians and Campanians defended it. Committing to a siege, however, would bog down Fabius' army, leaving it vulnerable to enemy harassment. A second army was needed to protect the first, so Fabius wrote to Marcellus at Nola: either he should leave Nola under adequate guard and trek with the remainder of his army to Casilinum, or he should instruct the proconsul Tiberius Sempronius Gracchus at Beneventum to come in his stead. Marcellus opted to answer the summons; together the strength of the armies sufficed to ward off Campanian raiders. The Romans probed the walls of Casilinum, hoping to launch an assault, but Livy says the Roman soldiers 'rashly approached the walls' and suffered significant wounds as a result. The consuls conferred. Fabius reckoned that Casilinum was not important enough to warrant the time and lives spent. Marcellus, however, reportedly convinced his colleague that they should stay the course; their reputations would suffer if they yielded here, and this would have a dangerous impact on the Roman war effort. Was this an overheard conversation? More likely Livy and his sources simply wrote up this aside according to the character assigned to Marcellus, the 'sword' – fiery and bent on honour – and Fabius, the 'shield', practical and cautious. Either Fabius consented or there was little disagreement to begin with, and the armies erected siege works. Alarmed by this development, the Campanian garrison in the city sought shelter with Fabius. The soldiers received the consul's permission to withdraw to Capua. This was a seeming act of mercy discordant with Roman values, but expediency, not mercy, likely drove Fabius: letting the Campanians go would weaken the city defences and shorten the siege. He could deal with these particular rebels later.[14]

Marcellus apparently was not privy to this meeting, for as some Campanians left the town, he blocked their exit. Then the Roman soldiers at the gate carved into the Campanians, and the slaughter spread into the town. A small group of Campanians, fifty Livy says, struggled their way to Fabius, who sent them under safeguard to Capua.[15] This is an odd enough detail that perhaps it represents an authentic episode. It certainly corroborates the rivalry of the two Romans, but could also simply have been the result of confused communications.

Marcellus returned to Nola, while Fabius journeyed south-east to collect a pound of flesh from the rebellious Samnites. Collect he did: Fabius' soldiers torched fields, successfully assaulted a handful of presumably less well-defended towns and besieged another two presumably better-defended settlements in the region. In the final tally, Livy calculates that 25,000 enemy soldiers were captured or killed. But that was not all: Fabius arrested 400 deserters from the Roman armies in the process. An especially brutal fate awaited them. All were publicly beaten in the Campus Martius, then hurled headlong off the Tarpeian Rock like so many who had run afoul of the Republic.[16]

Hannibal's army, meanwhile, exacted its own vengeance against territories still loyal to Rome, ravaging a trail all the way to Tarentum. Eager to gain Tarentine support, however, Hannibal curbed his army from damaging that city's hinterlands. Camping about a mile from Tarentum, he waited for the promised revolution in the city: vainly, as it happened, for the Roman fleet commander at Brundisium had dispatched Marcus Livius to shore up support in the city. Livius charmed the fickle young nobles who had pledged support to Hannibal and placed a close watch on gates and walls to check any attempts to betray the city. A few days passed, and it became increasingly clear to Hannibal that the town would not be his, or at least not yet. No doubt considerably frustrated, the Carthaginian marched his army north-west to the town of Salapia and collected grain for winter quarters. Numidians scoured the countryside but found little except for some horses, which were turned over to the cavalry for training.[17]

The son of Fabius Maximus Cunctator wins the Consulship (213 BC)

The year passed and the time for consular elections crept up. Fabius' son, Quintus Fabius Maximus, and Tiberius Sempronius Gracchus were elected.[18] The elder Fabius was not assigned a proconsular command for the year; instead he served his son as a legate in his army. It is interesting to ponder how this came to be. Did the younger Fabius ask his father, the famed aristocrat, to serve as his lieutenant? Did the elder Fabius impose himself on his son? One can imagine it would have been very difficult to exercise consular authority with one's father hanging about, as their ancestor Fabius Maximus Gurges well knew from service with his father Rullianus. Perhaps Livy was aware of the awkwardness when he reported the following anecdote. The elder Fabius rode to Suessula to rendezvous with his son, the consul. When he neared, convention dictated he should dismount and approach the consul on foot. The elder Fabius stayed in his saddle, however, and rode past eleven of his son's lictors. Finally, the consul Fabius ordered the twelfth to make his father dismount and approach on foot. The elder Fabius gladly did so, exclaiming, 'My son, I wanted to see if you were firmly aware that you are a consul.'[19] This sounds rather like the exchange between the elder Fabius and Servilius back in 217, but perhaps Fabius Cunctator had a penchant for public tests of power.

Son and father camped with the army at Suessula. One night a figure slipped into the Roman camp: Dasius Altinius from the city of Arpi in Apulia. The Arpinian had served in the Roman army at Cannae, as it happened, and been part of the revolt when Arpi joined forces with Hannibal. His proposition: in return for a reward, he would secure Arpi for the consul Fabius. The consul disclosed this scheme to his council of officers. Some denounced Altinius outright as a mere opportunist who should, by all rights, be scourged and executed. Who could trust a man who would so readily switch sides? They should make an example out of him to deter others from abandoning the Romans.[20] The elder Fabius, however, in his role as legate, noted that such principles and hurt pride had little place in war. The question that should fully occupy the officers was how to keep their allies from revolting. Turning Altinius into an object lesson for defectors would quash any hopes other wayward peoples would have of returning to the Roman fold. Fabius' plan was to place Altinius in the nearby town of Cales, free to roam the town during the day, but under guard at night. The Romans could decide what to do with him after the war. And so it happened. His absence from Arpi aroused suspicion, however, and the city leaders sent word to Hannibal that Altinius had disappeared. Hannibal, reportedly, was pleased. Something about the mercurial man did not sit well with the general, and, in any event, he wanted to commandeer his wealth for the war effort. Investigating the matter, Hannibal brought Altinius' family to camp for questioning. Livy is not exactly clear whether they revealed the plot, but he is clear what Hannibal did next. The general burned Altinius' family alive.[21]

Though the murder of Altinius' family must have grieved the defector, it did not slow the younger Fabius. The consul put his army into motion, marched to Arpi and began a siege. He studied the defences and pinpointed a section of wall that seemed the least well-defended, lying next to an abandoned section of the city. His most trusted tribunes and centurions gathered to form a strike force. They would lead 600 soldiers, equipped with ladders, to scale the wall, enter the city and destroy the nearby gate. Once they achieved this, a horn blast would alert the rest of the army on the outside that it was time to attack. Heavy rains came that night, a blessing for the Roman commandos; they muffled sounds and compelled guards to take shelter. The infiltrators entered the city and broke down the gate. The remainder of the Roman army stirred to action when they heard the horn blasts and flowed through the wrecked gate.[22]

The grim business of urban warfare was at hand, with close-quarter melees from street to street and house to house. The garrison of 5,000 Carthaginian troops and 3,000 Arpians would offer stiff resistance; or so it must have seemed at first. The Romans secured a foothold in the empty streets and houses nearest the wrecked gate. They soon encountered some Arpians, but both sides kept their cool. The word on the streets indicated only the city nobles supported Hannibal; the rest were forced to follow suit. Someone fetched a pro-Roman city official and an arrangement was reached. The town turned on its Carthaginian garrison. Some Spanish soldiers in the garrison subsequently agreed to defect if Hannibal's remaining troops could exit the city safely. The bargain was struck, and several thousand troops left the city and rejoined Hannibal.[23] The younger Fabius had won a solid victory.

Tarentum Revolts

Neither Fabius held a command in 212. Meanwhile, Hannibal's army continued to campaign in the heel of Italy in 213 and 212, keeping close to Tarentum, hoping it would defect. At some point Hannibal's prayers were answered, and Tarentum left the Roman fold.[24] Livy supplies this origin for Tarentum's revolt:

> 'Phileas had been a long time in Rome, ostensibly as the Tarentine envoy. He was a restless character and chafed under the inaction in which he seemed likely to spend the greater part of his life. The hostages from Tarentum and Thurii were kept in the Hall of Liberty … Phileas found means of access to them.'[25]

This is the first time Livy mentions such hostages in his narrative. It is not surprising that Rome did take hostages, given the Tarentines were the ones who had invited King Pyrrhus of Epirus to invade Italy about seventy years previously. Still, there is so much more we should like to know. When were these hostages taken? How many hostages were there? How extensively did the Romans normally take hostages to inspire otherwise less-than-loyal allies in Italy? Sadly, there are no conclusions beyond the initial one: at some point prior to 212, the Romans assayed to secure Tarentine loyalty by taking hostages.

Phileas began to visit these Tarentines, who were housed at the Temple of Liberty on the Aventine Hill in the city. The hostages apparently had little desire to flee, since they saw it as in their best interests for Tarentum to remain loyal to Rome. Phileas insinuated an alternative. The hostages could flee and their home city could then safely abandon the Roman cause without fear for their lives. How exactly he made that hard sale is a mystery. That he did is clear from subsequent events: he arranged an escape and fled the city with the hostages. The Romans were not amused, to say the least, and a group soon left the city to hunt the fleeing Tarentines. Angry and vengeful, the Romans inflicted a stern penalty. Each of the hostages was beaten in the assembly grounds and given a terminal trip off the Tarpeian Rock.[26]

The strong response alienated many Tarentines. Two in particular, Nico and Philemenus, gathered a band of nobles and forged a conspiracy. Under cover of a sham hunting trip, the leaders would exit the city and meet with Hannibal, who was in the vicinity. As it happened, they safely slipped out of Tarentum, but Carthaginian sentries challenged the would-be turncoats. They persuaded the watch to escort them to Hannibal so they could proffer their plan. Hannibal, reportedly, was most receptive and gave the plot his blessing. To lend further authenticity to the conspirators' deception, Hannibal gave them some cattle to claim as the spoils of their night-time hunt. Undetected the first time, Philemenus ventured out to meet with Hannibal again, and the two sealed the bargain.

The rebels would surrender the Roman garrison to Hannibal, they would live under their own laws and they would neither pay taxes to Carthage nor have a Carthaginian garrison imposed on them against their wishes.[27]

Philemenus set the stage, accustoming the city guards to his regular night-time exits, all purportedly for hunting expeditions. Meanwhile, Hannibal struck camp in the early hours before dawn with a select force of infantry and cavalry, perhaps 10,000 all told. Numidian cavalry acted like raiders but actively scoured both sides of the main road to apprehend anyone who might see and betray them to the city garrison. In this way, Hannibal's force covered ground and camped about 15 miles away from Tarentum. He even took the precaution of hiding his plans from the strike force. They were instructed to keep to the main road and to be ready to act when the command came. Hannibal's clandestine approach worked. The Roman prefect of Tarentum heard word of the Numidians and supposed they were simply a raiding party, certainly not a threat to the city.[28] Polybius suggests the prefect was also drunk, a detail Livy patriotically omits.

Nico then went to a certain part of the city, lit a beacon for Hannibal and murdered the nearby city guards in their sleep, though why the guards were asleep is anyone's guess. He opened the gate to admit the greater part of Hannibal's infantry. Philemenus, meanwhile, had work of his own. He approached the gate he normally used for his hunting trips. The guards, familiar with his nightly peregrinations, opened the gates when he whistled. Philemenus entered with three members of his sham hunting party, two lugging a slain boar. The guard was at ease and just distracted enough for Philemenus to get the upper hand, murdering him with a spear thrust. A small Carthaginian squad flowed through the open gate, killed the remaining guards and secured the way for the soldiers lying in wait.[29]

Quietly – it must have been so quietly – Hannibal's infantry collected undetected in the city forum. They had successfully infiltrated the city without incident. Now the Tarentine turncoats led detachments of Gallic soldiers to secure the streets that received the most traffic. Fights broke out – one-sided really – as the soldiers spared townspeople but slaughtered any Romans they encountered. There was no way to accomplish this silently. Noise from the struggles travelled around the city, though the source was not clear to any but the occupiers. The Romans in the city began to suspect treachery brewing, and the garrison prefect, Marcus Livius, worked his way to the port and found a boat to ferry him safely to the citadel. There, Roman troops and still-loyal Tarentines gathered. The light of day revealed the slaughtered Roman soldiers and the Carthaginian occupation of the city. Except for the citadel, held by the Roman garrison and some Tarentines, the Carthaginians controlled the city.[30]

When the urban brawl had abated, Hannibal assembled the Tarentines. He spoke in the words of a liberator and charged the citizens with a simple task: they should write their names on their house doors. Houses with no names attached clearly belonged to the Roman occupiers and would be plundered by the new masters of the city. The citizens complied, and the Carthaginian forces looted.[31]

The citadel with its Roman garrison remained a thorn in Hannibal's side. When the looting was finished, he moved to pluck it. The defences were formidable. The citadel jutted into the bay, with high rocks and the sea protecting it on three sides. On the landward side the citadel was protected from the city by a trench and wall. This presented Hannibal with a dilemma. Protecting the Tarentines from the entrenched Roman garrison would require him to syphon off manpower to provide a guard. In an effort to close in the citadel, Hannibal decided to excavate a ditch and construct a rampart by the landward wall of the citadel. A Roman thrust at the work in progress was easily blunted by the Carthaginians on hand, and the builders finished their work. The success of this construction even persuaded Hannibal that an assault might still be possible, and siege engines were lugged into position for the task. This prompted another Roman raid, more successful than the last, and the siege works were largely burnt and demolished. The tenacity of the defenders and their excellent defences made storming the citadel wall out of the question. By now, however, the landward side of the citadel was hemmed in by the Carthaginian fortifications. Hannibal, no doubt chafing to get back into the field and stay mobile, instructed the Tarentines to employ their navy to blockade the citadel and starve the garrison out. The Tarentines obliged and put their navy into action. Hannibal left them to it and returned with his army to winter quarters.[32]

The Roman Senate knew well the importance of Tarentum, and while they were not immediately ready to launch a recovery expedition that year (212), they did not abandon the resolute garrison. Following senatorial guidance, the legate of a praetor in the region, Gaius Servilius, ran the Tarentine blockade and supplied the beleaguered garrison with grain and hope.[33] And so as the year passed, the situation at Tarentum had not resolved in either Hannibal or the Republic's favour.

Hannibal Marches on Rome and Capua Surrenders

By 211 BC Hannibal faced another dilemma. The Roman garrison at Tarentum had not faltered, and the blockade runners had strengthened them with supplies. Carthaginian support would be needed to capture the citadel. At the same time Capua, a city whose support was critical to the Carthaginian war effort, struggled under a Roman siege – begun in 212 – and needed relief.[34] He could not attend to both. Ultimately, Hannibal opted to defend Capua, since it was in more immediate danger and, until now, stood as a symbol that Italians could successfully rebel against Romans. To facilitate a quick march, the Carthaginian army left most of its baggage train and its heavy infantry in Bruttium. The rest headed for Campania. Arriving at Mount Tifata, Hannibal occupied a local fort and prepared for operations against the Romans besieging the city. This involved harrying operations, presumably, since Hannibal could not hope to win a pitched battle without his heavy infantry. Communicating with his Capuan allies, he coordinated a sortie from the city to coincide with his raid on the outer siege works. The Roman commanders, proconsuls Fulvius Flaccus and Appius Claudius, successfully fought off both sides. The gambit had failed.[35]

Confounded, Hannibal took a new tack, a feint against the city of Rome. The hope was that threatening the capital would dislodge the Roman armies from their positions around Capua. He warned the Capuans of his plans so that they would not believe they had been abandoned, and headed north.[36] Carthaginian deserters approached the proconsul Flaccus and divulged Hannibal's plans. The resulting report stirred up the Senate considerably. One senator, Publius Cornelius Asina (his unfortunate *cognomen* was 'ass') proposed that Hannibal's threat took precedence over all Roman operations in Italy. Every army and commander should be recalled to protect the city. Fabius exerted his influence in the Senate. He urged calm and insisted the siege of Capua must continue: jumping at shadows and abandoning sound strategy was no way to conduct the war. A third speaker, Publius Valerius Flaccus, persuaded the Senate to err on the cautious side of Fabius' determined plan. Send word to the proconsuls at Capua and let them judge whether the siege operations could safely spare any troops to protect Rome.[37]

Flaccus and Claudius calculated that a significant force, two legions and their allied contingents, could safely leave the siege. Claudius' wound, which would prove the death of him a few weeks hence, prevented him from coming, so Flaccus commanded the relief force that followed in Hannibal's tracks. When he had crossed the Volturnus River, the proconsul determined that Hannibal had taken the Latin Way to Rome. Accordingly, he took the complementary road, the Appian Way, perhaps hoping to pass Hannibal along the way. Flaccus sent word ahead to the allied towns along the route, instructing them to put food near the road to supply the fast-moving Roman army.[38] Ultimately, Flaccus arrived with his army in time to meet Hannibal's forces outside the city. Though the two armies stood off for a few days, Hannibal opted to retire from the vicinity of the city. The siege of Capua continued, and the city ultimately surrendered in 211.[39]

During 212 and 211, Fabius the elder held no office, though judging from his part in the defence against Hannibal, he clearly continued to play his influential role as one of the leading men of the Senate. For a moment, as Livy reports it, Fabius was almost elected consul in 210. It was another unconventional election. The Veturian junior century got to vote first and named Titus Manlius Torquatus and Titus Otacilius. Hearing his name, Torquatus strode to the consuls' tribunal and sought leave to address the assembly before further voting. Something extraordinary was up. Torquatus asked, demanded really, not to be elected consul. His sight was failing and he simply could not carry out the duties of office effectively. But the men of the prerogative century were not so readily deterred. They persisted in their choice and shouted out as much to Torquatus. Reportedly, he uttered a simple retort: 'I shall not be able to tolerate your manners and conduct, nor will you submit to my authority. Go back and vote again, and bear in mind that the Carthaginians are carrying war in Italy, and that their leader is Hannibal.'[40]

The Veturian juniors were persuaded. They asked leave to meet with the Veturian senior century, the older men, and seek their advice. According to Livy, the seniors suggested three names: Marcellus, Fabius or, if they wanted someone new to the consulship, Marcus Valerius Laevinus. The juniors' respect for their elders was too much for Livy, who felt compelled to break the fourth wall and address readers directly:

> 'So much for those who ridicule admirers of the past! If there does exist a philosopher-state somewhere – a product of our scholars' imagination rather than their knowledge – I certainly would not believe its leaders could be more serious-minded or restrained in their political ambition, or the commons more principled, than in this case. That a century of younger men should have wanted to consult their elders about whom they should invest with power by their vote seems very implausible these days, when the influence that even parents have over their children is slight and ineffectual.'[41]

So Fabius was reportedly in the mix, but Marcellus and Valerius were elected consuls. The consular year saw continued campaigns in Italy and Sicily. Marcellus took the important city of Salapia through a conspiracy with some inhabitants, along with some towns in Samnium. Valerius operated in Sicily and captured Agrigentum, the last serious resistance on the island.[42] Reports from Tarentum for 210 indicate that the Romans were getting very good at running the Tarentine blockade. Livy mentions another effort. Legates purchased grain from Etruria, and supplied it and 1,000 additional soldiers to strengthen the citadel garrison.[43]

An Eventful Year (209 BC)

The elections for the consulship of 209 promised to be just as contentious as any other. First, there was the matter of holding the elections. Marcellus was in the field. Valerius had returned to the city to report on matters in Sicily and North Africa. The Senate decided he needed to return to his province immediately. They instructed him to summon the popular assembly to name a dictator to hold elections. Valerius refused, claiming that it was his right as consul to choose a dictator; it did not belong to the people to do so. The claim reads oddly. Strictly speaking, he was quite right, but why not simply name a dictator before he left

Italy? It is not at all clear, but apparently Valerius skipped town and returned to Sicily so he could not be forced to hold an election for dictator. Exasperated, the Senate sent a missive to Marcellus, currently in southern Italy. He selected Quintus Fulvius Flaccus to be dictator and hold elections.[44]

The Senate must have held its collective breath when the prerogative century voted this year, so frequently had the consular elections been disrupted. But it did not help. The century voted for Fulvius and Fabius. At this point, the tribunes Gaius and Lucius Arrenius, brothers as it happened, imposed their veto and suspended further voting. Their complaint was that Fulvius was an improper choice for the consulship. Holding two consecutive magistracies, they argued, violated the established civil procedures of the Republic. What's more, the precedent of electing consul the person who presided over the elections was dangerous. Presumably, they meant that it would not do to have the president of each assembly orchestrate matters so that he got elected.[45]

The tribunes' ultimatum was simple enough: Fulvius had to withdraw his name from the running or they would continue to veto the elections. Fulvius bristled at their threats and they locked horns. He tried to dismiss the tribunes' claims as spurious. Worse still, they were violating the right of the plebeians they were supposed to protect by suspending the assembly in action. After all, it was just after the disaster at Trasimene that a law had been passed dictating that 'as long as there was war in Italy the people had the right to reappoint as consuls, any who had been consuls, as often as they pleased'.[46] Nor were precedents lacking for electing as consul the magistrate presiding over an assembly. One could look at the election of Fabius Maximus in 214. Surely no one had claimed the great Cunctator had violated the rights of the people?

The wrangling continued as Fulvius and the tribunes each pleaded their case to the paralyzed electoral assembly. At last both parties agreed to let the Senate make the call. The Senate, in turn, declared that the election of Fulvius was acceptable, and – a reprimand it would seem – it was important to conduct these elections expeditiously so the new commanders could get ready for the war effort. The Arrenius brothers yielded the point, elections resumed, and Fulvius and Fabius were named consul, Fulvius for the fourth time and Fabius the fifth.[47]

At the start of the consular year of 209, an incident shook the foundations of Roman power in Italy. Fabius ordered his son, apparently serving as a legate, to gather the remnants of Gnaeus Fulvius Centumalus' army, which had been routed by Hannibal at Herdonea,[48] and ferry them to serve in Sicily. Most of these troops happened to be Latin allies, and their deployment far away in Sicily seems to have been the final straw for some of their home cities. Over the course of the past century and a half, the Romans had planted thirty Latin colonies. This year twelve colonies, after discussing the matter in detail with the delegates from other Latin colonies, announced to Fulvius and Fabius that they could supply neither more troops nor money – both were exhausted. This was little short of open rebellion, and the consuls handled the matter with care. They urged caution upon the delegates, emphasizing the enormity of their refusal. But the colonial ambassadors would not budge, leaving the consuls little choice but to pass the matter to the Senate. The Senate was reportedly terrified, and rightly so. Manpower was the foundation of Roman power in Italy and an important reason why the Romans defeated the Carthaginians in the First Punic War. No allied contributions meant fewer soldiers and less geopolitical power. It also meant that the Latin colonies essentially had no obligations to Rome, and if they had no obligations, what did Rome really control in Italy at all?

Fabius and Fulvius calmed the senators. Ultimately, the Senate authorized the consuls to handle the delicate matter as they thought best. Cautiously, the consuls first assessed the temper of the other Latin colonies. The delegates from the remaining eighteen confirmed that their men were ready to serve, and if necessary, they could provide even more. The consuls thanked these colonies publicly by bringing the delegates before the Senate and assembly, both of which voted public thanks to them. In a nice touch, Livy notes that even in his day, close to two centuries later, the loyal colonies would not be overlooked, then proceeded to name them. The twelve colonies in default of their obligations, on the other hand, were simply shunned; no one, consuls included, spoke to the delegates.[49]

It would hardly seem like a new consular year had dawned if there were no omens to address, and Livy does not disappoint:

'On the Alban Mount a statue of Jupiter had been struck by lightning, also a tree near the temple; at Ostia a fountain had been struck, at Capua the wall and the temple of Fortune, and the wall and a gate at Sinuessa. In addition to this it was reported by some that the Alban Lake had flowed red, like blood, and in Rome, inside the shrine of the temple of Fors Fortuna, a figure fixed to the wreath round the head of a statue fell without apparent cause into the statue's hand. It was common knowledge that at Privernum an ox talked and a vulture, while the forum was full of people, flew down on to a shop, and that at Sinuessa a child of ambiguous sex was born, half male half female – an androgynous child, to use, as often, the popular term, Greek being better adapted than Latin for the formation of compound words. At Sinuessa it also rained milk and a male baby was born with an elephant's head. These odd phenomena were atoned for by sacrifices of full-grown victims, and a decree was issued for prayer at all the "couches" and for one day of special entreaties; it was also decreed that the praetor Hostilius should vow and celebrate the Games in honour of Apollo according to the procedure of that period.'[50]

The report is a good reminder of the Roman world-view where gods spoke in omens and demanded honour and sacrifices in return for their blessings.

No less than religious obligations, political wrangling was alive and healthy in the Republic. Fulvius, now consul, held the elections for the censors. Two men who had not yet held the consulship were named, though traditionally the post was reserved for former consuls. It was another instance of a flexibly applied Roman convention. The two censors, Marcus Cornelius Cethegus and Publius Sempronius Tuditanus, grappled over the choice of *princeps senatus*. This 'leading man of the Senate' was a position created early in the third century BC.[51] The *princeps* had a position of high status and honour, marked by the privilege of offering his opinion first during any senatorial deliberations.[52] The censors used lots to determine which of them would pick the *princeps*. The lot favoured Sempronius, who selected Fabius to be *princeps*, and Cornelius protested. According to the *morem traditum a patribus*, the 'customs passed on by the ancestors' – a claim made on many occasions – the living senator who had held the censorship earliest should be chosen *princeps*. In this case, that was the myopic Manlius Torquatus. Sempronius countered: the lot had fallen to him, the gods had sanctified his choice, and he chose Fabius. Clearly, Sempronius opined, Fabius was the first among all citizens, regardless of Manlius' claim to have held the censorship first. The squabble dragged on in this vein for a while, but, ultimately, Sempronius got his way. Custom had yielded again to current practicalities.[53]

Tarentum Recovered

Sacrifices complete and political wrangling reduced to a simmer, the consuls departed to join their armies. Fabius overtook Fulvius, who had gone ahead, at Capua, and the two held a war council. Marcellus received word of their deliberations by letter. Fabius indicated it was time for Tarentum to return to the fold. While Fulvius and Marcellus occupied Hannibal, he would conduct the necessary siege. Accordingly, Marcellus dogged the Carthaginian forces in Apulia. He certainly occupied Hannibal; whether he won a tactical victory is far less clear. Livy details that Marcellus' army clashed with Hannibal's in Apulia. Marcellus' troops, allegedly, lost the first engagement but, bolstered by Marcellus' harangues, ultimately defeated the Carthaginians. This may be fabrication by a writer inclined to favour Marcellus. Strategically, however, the goal was to entangle Hannibal's army and leave Fabius free to take Tarentum. In this, Marcellus succeeded.[54]

Meanwhile, Fabius set about his own task. His soldiers first stormed Manduria, a town south-east of Tarentum. Perhaps its position nearby made it an unacceptable threat to Fabius' siege. Perhaps he wanted to boost his soldiers' morale before they settled into the drudgery of a siege. To a siege, however, they did turn, camping at the mouth of Tarentum's harbour. First, however, Fabius wanted to test the sea defences of the city. He outfitted his quinqueremes accordingly, some with scaling equipment for the sea walls, others with stone and bolt-throwing engines to assist the assault. It can be chalked up to simple good fortune that the Punic fleet that might have fouled this operation was away in Greece aiding Carthage's Macedonian ally, King Philip.[55] Nothing is reported, however, about the success of this operation. Livy states simply that while Fabius had Tarentum under siege, something happened within the city. He dismisses it as a 'trivial circumstance', but this is likely just an attempt not to diminish Fabius' record, because it changed everything.

It seems that a love story intertwined with the recapture of Tarentum. Hannibal had assigned a unit of Bruttians – allies from the toe of the Italian peninsula – to help protect Tarentum. The commander of that unit loved a woman whose brother served in Fabius' army. That brother learned about this relationship and brought the matter to Fabius' attention. They agreed the Bruttian commander's crush could prove useful and crafted a plan. The brother made a show of deserting the Roman army and sought the protection of Tarentum. Once harboured by the city, the brother insinuated himself into the Bruttian officer's good graces, leveraging the officer's love for his sister. When the opportunity arose, the Roman double agent persuaded the Bruttian commander to betray the city to Fabius. They sent word to the consul and coordinated a plan.[56]

Fabius somehow communicated with the garrison in the citadel, unsurprisingly given that the Romans had managed to run the Tarentine blockade more than once. He also gave instructions to the troops outside the city and those patrolling the harbour itself. Then he took a segment of the army to the east side of the city wall and hid them from sight. When all was ready, trumpet blasts rose from the citadel, the harbour and the Roman ships on the water, shattering the quiet of the dawn. Then came shouts. The effect was cacophonic. With all the noise in the city, the Tarentines could not pinpoint exactly where the greatest threat lay. The real threat, Fabius' assault troops, kept deadly silent. The Tarentine commander, Democrates, followed the cries to the citadel, mistakenly judging the threat to be there. He led his troops there, leaving the eastern portion of the city, where Fabius lurked, relatively undefended. Fabius issued orders for his men to scale the city walls in a place where, by pre-arrangement, the Bruttian guards would be stationed to welcome them. Once over the top, the Romans and Bruttians demolished a nearby gate to allow the rest of the Roman force easy access.[57]

Now the Romans in Fabius' command added their own shouts to the mayhem. They occupied the central marketplace without incident. The sun rose and the distracted Tarentine garrison soon learned of the real threat. Alerted, the Tarentine guards swarmed against the Roman invaders in the market. Not surprisingly, Livy cannot resist a bit of prejudicial pride here: 'The Tarentine was no match for the Roman in courage, in arms, in the art of war, in bodily energy and strength.'[58] Perhaps that was true, though it may be that the Romans simply had the advantage of surprise. Allegedly, in any event, the Tarentines simply cast their javelins and fled. But this does not seem to quite fit with Livy's report that Nicon and Democrates fell 'fighting bravely'. The market skirmish may, in fact, have been a grim affair. Whatever the reality was, Philemenus abandoned the scuffle on horseback. When the killing was done, the horse was found, but not its rider. Rumour had it that Philemenus dived into a well to end his life.[59]

So much for the Tarentine detachment of the garrison. Carthalo commanded the Carthaginian contingent. Fabius and his father were bound by guest-friendship. He had apparently noted this to some Romans, surrendered his arms and made his way to Fabius. Sadly, a Roman soldier who either did not know or did not care about Carthalo's family connections, slew him. There apparently were a number of similar episodes. Livy and Plutarch refer to the slaying of numerous defectors.[60] Plutarch adds a disturbing detail: Fabius killed all the complicit Bruttians, scheming to bury the fact that he had won the city through treachery. But this cruel act did not cover his tracks.[61] Livy, the earlier source, mentions the slaughter of the Bruttians and agrees that the Romans may have been motivated to hide the help they received from them. He does not, however, suggest Fabius specifically targeted the Bruttians.[62] Was Livy omitting a connection that would only tarnish Fabius' reputation, or did Plutarch's source unfairly pin the slaughter of the Bruttians on Fabius? We simply do not know.

'After the carnage followed the sack of the city,' says Livy, leaving perhaps too much leeway to the imagination for the student of Roman history.[63] The likely horror would shock modern sensibilities. Rape, slaughter, theft and destruction happened more or less indiscriminately, depending on the commander's inclination and the mood of the soldiers. Regardless of whatever protocols they may have followed when sacking cities, the carnage made a virtual Hell on Earth.[64]

The results of the sack are difficult to know for certain. The sources used Fabius' treatement of Tarentum to illustrate that he was more moderate than his rival Marcellus. Though the precise numbers Livy gives are hardly trustworthy, it is reasonable to suppose the sack of Tarentum brought the Roman soldiers a great deal of loot. Livy, and likely his sources, cannot stop themselves from using this moment to praise Fabius:

'After the carnage followed the sack of the city. It is said that 30,000 slaves were captured together with an enormous quantity of silver plate and bullion, 83 pounds' weight of gold and a collection of statues and pictures almost equal to that which had adorned Syracuse. Fabius, however, showed a nobler spirit than Marcellus had exhibited in Sicily; he kept his hands off that kind of spoil. When his secretary asked him what he wished to have done with some colossal statues – they were deities, each represented in his appropriate dress and in a fighting attitude – he ordered them to be left to the Tarentines who had felt their wrath.'[65]

Aware of that rivalry, the ancient sources dwelt on the difference between Marcellus' sack of the great city of Syracuse in 211 and Fabius' capture of Tarentum. According to the sources, Marcellus lavished the captured wealth from Syracuse on the Romans: his temple to Honos and Virtus – which was an addition to the very same structure that Fabius had originally constructed for Honos – became a spectacle of Greek art, as did many other places throughout the city.[66] But Marcellus earned the criticism of the sources for this allegedly un-Roman attachment to Greek art.[67]

The sources transmitted to us decidedly did not approve of Marcellus' treatment of Syracuse, and suggested Fabius was the better man for his restraint at Tarentum. Polybius, the earliest surviving commentary, does not directly compare the two commanders in the remaining excerpts of his work, but certainly criticizes Marcellus. For Polybius, the issue seems to be that Marcellus despoiled Syracuse of a great deal of artwork – 'paintings and reliefs', he specifies – and could have exercised a much more dignified restraint in this matter. Coming later, Livy adds some prejudice at the Greeks' expense, expanding on Polybius' criticism and adding that the Greek art corroded Roman virtue:

> 'As regards the adornments of the city, the statues and paintings which Syracuse possessed in abundance, he carried them away to Rome. They were the spoils of the enemy, to be sure, and acquired by right of war. Yet from that came the very beginning of enthusiasm for Greek works of art and consequently of this general licence to despoil all kinds of buildings, sacred and profane, a licence which finally turned against Roman gods and first of all against the very temple which was magnificently adorned by Marcellus. For temples dedicated by Marcus Marcellus near the Porta Capena used to be visited by foreigners on account of their remarkable adornments of that kind; but of these a very small part is still to be seen.'[68]

But that is not all that Livy is saying. When he says Marcellus' actions set the precedent for despoiling 'all kinds of buildings, sacred and profane', he clearly implies that Marcellus did not limit his soldiers to sacking mundane buildings but allowed them to target religious objects and structures. A century later, Plutarch made this contrast between the so–called 'Sword' and 'Shield' of Rome explicit:

> 'When Marcellus was recalled by the Romans to the war in their home territories, he carried back with him the greater part and the most beautiful of the dedicatory offerings in Syracuse, that they might grace his triumph and adorn his city … Therefore with the common people Marcellus won more favour because he adorned the city with objects that had Hellenic grace and charm and fidelity; but with the elder citizens Fabius Maximus was more popular. For he neither disturbed nor brought away anything

of the sort from Tarentum, when that city was taken, but while he carried off the money and the other valuables, he suffered the statues to remain in their places, adding the well-known saying: "Let us leave these gods in their anger for the Tarentines." And they blamed Marcellus, first, because he made the city odious, in that not only men, but even gods were led about in her triumphal processions like captives; and again, because, when the people was accustomed only to war or agriculture, and was inexperienced in luxury and ease, but, like the Heracles of Euripides, was "Plain, unadorned, in a great crisis brave and true", he made them idle and full of glib talk about art and artists, so that they spent a great part of the day in such clever disputation.'[69]

Now the ancient analysis suggests that not only did the art corrupt, not only was sacking the statues and paintings of gods from their temples blasphemous, but the elder citizens among Fabius' contemporaries actively supported Fabius' approach over that of Marcellus.

But did Fabius or his adherents at the time contrast his supposedly more dignified behaviour with Marcellus' coarse plundering? Did Fabius refrain from despoiling Tarentum? Apparently not. Several sources refer to a colossal bronze statue of Hercules that Fabius seized from Tarentum and installed on the Capitoline Hill in Rome, no doubt another effort to reinforce the Fabii's connection to that legendary hero.[70] Plutarch elaborates, noting that Tarentum,

'was plundered by the Roman army, and three thousand talents were thereby brought into the public treasury. While everything else was carried off as plunder, it is said that the accountant asked Fabius what his orders were concerning the gods, for so he called the pictures and statues; and that Fabius answered: "Let us leave their angered gods for the Tarentines." However, he removed the colossal statue of Heracles from Tarentum, and set it up on the Capitol, and near it an equestrian statue of himself, in bronze.'[71]

It appears that Fabius' army did loot Tarentum, but that perhaps Fabius or one of his adherents tried to make the case that he had left the Tarentine religious statues untouched. It was a shaky claim at best, but perhaps it was tossed around in the years after Syracuse and Tarentum were recovered.

The Political Aftermath of Tarentum

Fabius returned to the Senate after his successful consulship. The assembly elected his rival Marcellus consul for 208, along with Titus Quinctius Crispinus.[72] Once the Senate had distributed the consuls' provinces and tended to the military decisions within its competence, that august body came to scrutinize important matters related to Tarentum. How to treat the prodigal Tarentines was the first order of business. Tempers flared as senators fenced about the matter. As the *princeps senatus*, Fabius offered the first opinion on the matter.[73] He urged, Livy records, a lenient approach to the captured Tarentines. Others insisted that Tarentum should meet the same fate as Capua. When that city had been recaptured after a lengthy siege, the Romans summarily executed, enslaved or imprisoned many leading Capuans. The city and its hinterlands were declared to be Roman property, and Capua lost municipal status and became territory directly administered by Roman officials. All the Capuans lost their Roman citizenship, and, of course, the city was plundered.[74] The Senate was fractured on the matter until Manius Acilius successfully moved that, for now, Tarentum should come under Roman guard and the Tarentines remain confined within their city walls. The Senate would revisit the matter later at the more appropriate time when Italy was pacified and there was room to deliberate more fully.[75] Though strictly speaking Acilius' motion was not what Fabius had recommended, the outcome was something of a victory for Fabius. He had consistently urged moderate responses to Rome's defected allies, to avoid alienating them further. He achieved this in the Tarentum debate: those most opposed to his motion had not carried the Senate and Tarentum would not be subjected to the horrors the Capuans had experienced. At least, not yet.

The debate was no less animated when it came to the Roman commander of the garrison at Tarentum, Marcus Livius. Depending on who framed the issue, he ranged from a hero to a blunderer. Under his command the Romans had lost Tarentum, and then there were allegations that he was drunk when the city changed hands. But under his command the citadel also resisted capture for years. As the estimation of Livius' tenure differed, so did his suggested recompense. At the two extremes were those who wished to vote him rewards and those who wished him stigmatized by senatorial decree. Fabius, however, who must have led the debate here too, opted for a moderate path. It would be the next censors' task to judge whether Livius had behaved admirably or deserved censure, not the Senate. Despite his moderate path on the matter, Fabius could not resist a jibe at Livius' expense. After his supporters had repeatedly offered that Tarentum was recovered due to Livius, Fabius noted that, strictly speaking, this was true. If Livius had not lost Tarentum, Fabius would not have needed to recover it.[76]

The debate in the Senate was followed by more political wrangling. The board of priests detained Marcellus before he could depart to his consular province in southern Italy: there was the matter of his temple to Honos and Virtus, which he had vowed more than a decade earlier for outmanoeuvring the Gauls at Clastidium.[77] Marcellus, apparently, simply wanted to take the existing temple to Honos, the one Fabius had dedicated some twenty or more years before, and dedicate it to both Honos and Virtus. The pontiffs – Fabius was one of them –

insisted this would not do. More precisely, they noted that one *cella* – the name for the inner chamber of a Roman temple where the statue of the divinity lived and gifts could be dedicated – could not be dedicated to two gods. If any omens occurred such as lightning striking the *cella*, the priests would be unable to determine which god had crafted the message and which god required atonement. Marcellus was stuck, and it is difficult not to imagine Fabius smiling, at least inwardly, at this obstacle to his upstart rival's plans. Marcellus' only option was to rush construction of a second *cella*.[78] He was pressed for time, however, and could not dedicate the final complex personally. He never got the chance. That very year he and Crispinus led a scouting party straight into a Carthaginian ambush, and Marcellus died in the ensuing fight.[79]

The scrap over the temple dedication illustrates vividly the connection between religion and politics in Republican Rome seen on many occasions in this book. It would be a misunderstanding to declare that Fabius had somehow manipulated the state religion for his political ends, if we suppose that to mean that there really was no religious issue at stake. It was the pontiffs' task to make sure that the Roman state and its magistrates acted in ways that were pleasing to the gods. In a world where the gods could communicate in so many ways and have such serious impact on the fortunes of humans, this task required a fair measure of interpretation. But it was critical that the signs from the gods be understood correctly and the appropriate measures be taken to patch the relationship. Both pontiff and augur, Fabius, appropriately enough for one in those positions, insisted obligations to the gods must be taken very seriously. So far as we know, he always had: the consistency in the sources likely reflects Fabius' real position. There was a case to be made that the dual dedication confused affairs and would make it difficult to placate the gods properly. It was the obligation of the pontiffs to rule on such a case. None of this, however, means that Fabius approached this matter dispassionately. Doubtless he found some satisfaction that he could twist the knife into Marcellus, if metaphorically only, concerning what he and a sufficient number of his priestly colleagues held to be a legitimate religious objection.

The ambush that killed Marcellus also mortally wounded Crispinus, who died within a few weeks. Though the damage to Marcellus and Crispinus' armies had been limited and the armies were still safe, 208 was a sombre year. It was bad enough that both consuls perished; worse still, they had died in a trap, taken as testimony to their impulsivity and arrogance. Election of new consuls to take the leaderless armies in hand was a top priority. Livy makes it seem as if the Senate was united in its choices for candidates to the office. Gaius Claudius Nero appeared a fit enough patrician candidate, but this left the question of a plebeian who might serve as his colleague. Obvious choices for candidates were patrician: Fabius Maximus, Valerius Laevinus and so on. Marcellus was dead. Someone in the Senate seized on Marcus Livius Salinator. The suggestion garnered sufficient approval in the Senate and the electoral assembly was willing enough to choose these candidates.[80]

Claudius Nero and Livius Salinator: the Hostile Consuls and the Battle of the Metaurus (207 BC)

There was a bit of a problem though, as Livius did not want the position. More than a decade ago, the assembly had convicted him for misconduct while consul.[81] Humiliated, he retired from public life, subsisting in quiet disgrace in the countryside. In 210, the consuls Marcellus and Laevinus decided the outcast should return to public life at Rome. Still, Salinator nursed his indignation, wearing shabby clothing and sporting long hair and a beard to indicate his grief. Then the censors stepped in, forcing him to shave, dress appropriately and return to his senatorial duties. Salinator remained in ill-humour, refusing to offer anything more than his assent by a single word or by walking across the Senate chambers to the mover's side. When his relative, Marcus Livius Macatus, was investigated for his command at Tarentum, however, Salinator shelved his grudge long enough to deliver a speech in his defence. His words stirred the admiration of many senators, who now felt he was exactly the sort of Roman they needed to serve as Nero's consular colleague. When he heard news of his election, Livius Salinator bitterly mocked the inconstancy of the people. They had once convicted him, but now judged him worthy to hold the consular office again. Somehow, the leaders of the Senate persuaded him to drop his grudge and serve in the best interests of the Republic.[82]

Their choice of Salinator's consular colleague had not helped matters. Nero had testified against Salinator, and the two were enemies.[83] The Senate and people, however, seemed determined to keep these two in office. One wonders what credentials, or connections, Livius Salinator had to warrant all this effort to make him consul. In any event, it would hardly do to have two bitter enemies commanding Rome's armies. Fabius, therefore, proposed to reconcile the two consuls, and his motion gained the approval of the Senate. It should come as no surprise at this point that reconciliation was a tough sell. Livius insisted no reconciliation was needed; on the contrary, competition with his foe, Nero, would keep him sharp in office. Fabius was negotiating with the collective authority of the Senate at his back, however, and the two ostensibly surrendered their grudges.[84] If Livy can be believed, however, there was no fury like that of an aristocrat whose pride had been wounded. As the consuls set out to their armies, Fabius reportedly warned Livius to study the enemy before engaging him rashly. Livius demurred. He would attack the Carthaginians on sight, reasoning that then he would either win glory against the enemy or the pleasure of seeing his fellow citizens defeated.[85]

It strains belief, however, that Livius could have walked about saying things like this and still be elected consul, or once elected remain in office without a murmur. This is probably a case where Livy's excess needs to be ignored without losing the point: the man was proud, and that pride had been seriously wounded. Livy or his sources took the opportunity posed by the episode to have Fabius preach again to a Roman commander. They may not have fabricated this. After all, Fabius was *princeps senatus* and now five times a consul. It is no stretch to suppose he helped reintegrate Livius Salinator, and felt free to preach in the process.

As it happened, Livius Salinator and his colleague, Claudius Nero, would fight one of the most important engagements of the war. Hannibal's brother, Hasdrubal, had left Spain and the fight there against the Romans in 208, and made his way to northern Italy by the long trek along the Spanish and French coasts. Along the way he recruited various Gauls until he had a sizeable force, perhaps 30,000 soldiers in all. He aimed to join forces with Hannibal in southern Italy. Through their soldiers' feat of will and military discipline, however, the two consuls prevented this happening. Claudius Nero, facing Hannibal in the south, took a detachment of 6,000 infantry and 1,000 cavalry, left his subordinate in charge to keep Hannibal occupied and travelled at lightning speed some 280 miles in six days to join Livius Salinator's force at the Metaurus River. Together, the two consuls and an additional force under praetor Lucius Porcius Licinus defeated Hasdrubal at the Metaurus, killing 10,000 men, capturing 5,000 and scattering the rest. As a side note, Fabius' son, the consul of 213, served as one of Livius Salinator's legates at the Metaurus.[86] After the battle, Claudius Nero and his detachment returned to the south. Hannibal had been duped. He never realized the consul had left a smaller force facing him or that a battle had been fought in the north until a Roman patrol threw Hasdrubal's severed head at the Carthaginian pickets.[87] The victory at the Metaurus was certainly a turning point. Hannibal withdrew his army to Bruttium, and though it is only through hindsight that we can see he never again took the offensive in Italy, remaining instead in his corner of the peninsula, it was clear at the time that this victory was crucial.[88]

Business as usual followed in Rome. Lucius Veturius Philo and Quintus Caecilius Metellus had distinguished themselves as legates in the Metaurus campaign, and their resulting good reputation propelled them to the consulship for 206.[89] The Senate declared Bruttium to be the consular province of the year. As usual, the gods' grievances, revealed through ill omens, were dutifully addressed. But there was something different in the air: the tides of war had ebbed. The Senate charged the consuls to return Roman farmers to their ploughs and their crops. The consuls issued an appropriate proclamation, and the northern colonies of Placentia and Cremona received special attention. These two settlements had suffered greatly under Punic and Gallic predations, and many of their colonists had scattered, leaving farms abandoned and the town forums quiet. These colonies were critical to the projection of Roman power in northern Italy, and their condition had to be addressed. This year the praetor Mamilius marched with troops to protect the colonies, and the consuls declared that all the colonists from these settlements should return.[90] Events for the year reinforced the decision to get farmers back to their farms. Hannibal stayed quietly in Bruttium. For the first year since the invasion of Italy, the great general simply sat and waited. For their part, the Roman consuls did nothing to provoke him. Livy notes, perhaps drawing from Polybius, that the real miracle in all of this was that Hannibal's troops remained loyal while inactive. Loyal they were, however, and the year passed without major incident.[91]

The Second Punic War in Spain

To understand the final years of the war in Italy and Africa, we need to backtrack, shift theatres and consider the course of the Second Punic War in Spain. The Carthaginians had carved out an empire there in the years between the First and Second Punic Wars, and Hannibal had launched his invasion from the peninsula. When Publius Cornelius Scipio remained in northern Italy in 218 BC to check Hannibal, his brother, Gnaeus Cornelius Scipio Calvus ('baldy'), continued with forces to Spain to attack the Carthaginians there. Once he was reinforced later in the year by his brother Publius, the two drove into Carthaginian territory and began a long, slow war to wrest territory from the Carthaginian empire. The exact chronology and details of the Scipios' campaigns are far from clear. Still, they seem to have met with some success in between long standstills in hostilities. Then disaster struck in 211. Roman forces were routed and the Scipio brothers died in action, Publius at the Baetis River and Gnaeus at Ilorci. Surviving soldiers gathered together under the impromptu leadership of an officer, Lucius Marcius. Marcius managed to collect a small army – 8,000–9,000 soldiers – retreat to the Ebro River in northern Spain and hold firm. The Senate responded to his missives, dispatching propraetor Gaius Claudius Nero to supplement the small Spanish army with an additional 12,000 infantry and 1,000 cavalry. Claudius, now in command of Rome's Spanish forces, seems to have remained on the defensive in 210.[92]

Then something rather striking happened at Rome. Claudius was clearly meant to be a provisional solution to the Spanish problem, and there were many suitable commanders to take the reins in Spain for the longer term. At this point the young son of Publius Cornelius Scipio, also named Publius Cornelius Scipio, stepped into the spotlight. Though only 25, he had probably seen a great deal of military service, though all we know for certain is that he served in northern Italy in 218 and was at Cannae in 216. He had been aedile in 213. He was too young to be a praetor, certainly too young to be a consul, and accordingly lacked all the necessary prerequisites for commanding the Spanish army. Yet he presented himself to the voters of the centuriate assembly anyway and staked his claim on his parentage; what more legitimate successor to the campaigns of the Scipios than the son of Scipio? For this to happen, however, a number of constitutional irregularities had to be sustained. Not only was Scipio too young to hold high command, and not only had he not served in offices traditionally required before holding high command – praetor, consul – but at the time of his appointment, Scipio was a private citizen, not a government magistrate at all. And yet the centuriate assembly voted to give him proconsular imperium and dispatch him to command the Roman army in Spain.[93]

Ultimately, Scipio rewarded the extraordinary confidence of the assembly. He imposed rigorous training regimes on his soldiers and seems to have employed some army reorganization to make his forces more effective. He conducted a series of successful campaigns in Spain, capped in 209 with the capture of New Carthage, the bastion of Carthaginian strength in the peninsula. Further victories followed and, by 206, with the striking victory – and tactical innovations – at Ilipa, Scipio had shattered the Carthaginian forces in Spain and effectively commandeered Carthage's Spanish empire for Rome.[94] Then Scipio returned to Rome, his sights set on the consulship for 205.

The Warhorse and the Upstart: Fabius and Scipio at Rome

Now Fabius, a credit to his lineage, an aristocrat whose record outshone almost all his rivals, who shaped the military and diplomatic policies of the Republic during the critical war years, faced a political battle he could not win. The immovable object was about to be sidestepped by the up-and-coming Publius Cornelius Scipio. His achievements in Spain had been nothing short of astonishing. He left for Spain as a young man with no major offices to his credit, too young for a Roman to hold a command. Yet command he did. Denied a triumph for his victories in Spain, Scipio did not press. He had his eye on greater *gloria*, a chance to defeat the mighty Hannibal himself and end the war. Because a proconsul had to surrender his *imperium* before he could enter the city of Rome, Scipio came as a private citizen, but by no means an ordinary one. As he entered the city on foot, he was preceded by 14,342lb of Spanish silver and a horde of silver coins, all of which he deposited in the state coffers. It would not be surprising at all to hear that word of his entry was circulated through the city before the event itself. However things may have been, Scipio was popular enough to win election to the consulship alongside Publius Licinius Crassus, despite his youth and the fact that he had not been praetor.[95] The buzz was everywhere, the assembly packed with people who just wanted to catch a sight of the youthful imperator who had pacified Carthaginian Spain.

With the consuls duly elected for 205, the Senate established the provinces for the year: Sicily and Bruttium. There was no need to cast lots: Crassus, as *pontifex maximus*, had to remain in Italy to fulfill his obligations to the gods. The consuls made the necessary arrangement. Then the Senate convened on the Capitoline Hill. Scipio, however, queried the Senate about their allocation of provinces, along with other matters. He had vowed public games in honour of the gods when his soldiers had mutinied in Spain at the end of his campaigns – a slight stain on his otherwise superlative record. The mutiny quelled, Scipio wished to draw from the deposits he had made to the treasury to underwrite the games. The Senate issue a decree to make it so.[96] Then matters shifted to the ambassadors from Spanish Saguntum. They brought praise and thanksgiving to the Romans, along with the more substantial gift of a golden wreath to symbolize the victories in Spain.[97]

The time came for levying and allocating troops. But Scipio had set his sights on Africa and had made little, if any, attempt to mask the fact. On the contrary, he let it circulate that, if the Senate would not willingly assign him the province of Africa that year, he would bypass their authority and seek the people's approval to invade Africa through a special assembly. Apparently, he put the question to the Senate: would they acquiesce and change his sphere of operations to Africa? As Livy had it, the leading senators strenuously censured the motion while the rest remained quiet, fearful of upsetting Scipio. If indeed it was fear that locked their jaws, it did nothing to prevent Fabius from launching into a tirade. As the *princeps senatus*, he was rightfully the first to respond.

And respond he did. Livy presents Fabius' speech, a lengthy, blistering oration. As usual, we should suspect it may be fabricated. Yet it is possible that Fabius' speech survived the centuries. Roman speeches from the time certainly survived and were circulated by the literati. Ultimately, we cannot assume, without good evidence, that this was one of those speeches. That Fabius spoke that day and that he opposed Scipio's proposal are reasonably supposed. The question is, did Livy capture the contents of the speech, the heart of Fabius' opposition, successfully?

It would seem so. As Livy has it, Fabius began by noting that for most of the Senate, it probably appeared certain that Scipio would invade Africa. There would have been reason to think so. The Senate had assigned the province of Sicily to Scipio without the customary drawing of lots. There would have been absolutely no reason to do this, to send the spectacularly successful general to the pacified Sicily, unless the assumption was that he would use the island to stage an invasion of Africa.[98] But to Fabius this invasion was anything but certain, and he would demonstrate that Africa should by no means be Scipio's province. He began by anticipating objections others might make. The easiest path was to criticize him for being Cunctator, the consummate delayer. An inexperienced Roman could call him timid. It mattered not to Fabius; his strategy had proved sound enough. Still others might suspect that Fabius was no more than an elderly jealous critic of a young man whose star was on the rise. But, Fabius responded, his reputation and his record – five consulships – should suffice to squelch any charge of jealousy.[99] Then he completed his offensive: even if Fabius had no such record, Scipio could not seriously be considered his rival. He was little more than a boy, younger in fact than his son. Covering his bases, Fabius opined that he certainly did not wish for the African command himself, he who was in fact elderly and tired. No, he would have to be content with his record in the competition for glory.[100]

His rhetorical foundation laid, Livy's Fabius moved to the core issue. Hannibal remained in Italy with an army, and that was more than enough reason to keep both the consuls at home. For Hannibal did not lack teeth, and he had to be met in Bruttium, not lured to leave by an attack on Africa. What if Hannibal made an attack on Rome again: would Scipio return from Africa to protect Rome like Fulvius had returned from Capua? This was certainly a worthwhile topic to bring up for someone in Fabius' position, but it seems odd for Fabius himself to have made it. Recall that he had opposed recalling Fulvius from Capua at the time, arguing that Hannibal did not pose a threat to the city. Livy could have been mistaken here, but it's also true that Fabius may not have been consistent or even that he did not expect anyone to notice. Then Fabius moved on to historical examples, specifically Marcus Atilius Regulus' failed invasion of Africa in 256 BC, which ended with his army defeated and the commander himself captured.[101] Then Fabius turned to contrasting Spain with Africa. In Spain the Romans had allies and safe havens in their campaign from the very beginning. In Africa there would be none. Building on a prior point, Fabius noted that not only was Hannibal still a threat, but the Carthaginians could take advantage of Scipo's absence from Italy to reinforce Hannibal's army.[102] In short, it was simply rash to have Scipio, a youth with delusions of grandeur, invade Africa. Fabius concluded:

> 'Scipio was elected consul not for his own private ends, but for us and the commonwealth, and … armies are raised to guard this city and the soil of Italy, and not for consuls to transport to any part of the world they please in the arrogant style of kings and despots.'[103]

Message delivered, Fabius waited to see its impact.

As Livy had it, Fabius' speech resonated with the Senate, especially the elder senators.[104] As with Fabius, Livy constructed a speech for Scipio. In Livy's recount he respectfully, but pointedly, accused Fabius of the very jealousy the older man denied. For Scipio, Fabius was a rival; he was at the top and that was exactly where Scipio planned to be. Truly, he hoped to have even greater fame than Fabius.[105] He conceded that Africa was dangerous, but noted that no one seemed particularly concerned with the danger when they sent him, a youthful private citizen, to succeed to the command of his slaughtered father and uncle in Spain. Yet look at what he did in Spain: stormed many cities and veritably shattered Punic armies. Scipio provided his own historic examples to challenge those of Fabius. Further, he predicted that once the Romans won an early victory in Africa, the Carthaginians' allies would abandon them. Most of all, he argued that Africa should now suffer the ravages of war, not Italy. He would indeed fight Hannibal, but fight him in Africa.

Livy notes that the Senate was hardened against Scipio's rhetoric because he had clearly indicated he would petition the assembly if the Senate denied him Africa. Fulvius was, presumably as a consular, very high on the list of senators giving opinions, for he spoke next. Rather than offering an opinion, however, he called out Scipio on his shameful lack of deference to senatorial authority. He then heightened the political theatre, calling on the tribunes of the plebs to excuse him from the responsibility to utter an opinion when it was his turn to do so. Scipio – the consul in this debate – countered that tribunes had no power to excuse a senator from the obligation to offer his opinion at the correct time. The tribunes, hardly the firebrand populists some of their successors would be a century later, ruled that Scipio indeed must abide by the Senate's assignment. If he tried to circumvent the Senate's will and propose a motion about consular assignments to the assembly, the tribunes would block the motion.[106] This determination decidedly threw Scipio off-balance. He asked for a day's recess to confer with his consular colleague. The next day, Scipio submitted: he would honour the Senate's decision. This was hardly a victory for Fabius or a defeat for Scipio, however. The Senate determined that Bruttium and Hannibal would remain a province. Scipio would be assigned Sicily, but with a critical proviso: the consul was authorized to lead his army to Africa, 'if he should consider that to be to the advantage of the state'. No one that day could reasonably doubt, however, that Scipio would indeed think it to the state's advantage to invade the southern continent.[107]

Still, it appeared Fabius' views had some traction, for the Senate did not authorize a troop levy for Scipio. Given a command but no additional troops other than those garrisoning Sicily, Fabius and the other senators opposed to Scipio's invasion exercised their powers to check the young commander. In vain, it turned out. Scipio did receive permission to take volunteers with him to Sicily and, when he made a call for soldiers, some 7,000 flocked to him. Desiring to expand on the small fleet of thirty quinqueremes he received from the Senate, he again received permission to seek donations from the allies. Once again the buzz surrounding Scipio paid off, for a number combined gifts to supply enough timber, resources and men to construct and equip an additional thirty ships. These were completed swiftly, in about six weeks. At that point, the summer of 205, Scipio, his 7,000 volunteer soldiers and thirty new warships crossed to Sicily.[108]

The Pleminius Affair

The view, clarified by hindsight, might make one suppose that the war was winding down in Italy. Indeed, the efforts to return farmers to their fields might suggest the Romans thought so too. If anything, however, the events of 205 rudely reinforced the blunt fact that the war had not ended and the danger had not past. In the summer of 205, while Scipio was making various preparations in Sicily, Hannibal's brother, Mago, crossed from the Balearic Islands with thirty warships and transports bearing 12,000 infantry and 2,000 cavalry. He seized the coastal town of Genoa in northern Italy, then trekked north into the region of Liguria to stir up Gallic rebellion. When he heard of Scipio's preparations in Sicily, he sent twenty warships back to guard the African coastline but kept to his purpose in northern Italy. This decision suggests several things. First, the Carthaginians, Mago at least, did not see Scipio's invasion as a catastrophic threat, or at least not so catastrophic that it compelled him to abort his efforts in northern Italy. Second, the Romans at the time still potentially had plenty to worry about in Italy. The war had not been concluded there. The fear in the air, according to Livy, was that the celebrations after the victory at the Metaurus were premature. For here were more Carthaginian forces causing who-knew-what chaos in concert with the Gauls.[109]

In response to this new threat, the Senate dispatched the proconsul Livius to take the army of volunteer slaves to Ariminum while Marcus Valerius Laevinus took the two city legions to Arretium.[110] Scipio spent the remainder of the year involved with preparations and duties. Once in Sicily, he supplemented his volunteers with choice veterans from the legions on the island to form an army. He drydocked his new ships so that their green timbers could weather. He also went to Syracuse to adjudicate all manner of grievances that had simmered since the city's capture by Marcellus six years before. Rather than decrease the pressure on Carthage while he prepared, Scipio sent his legate Gaius Laelius with the Sicilian fleet of thirty ships to raid the coast of Africa.[111] In other news, a Spanish revolt was quashed within a few days of its start.[112]

While Scipio administered affairs in Sicily, an opportunity arose to seize the southern Italian port of Locri. Scipio took advantage, occupied Locri and placed a certain Gaius Pleminius in charge.[113] Then he crossed the straits of Messina and returned to Sicily. Pleminius proved to be an unfortunate choice of legate; he apparently manhandled the Locrians. Livy provides a diatribe:

'[I]n terms of unscrupulous and rapacious conduct Pleminius so outdid the garrison commander Hamilcar, and the Roman occupying force so outdid the Carthaginians, that it seemed like a contest in villainy, not arms. Of all the things that make the weak hate the strength of the powerful, there was not one that was not inflicted on the townspeople by the commander or his men. Unspeakable abuse was inflicted on the men themselves, on their children, and on their wives. Soon the greed of the Romans did not shrink from the desecration even of the sacred, and it was not simply a matter of the violation of ordinary temples. Even the treasures of Proserpina suffered this fate.'[114]

Unfortunately, except for the charge of looting temples, particularly the Locrians' most distinguished one belonging to the Queen of the Dead, we are left with few specifics. Still, these were the sorts of activities that posed serious diplomatic problems.

It's not clear whether anything would have been done to curb Pleminius' rapacity by itself. But soon, all Hell broke loose. It seems that although Pleminus was the ranking officer in Locri, there was an independent detachment of sorts, under the command of a pair of military tribunes. One of Pleminius' soldiers pilfered a silver cup from a Locrian. He fled the crime scene but encountered the two military tribunes, Sergius and Matienus, along the way. They decided to apprehend the soldier and return the cup to the Locrian. The thief lacked discipline, however, and challenged the tribunes' order. Some of the soldier's comrades – Pleminius' men – joined the dispute, as did some of the tribunes' men. Harsh words were followed by a street brawl. Pleminius' soldiers got the worst of it and hightailed to Pleminius to complain. Pleminius saw that his men had been bloodied, heard the details and overreacted.

Leaving his house, Pleminius commanded the tribunes to be dragged before him. His lictors obeyed, and he had Sergius and Matienus stripped down and prepared for a beating. The two tribunes resisted arrest, however, and called for the help of their men. Men loyal to the tribunes arrived, stopped the lictors in their tracks and, enraged, went for Pleminius himself. Pleminius was now surrounded by irate soldiers, who cut and beat him. In a final act of cruelty, they mutilated Pleminius' ears and nose and cast him aside like so much refuse.[115]

Word reached Scipio of his soldiers' atrocious behaviour, and it is no stretch to say he was displeased. Hopping on a ship from Syracuse, he sailed to Locri – probably a couple of days' trip – and investigated the incident. Pleminius was cleared of any wrongdoing and kept his post. Scipio shackled the tribunes and ordered them sent to Rome for the Senate to judge. As far as Scipio was concerned, the matter was done. He returned to Syracuse. But he badly misjudged Pleminius, and, worse still, failed to send off the tribunes before he left Locri, trusting all would be handled as he had ordered. With Scipio gone, however, Pleminius was back in charge. He bore the permanent scars of a disfigured face and felt the tribunes had escaped a justly harsh punishment. Summoning the tribunes before they could be escorted from the city, he had his revenge. Pleminius tortured them brutally and, when he had satisfied his rancour, executed them. Yet still his malignant rage drove him, for he cast the corpses out in the street to lay unburied. Nor was he finished. According to Livy,

'He [Pleminius] exercised the same savage cruelty upon the leading citizens of Locri, who he learnt had gone to Scipio to complain of his misconduct. The shocking proofs he had already given of his lust and greed amongst the allies of Rome were now multiplied in his fury, and the shame and odium they created recoiled not only on him but on his commander-in-chief as well.'[116]

Unsurprisingly, given the fractured loyalties at Locri, word soon reached Rome.

While the Senate was engaged in a variety of affairs, including the arrival of a new goddess and priestly cult from Asia Minor, word arrived of Pleminius' savagery in Locri. The Locrians sent ten ambassadors, who petitioned the consuls and received leave to address the Senate.[117] According to Livy, one core complaint was this:

'[The Roman garrison troops] are all given to robbery, pillage, assault, wounding, murder. They rape married women, girls, and free-born boys torn from their parents' arms. Every day our city suffers capture; every day it is pillaged. Day and night every corner of it rings with the wailing of women and boys being violated and carried off.'[118]

But that was not all; the Roman occupiers had violated the goddess Proserpina. She had a temple at Locri with a substantial treasury. The Locrians had explained to Pleminius that the treasury was sacred. They warned him that the King of Epirus, Pyrrhus, had once dared to touch the sacred funds and was cursed with defeat and death. Evil things awaited those who had dared to seize Proserpina's wealth. The Locrians had reported the Roman soldiers' crimes to their commanding officers. They warned the Romans about the power of Proserpina to curse those sacrilegious enough to handle her possessions. It mattered not at all; the Roman soldiers desecrated her temple by stealing her treasury anyway. The garrison's blasphemy had triggered divine vengeance. That was clear, the Locrians said, to anyone who had seen the Roman street brawl, the mutilation of Pleminius and the torture and murder of the tribunes.[119]

Their report concluded, the envoys responded to senatorial questioning. *Princeps senatus*, Fabius, took the lead. Had the envoys presented their complaints directly to Scipio, he queried? They replied that the proconsul was already immersed in plans for Africa. More importantly, Scipio had already shown that he favoured Pleminius, so little satisfaction could be had going down that path. The envoys revealed in this answer the whole affair between Pleminius and the now-murdered tribunes. The senators had heard enough. The envoys were excused so that the Senate could debate the matter in earnest.[120] Scipio's opponents in the Senate seized this opportunity to condemn the young consul's conduct. Fabius took his rightful lead, questioning Scipio's fitness to command and arguing that Scipio bred indiscipline among his troops. Then he moved to drag Pleminius before the Senate to answer for his crimes; recall Scipio for leaving his province of Sicily and going to Locri in the first place; and have a tribune abrogate Scipio's command. Finally, Fabius proposed a host of compensations to assure the Locrians that Rome condemned the wrongs inflicted on their gods and them.[121]

The air was charged. Many supported Scipio, the prodigy who had won Spain and now was poised to win the bitter war against Carthage. Many others saw him as a mere upstart, a successful one to be sure, but one who promoted laxity among his troops and did not respect the proper authority of the Senate. Passions for and against Scipio reportedly made senators so eager to speak that all could not register their opinions that day. Additional grievances arose, as they so often did when one's rival was vulnerable: Scipio was not only soft on his troops, he was too Greek in his clothing and manners, by which, among other things, his detractors meant to suggest that he was effeminate.

Ultimately, Scipio's detractors did not carry the day. Not Fabius' motion but that of Quintus Metellus prevailed. Rather than summarily condemn Scipio, senators sent a commission to investigate. If Scipio indeed had authorized Pleminius' crimes against the Locrians, they could retire him from his command. If not, they would let him go about his task, the invasion of Africa. The Senate came to some consensus and issued the necessary decree. A commission formed and departed for Locri.[122] When they arrived in the city, they worked to make amends and to investigate. The Locrians maintained that Pleminius, not Scipio, was the villain. Livy has the Locrians also suggest that Scipio was far too lax an overseer, but that he was far better a friend than an enemy. That the Locrians concluded this is practically certain, though it seems far less likely they would have openly vented that conclusion to a Roman investigation. Still the commission found no cause to try Scipio and absolved him of guilt. Pleminius, on the other hand, cooled his heels in prison for a time but died before his trial finished.[123]

The Death of Fabius Maximus Cunctator

Fabius had not managed to turn this scandal into what he had hoped, the end of Scipio's command and his plan to invade Africa. He had not checked the youth. And here, just within reach of the finale to the great war against Hannibal, the second of two long and costly wars against Carthage – the one that essentially broke Carthaginian power and set the stage for Rome to dominate the Mediterranean – the story of Fabius Maximus Ovicula Verrucosus Cunctator ends. It is an end not without some tragedy. Fabius, the old man, seems to have been eclipsed by young Scipio, though this may be just hindsight; at the time, Fabius was the most distinguished senator alive, with laurels to rest on in his waning years. Almost assuredly, the greater tragedy was that his son, the consul of 213, did not survive him. The last clear reference Livy makes to Fabius Cunctator's son is in 207. The Roman custom of using a limited number of first names makes matters confusing, but Livy refers to 'Quintus Fabius, son of Quintus Fabius Maximus',[124] which must be the great Cunctator. Fabius' son at this particular moment was mentioned because he was sent by the Senate as a special messenger to the consul Livius Drusus. All that we hear about the son of Cunctator after this is that he died. To be more precise, Plutarch and that famous senator of the late Republic, Cicero, refer to the fine eulogy Cunctator gave for his son, which of course can only mean the son died before the father.[125] This must have been sometime between 207, the last reference to the son, and 203, the year when the great Cunctator himself died.

By 203, the war against Carthage was in its final stages. Scipio had invaded Africa in 204 and began to raid and ravage Carthaginian homelands. Hannibal had left Italy to defend his home. A temporary truce was soon aborted. Finally in 202, the great generals Hannibal and Scipio clashed with their armies on the plains of Zama. The result was a crushing Roman victory and the end of the Second Punic War.[126] In 203, however, Fabius died. Livy's notice upon the Cunctator's death, though not particularly long, is more substantial than that he gave to many an aristocrat posthumously:

'This year also saw the death of Quintus Fabius Maximus. He had reached a very great age, if it is true, as some writers have stated, that he held the office of augur for sixty-two years. What is indisputable is that he was worthy of the name Maximus, and would have deserved to be the first of his line to bear it. He held more magistracies than his father, and the same number as his grandfather. His grandfather Rullus enjoyed the fame of more victories and greater battles, but to have had Hannibal as one's enemy is enough to equal or outweigh them all. Fabius has been stigmatized as a cautious soldier, never quick to act; but though one may question whether he was a "delayer" by nature or because delaying tactics happened to suit the campaigns he was engaged in, this, at least, is certain, that, as the poet Ennius wrote, "One man by his delaying saved the State." His son Quintus Fabius Maximus succeeded him as augur, and as pontifex (for he had held two priesthoods) he was succeeded by Servius Sulpicius Galba.'[127]

Yet when Livy says Fabius' 'son', Quintus Fabius Maximus, took over his position as augur, he must be mistaken for, as we have seen, the son died before the father. Accordingly, this Quintus Fabius Maximus must have been the grandson of the Cunctator. Yet the grandson too slips through our fingers and no source refers to any office he held other than the augurate. Scion of a most prestigious family, he did not escape an early death. In 196 BC he died, Livy says, while still very young and before holding any elected office.[128]

Though the untimely death of Fabius Cunctator's son and grandson could well have been the end of the Fabii Maximi, the family whose progenitors stretched back as much as half a millennium, the clan survived. And while the great Cunctator's descendants would never reach his level of fame and distinction as the veritable saviour of the Republic in this, its moment of crisis, there were still wars to be fought and laurels to be earned for the great family of the Republic.

Chapter 7

Spanish Wars, Gallic Wars, Civil Wars and the End of the Line

The End of the Line Averted

The last chapter left the line of the Fabii Maximi faltering. Cunctator had lived past his son. The son of that child, grandson of Cunctator, survived his father by no more than a decade, dying in 196 without any elected office to his name.[1] A little less than a decade later, another family member surfaces briefly in the sources. This particular Quintus Fabius was a quaestor under Manlius Accidius in Farther Spain, one of the two Spanish provinces Rome created after the war against Hannibal. He served as praetor in 188 and was propraetor as late as 186 BC. Livy does not provide his *cognomen*, however, and it is not clear whether this Quintus Fabius was a Maximus or a Buteo, another somewhat less distinguished but still notable branch of the clan.[2] Either way, Quintus Fabius went on, it seems, to be elected praetor for 181. To be more precise, two of the six praetors elected that year were named Quintus Fabius, one a Quintus Fabius Buteo and the other a Quintus Fabius Maximus. The lots assigned Fabius Buteo to Gaul and Fabius Maximus to the post of praetor *peregrinus*, charged with hearing suits between Romans and foreigners.[3] Livy only mentions that Fabius Maximus was instructed to levy soldiers for defence against the Ligurians. When the Senate felt the danger had passed, Fabius was ordered to cease the levy.[4] Hardly the sort of record that would move the stylus of an epic poet. And with that, another Quintus Fabius Maximus disappears from the sources.

'He is a noble, but no Cunctator, no Rullianus', many Romans must have thought about these Fabii Maximi in the decades after the Second Punic War. How these Fabii themselves felt about their records, trivial in comparison to their grandfathers Cunctator and Rullianus, is lost to time. But it cannot have been easy on them. Fabius Cunctator's landmarks, his equestrian statue in bronze and the

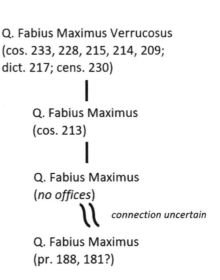

Q. Fabius Maximus Verrucosus
(cos. 233, 228, 215, 214, 209;
dict. 217; cens. 230)

|

Q. Fabius Maximus
(cos. 213)

|

Q. Fabius Maximus
(*no offices*)

    connection uncertain

Q. Fabius Maximus
(pr. 188, 181?)

colossal Hercules from Tarentum, graced the Capitoline Hill for all to see. The great war was still in living memory. The great Fabius Cunctator, as the most distinguished senator during that war, at least at the end when he was twice named *princeps senatus*, would have been something of a household name for any who paid attention to Roman affairs of the past twenty years. This stood in stark contrast to this series of relatively politically insignificant Fabii Maximi who remained, the most successful never going past the praetorship, a prestigious post to be sure, but nothing like the consulships that Fabii Maximi had held in the past.

Before long, it appeared that the line would end altogether. Sometime not too long after 180, all male heirs were apparently dead. Only a pact with the distinguished Aemilli Paulli averted the extinction of the line. Plutarch relates the following story. Lucius Aemilius Paullus, whose father of the same name earned great glory for dying in the thick of the fighting at Cannae in 216, had two sons with his wife Papiria. They divorced and Paullus had two more sons in a second marriage. Paullus presumably felt that four sons inheriting would strain his estate excessively, so he arranged for the two boys from his first marriage to be adopted. The younger was adopted by the great family of Cornelius Scipio Africanus. The oldest son of Scipio Africanus was Paullus' first cousin, and it may have been that the far wealthier Scipio was doing a favour for Paullus by taking on one of his sons to raise and support. Or, if Scipio was out of heirs, Paullus did him a great favour by allowing his son to be adopted. A Fabius Maximus, presumably the praetor from 181, adopted the eldest child of Aemilius Paullus. Equally presumably, that family lacked male heirs to carry on the Fabius Maximus branch to future generations.[5] For Roman aristocrats, adoption was a perfectly viable means to carry on the family name, the name of an aristocratic family being far more important than any specific biological ties. In this case, the adoption saved the Fabii Maximii from extinction.

Fabius Maximus Aemilianus and Cornelius Scipio Aemilianus

Paullus did not sever ties to his biological sons, now named Fabius Aemilanus and Scipio Aemilianus, the name Aemilianus indicating that they had been born Aemilii. Though Fabius and Scipio both legally bore the names of their adoptive families, they continued to have close ties with their biological father. When Aemilius Paullus won the consulship and command against the Macedonian King Perseus in 168, the two young men accompanied him to war. When Carthage surrendered at the end of the Second Punic War, the Republic became the most powerful state in the western Mediterranean. It now involved itself more frequently in the eastern Mediterranean, where a number of large Greek kingdoms, sprung from the ruins of Alexander the Great's short-lived conquests, vied for dominance. Macedonia was one of these states, and ever since

Philip V had joined Hannibal against the Republic, relations had been strained. By 171, the Republic went to war against King Perseus of Macedonia, uneasy with his power and influence in the Greek-speaking world.[6] Perseus defeated the first Roman army he encountered, in Thessaly, and the war bogged down until Aemilius Paullus defeated the king at the Battle of Pydna in 168.[7] Fabius, the elder son of Paullus, apparently served with some distinction in the Pydna campaign. In Livy's somewhat fragmented surviving narrative, supplemented by Plutarch, Fabius Maximus Aemilianus and Scipio Nasica, a relative of some sort due to all these adoptive ties, led some 5,000–8,000 troops on an operational feint that strategically encircled King Perseus' forces. Perseus dispatched some of those forces to meet the threat. Nasica, the main actor in Plutarch's version, though Fabius was a co-commander, routed the Macedonian detachment and rejoined with Paullus for the decisive victory against the now-weaker Macedonian army.[8] Perseus was taken prisoner and led in chains through the streets of Rome during Paullus' triumph.[9]

According to Livy, and quite likely true, Fabius Maximus Aemilianus and his younger brother, Scipio Aemilianus, both accompanied their biological father in his triumphal procession, a spectacular affair that lasted three days, according to Roman writers.[10] Tragedy then struck Paullus. It must have seemed a divine curse, as his two young sons from his second wife, the sons who were to carry on his family name, both died within days of his triumph, one just before and the other just after.[11] And so in a cruel irony, the family line of the Aemilii Paulli ended, though Paullus had had four sons. The Fabius Maximus and Scipio Africanus clans lived on.

If Livy did recount Fabius Aemilianus' career in the aftermath of this Third Macedonian War, there is no sign of it, for the surviving books of his history break off with the year 166, and that unknown author, whose summaries of Livy's books still survive, makes no mention of Fabius. There are, however, interesting bits and pieces of evidence that can add a little to his story. When the Romans had defeated the Macedonians, they also deported 1,000 Greek hostages to Italy to guarantee the Greeks' good behaviour. Among them was the politician, military commander and scholar Polybius, to whom we are indebted for his history of Rome. In this process of deportation, Polybius encountered Fabius and Scipio. He formed a bond with the two young men early on, and when so many of his fellow Greek hostages were detained in the Italian countryside, Polybius, at Fabius and Scipio's request, remained in Rome.[12] Polybius became the mentor and fast friend of Scipio, still a youth, though he speaks positively of Fabius and suggests that at least some contemporary Romans thought more of the elder than the younger brother.[13]

Polybius' greatest praise is reserved for his protégé and patron Scipio, and we only learn a little from him about Fabius Aemilianus and the house of Fabius Maximus. Apparently, not only did the Fabius Maximus branch lack sufficient

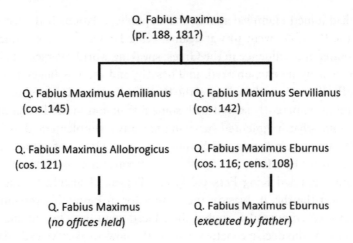

Q. Fabius Maximus
(pr. 188, 181?)

Q. Fabius Maximus Aemilianus
(cos. 145)

Q. Fabius Maximus Servilianus
(cos. 142)

Q. Fabius Maximus Allobrogicus
(cos. 121)

Q. Fabius Maximus Eburnus
(cos. 116; cens. 108)

Q. Fabius Maximus
(*no offices held*)

Q. Fabius Maximus Eburnus
(*executed by father*)

male heirs to carry on the family name, but they were also not particularly wealthy. To be more precise, not as wealthy as the incredibly wealthy family of Scipio Africanus, the defeater of Hannibal and the Carthaginians. When their biological father, Aemilius Paullus, passed away a few years after his Macedonian triumph, Fabius and Scipio became his heirs. Scipio, however, already had access to the greater riches of the Scipio family fortune and gave his portion of his inheritance from Paullus to Fabius.[14] Elsewehere, Polybius reports when Fabius Aemilianus could not afford to throw the kind of gladiatorial games he wished for his father's funeral, his younger brother, Scipio Aemilianus, covered the costs.[15] Other than these personal details that Polybius offered as testimony to the far-more-famous Scipio Aemilianus' generosity, we know little more about Fabius Aemilianus for a while. He appeared as a praetor in Sicily in 149, playing a minor role in Polybius' narrative.[16] Scipio Aemilianus, meanwhile, soon eclipsed his older brother. He sought to be elected aedile in 147. Breaking convention and by this date law, the Romans elected him consul instead. Scipio was assigned to finish the up-to-then unsuccessful siege of Carthage, for the third and final war against the city-state had broken out two years before. Perhaps Fabius Aemilianus was jealous – he probably should have been jealous from a Roman perspective – but the available evidence suggests the two biological brothers remained close all their lives. No doubt the shift in the fortunes of the Fabii Maximi and the Scipiones Africani, however, would have caused old Cunctator much distress had he known.

The Spanish Wars

When Fabius Aemilianus won the consulship in 145, two years after his considerably younger brother, he took part in one of the many brutal second-century wars the Romans fought in the Iberian peninsula. Rome acquired its first territorial interests in Spain during the war against Hannibal. At that war's end,

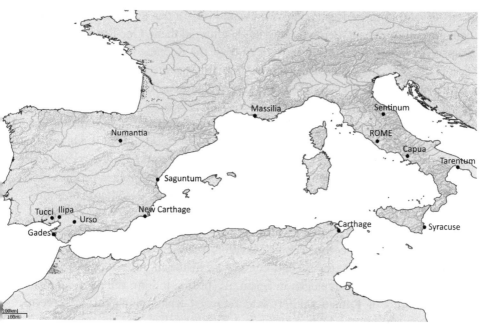

West Med.

they controlled territory that included the coastal strip along the Mediterranean and the Baetis River valley in the south (now the Guadalquivir River). Their control was far from secure; many Spanish tribes did not welcome the Romans, their rules or their taxes. Even in the wake of Scipio's Spanish victories, therefore, various groups contested Roman control. So the Republic steadily campaigned in the first half of the second century to pacify Spain. In 197, the Republic established two new praetors – raising the yearly total to four – to administer Spain, now divided into two provinces: Citerior, or 'Nearer', and Ulterior, or 'Farther'. War was the normal state of affairs in these provinces for quite some time as the Romans committed army after army to subjugating the Spanish tribes. Over time, the Republic increased its control in parts of the peninsula.[17]

In the middle of the second century, Roman troops in Hispania Ulterior faced a brutal war against the Lusitanians of south-western Hispania. In 155, the Lusitanian chief, Punicus, banded with the neighbouring Vettones tribe to attack the Roman province. They defeated the first praetor they encountered, then the second, slaughtering some 6,000 Roman troops. Punicus, however, died in one of these clashes, and an Iberian named Kaiseros succeeded him as chief of the Lusitanians. He kept up the resistance against the Romans and had some success against the next praetor in command, Lucius Mummius (153 BC). Mummius and his troops recovered, however, and the praetor earned a triumph at Rome for success against the Lusitanians.[18]

But war continued in Spain, one so brutal that even Roman historians noted it. In 150, for example, the praetor Servius Sulpicius Galba offered peace and grants of land to those Lusitanians who would obey a truce. Once he had lured them into surrendering their weapons, he slaughtered them. One Lusitanian who escaped the bloodbath and learned not to trust the Romans was Viriathus, who became the next chief of the Lusitanians.[19] Viriathus is introduced by the fourth-century summarizer of Livy as a shepherd turned hunter, then bandit, and finally general of 'a proper army'.[20] Diodorus adds that he was a sturdy boy and man, eating and sleeping sparingly, and excelling at combat against both humans and beasts; the sort of person who could give the Romans a hard time of it. He seized control of Lusitania, and, says Diodorus, shattered a Roman army under Vetillius, who was probably a praetor in Farther Spain in 147.[21] In the process Vetillius was captured; he did not live long after that.[22] Viriathus and his Lusitanians continued their string of victories, defeating several successive armies under the command of praetors. Stung by these defeats, in 145 the Senate dispatched a larger army to the province under the consul Fabius Maximus Aemilianus.[23]

Appian of Alexandria, the second-century AD historian, preserves an account of Fabius Aemilianus' campaigns in Spain. According to him, the previous year (146) thousands of Roman soldiers had returned from campaigns in Greece and at Carthage, and the Senate instructed Fabius to allow these veterans some relief and levy new recruits for the Spanish campaign. An army of raw recruits, some 15,000 infantry and 2,000 cavalry, sailed from Italy and disembarked at Urso in southern Spain. It appears Fabius had no plan of clashing with Viriathus immediately with green recruits. Accordingly, he deposited his army at Urso under a subordinate and continued on to Gades to make a special sacrifice to Hercules for the upcoming campaign. It was yet another glimpse of the Fabii Maximi both demonstrating religious piety and preserving their family status and prestige by cementing claims to descent from Hercules.[24]

While Fabius tended to these religious tasks, Viriathus harried the Roman foragers at Urso, drawing Fabius' legate into battle. Viriathus' warriors beat the Romans soundly.[25] Still, Fabius kept his command in Spain and seems to have been made proconsul for 144. His brother, Scipio Aemilianus, fresh from his destruction of Carthage in 146, may have had a hand in this. Valerius Maximus, who authored a tome of memorable anecdotes in Roman history during the first century of the Empire, describes a debate in the Senate. Apparently, the consuls for 144, Servius Suplicius Galba and Lucius Aurelius Cotta, argued who should be sent to Spain and the war against Viriathus, an odd argument to have since, presumably, the commander should be chosen by lot. In any event, Scipio Aemilianus reportedly spoke out critically against both consuls and, as a result, neither was sent to Spain.[26] This suggests Scipio Aemilianus played some role in extending his biological brother Fabius' command, consistent with the evidence we have suggesting the two remained close in their adult years.

Fabius made good use of the extension. He did not attempt to attack Viriathus directly when he returned to his army. Instead, he dispatched armed soldiers alongside future foraging parties, building up the stamina and confidence of his inexperienced soldiers through minor skirmishes with the enemy. Reports of the discipline that he supposedly instilled in his recruits left a trace in later sources. Velleius Paterculus, a Roman historian of the early first-century AD, notes that Fabius won fame in Spain by 'the severity of his discipline'.[27] When the spring arrived, Fabius' troops appeared ready to wage war. Of course, this all sounds like something old Cunctator might have done, and the training is possibly a fabricated detail, but it will hardly do to reject every story of a cautious Fabius as a copy of Fabius Cunctator's actions in 217. Whatever the truth of the matter, Fabius Aemilianus' army clashed with Viriathus and routed his forces, capturing two cities for good measure.[28] At some point after, he seems to have returned to Rome.

Checked, but not silenced, Viriathus sought more allies, persuading tribes like the Arevaci, Titthi and Belli to abandon their treaties with Rome and foster war. The result was the second phase of the Numantine War (143–133 BC), named after the important Celtiberian city of Numantia in north-central Spain that became a stronghold of Spanish resistance. Viriathus' warriors crossed swords with Romans under a commander Appius, only recognized as Quintius, or Quinctius as the Romans spelled it. This Quinctius successfully fended off Viriathus' first offensive, and the Spanish general retreated his forces to the safety of the mountains. Rallying there, the Spanish were more successful in their second attack on the Romans, killing some 1,000 of Quinctius' men, seizing some Roman battle standards and driving the fleeing army to the safety of its camp. Then Viriathus dislodged a Roman garrison from its position at Tucci, raiding and plundering in the region for good measure. Appian judged Quinctius harshly, saying the Roman commander failed to counter Viriathus because he was timid and lacked experience.[29]

At this point Viriathus had formed a Celtiberian and Lusitanian coalition that resisted Roman rule even more mightily. Rome, meanwhile, continued to churn out consular armies to deal with the threat. In 142, consul Quintus Caecilius Metellus Macedonicus, commanding 30,000 soldiers, had limited success against the Spanish. In 141, the praetor Quintus Pompeius moved against the stronghold of Numantia. Unsuccessful at first, Pompeius' command was extended for 140, but he failed to encircle Numantia fully and could not complete the siege.[30]

At this point in the Numantine War, another Fabius Maximus appears in the sources. Appian notes that Fabius Maximus Servilianus, Aemilianus' adopted brother, arrived in Spain to succeed Quinctius in 140. Clearly the older generation of the Fabius family had adopted not just one son in Aemilianus, but at least two, this second from the family of Servilius Caepio. His biological father was likely the Gnaeus Servilius Caepio who was consul in 169, and Appian attests that he was a brother of the consul of 140, Quintus Servilius Caepio.[31] Fabius Servilianus held the consulship in 142 and, reportedly, relieved Quinctius in Spain. The

Senate made him proconsul in 141, continuing his command in Spain.[32] It is not clear which campaigns took place during his consulship and which during his pronconsulship, but the rough sequence of events over the next two years seems to have been as follows. According to Appian, Fabius Servilianus brought two additional legions with him to Spain so that the force he commanded there numbered some 18,000 infantry and 1,600 horsemen. He reportedly even requested some war elephants from Rome's ally, King Micipsa of Numidia.

Viriathus waited for his moment to strike. While Fabius Servilianus' army was divided into several groups for the march to Tucci, Viriathus attacked with a force of some 6,000 men. Despite the element of surprise, the Roman contingent appears to have repelled the Spanish force, and Fabius Servilianus reportedly stood his ground bravely in the attack. Now the Roman army coalesced, along with the ten elephants and 300 Numidian cavalry for good measure. The soldiers constructed an appropriate camp, then sought out Viriathus. A battle ensued, and the Romans successfully drove the Spanish away. But Fortune was fickle, as the ancients said, for the Romans troops grew disorderly as they pursued their fleeing foes. Viriathus, in what must have been a magnificent display of leadership, managed to halt the Spanish flight, turn his forces against their Roman pursuers and drive the Romans back to their own camp, killing some 3,000 in the process. Somewhat inexplicably, the Roman forces, says Appian, were paralyzed by fear. A few defended the gates of the camp, but most cowered in their tents. It was Fabius Servilianus' moment of crisis, but he seems to have proven his command skills. He and his tribunes coaxed, cajoled and coerced Roman soldiers back into the fray, and with the help of approaching darkness, the camp was saved.[33]

Still, Viriathus continued to hound the Romans, light troops harassing them to the point that Fabius Servilianus drew his men back to the town of Itucca. The Spanish army grew short on supplies, however, so Viriathus burnt his own camp and returned his forces to Lusitania. Freed, momentarily, from the threat of Viriathus, Fabius Servilianus launched a punitive campaign against the towns in the Baetis River valley that had been loyal to the Spanish commander. After this, and an apparently small operation against the Cunaei, the Romans trekked to Lusitania in pursuit of Viriathus. Along the way, however, two 'captains of robbers', as Appian calls them, attacked the Roman force.[34] Robbers or not, they had amassed a force of 10,000, bloodied the Roman army and stole some of their loot in the process. Still, it was not a serious setback. Fabius Servilianus and his troops soon returned the measure, killing one of the robber captains in the process and recovering the booty. Continuing their momentum, the Romans captured several towns garrisoned by Viriathus and plundered here and there. In the process, Servilianus sold nearly 10,000 Spaniards into slavery.[35]

During these campaigns, Fabius Servilianus seems to have earned himself a reputation for brutality against Roman enemies in Spain. According to Valerius Maximus,

'[Servilianus] was very kind by nature, but he forced himself to put aside his merciful character for the time being and to adopt a harsh and severe policy. If he captured anyone who had deserted from the Roman garrison to the enemy, he had their hands cut off. As they went around with their mutilated arms, they made the others too terrified to desert. By cutting off the hands of rebels from their bodies and throwing them on the ground that was covered with their blood, he proved to the others that they should not dare to do likewise.'[36]

Frontinus also preserved the detail that Servilianus severed the right hands of Roman deserters.[37] Orosius, the fourth-century clergyman, suggests he exercised this brutality against the Spanish too, luring 500 Lusitanian leaders to him with a pledge of alliance, then lopping their hands from their arms.[38] The cruelty stood out, the mentions in the sources show, but there seems to have been no repercussions for Fabius; all was fair in war. Despite his brutal methods, however, Fabius Servilianus seemed unable to conclude the war. Appian provides the most positive version of his failure. He simply says Servilianus took his soldiers to winter quarters after successfully campaigning in Lusitania, then returned to Rome and was replaced in Spain by Quintus Pompeius Aulus.[39] There are different versions of the story, however. Diodorus asserts Viriathus and his army forced Servilianus to come to terms that embarrassed the Romans. Livy's summarizer, and thus almost assuredly Livy, essentially agree with Diodorus. He reports that Servilianus 'ended his successful accomplishments in disgrace, when he concluded a peace with Viriathus on equal terms'.[40] Ultimately it was Servilius Caepio, consul in 140, who defeated Viriathus decisively and imposed a peace upon him favourable to the Romans. Disgruntled traitors in the Spanish army then murdered Viriathus and ended his more-than-a-decade of resistance to the Roman occupiers.[41]

In a most Roman way, a reputation for battlefield brutality did not prevent Fabius Servilianus' success as a literary man, for he apparently achieved note as a historian. Dionysius refers to a history written by a Fabius Maximus, and this seems to have been Fabius Maximus Servilianus. If so, Dionysius' assessment that his work was a source the Romans themselves approved suggests that his history was indeed significant. It apparently began with Aeneas, as so many Roman histories did, but where it ended is simply unknown.[42] Equally lost is Servilanus' fate, for after his brief moments of record in the sources, he disappears.

But Fabius Aemilianus, consul of 145, biological brother of Scipio Aemilanus and adopted brother of Fabius Servilianus, had not yet disappeared entirely from posterity. His younger but far-more-successful brother, Scipio, won a consulship for 134 and campaigned against Numantia, the focus of Celtiberian resistance. Fabius Aemilianus accompanied Scipio as one of his legates. According to the sources, Scipio – and as his legate it is reasonable to suppose Fabius assisted –

first moved to restore order to a Roman army that he believed had grown soft. All sources of entertainment and leisure were removed: camp followers and peddlers of wares, even 2,000 prostitutes were sent on their ways.[43] In place of leisure, Scipio instituted drills and marches to build strength and discipline, no doubt to the dismay of at least some of his new soldiers. When he judged the army up to the task, Scipio began the final siege of Numantia.

The siege was an elaborate affair as Appian describes it. Two long-term camps, the stone foundations of which can still be seen today, were pitched and the army divided. Scipio commanded one camp and Fabius the other. The rebellious city was encircled by a ditch and palisade overlooked by seven towers. According to Scipio's instructions, soldiers facing an enemy sortie would raise a red flag to alert the two main camps and request reserves. Finally, a siege wall was built around most of the city, 3 metres high and 2.5 metres wide, punctuated by towers every 30 metres.[44] Scipio seems not to have missed a single detail. The Durius River that flowed through the fortifications, Scipio screened with two towers that anchored logs riddled with knife and spear points to catch any foolish enough to float downstream.[45] In some sieges, the Romans offered terms of some sort that might appeal to the defenders, but not this time. Scipio came with no terms for the defenders, no hope of a good deal. They would surrender completely, or die. His siege works emphasized that grim choice, designed as they were to crush all resistance. Earthworks, towers and artillery were erected to terrify and, ultimately, destroy the enemy.[46]

Once the siegeworks were complete, it was only a matter of time until the city was strangled. At first the Numantines attacked the siegeworks here and there, testing the cordon, trying to break out. They were swatted down by the Roman defenders, who easily converged on any point as needed.[47] Somehow, though, 400 Numantines escaped the cordon, but they found no shelter from their neighbours. When Scipio located them, he cut off their hands and left them to their fate.[48] Eventually the Numantines began to starve and panic. They attempted to negotiate with Scipio, to get some assurance of mercy if they should surrender. Appian reports the plea:

'The Numantines, being oppressed by hunger, sent five men to Scipio to ask whether he would treat them with moderation if they would surrender. Their leader, Avarus, discoursed much about the prestige and bravery of the Numantines, and said that even now they had done no wrong, but had fallen into their present misery for the sake of their wives and children, and for the freedom of their country. "Wherefore, Scipio," he said, "it is worthy of you, as a man renowned for virtue, to spare a brave and honorable race and to extend to us terms dictated by humanity, which we shall be able to bear, now that we have at last experienced a change of fortune. It rests not with us but with you whether you receive the surrender of our city on fair terms, or allow it to perish in a last struggle." When Avarus had thus spoken, Scipio (who knew from prisoners the state of affairs inside) said merely that they must surrender their arms and place themselves and their city in his hands.'[49]

The ambassadors returned empty-handed to their city, only to face the wrath of their fellow citizens:

'When [Scipio's] answer was made known, the Numantines, who were previously savage in temper because of their absolute freedom and quite unaccustomed to obey the orders of others, and were now wilder than ever and beside themselves by reason of their hardships, slew Avarus and the five ambassadors who had accompanied him, as bearers of evil tidings, and perhaps thinking that they had made private terms for themselves with Scipio.'[50]

And then, Appian asserts, true horror awoke within the city walls. The starving Numantines, those strong enough to do so, fell upon the weaker citizens and devoured them; the city descended into cannibalism. Only after this last monstrous gasp of resistance did the Numantines surrender completely to Scipio in 133 BC. Even then, many took their own lives rather than surrender.[51] It was of no matter to Rome; either way, the Spanish resistance in the region had been crushed. Scipio kept fifty Numantines to march in his predicted triumphal procession at Rome, sold the rest into slavery and destroyed the city.[52] Scipio did in fact receive the right to triumph when he returned to Rome.[53] Did the two Aemiliani, Scipio and Fabius, ride together in triumph, as they had in their father Paullus' victory three decades prior? It is certainly possible, given the close relationship the brothers seem to have had.

Fabius Allobrogicus and the Gauls

After Numantia, however, Fabius Aemilianus disappears from the sources. Fabius Aemilianus' son, who would earn the *cognomen* Allobrogicus for his exploits against the Gallic Allobroges, however, won enough distinction to stand as the third most famous of the Fabii Maximi, alongside his ancestors Rullianus and Cunctator. Of course, family tradition was preserved, and Allobrogicus began life as Quintus Fabius Maximus, the name so many of his ancestors had held since Rullianus acquired the nickname in the late fourth century BC. The number of references to him in the sources indicate that he had quite a distinguished reputation in his day and for several generations afterward. Yet for all those references, there is very little that is known about him. His early career, as so often is the case in Roman history, is something of a mystery. A couple of passages suggest he was a junior magistrate in Spain with his father Fabius Aemilianus and his biological uncle, Scipio Aemilianus. Valerius Maximus attests Scipio Aemilianus won his second consulship, the one that sent him to Numantia in 134, unintentionally. He came to the Campus Martius on election day to support his nephew's bid for the quaestorship and left with a consulship.[54] Though Valerius does not say whether Fabius succeeded in his bid for the quaestorship, it is as good a year as any to place him in this office, and Scipio's support could easily have been the tipping factor that won Fabius Maximus 'Not-Yet-Allobrogicus' the election. It is reasonable to suppose Scipio and Fabius Aemilianus remained close, and Scipio may very well have campaigned on his nephew's behalf. His endorsement should have been worth a great deal: he had won election to the consulship without having been even an aedile, and his conquest of Carthage presumably would have made him only more popular with the electorate.

If we suppose nephew Fabius joined his father and uncle in the Numantine War, it can help clarify an error in Appian's account. While still in Italy, Scipio amassed a sizeable force of volunteers, some 4,500, to take to Spain. He placed these troops under the command of Buteo, 'his nephew' says Appian.[55] It was reasonably suggested decades ago that Appian had likely mistaken Fabius Buteo for Scipio's certain nephew, 'Not-Yet-Allobrogicus'.[56] The fact that his father, Fabius Aemilianus, was also in Spain under Scipio's command only strengthens the possibility that the son came along. If this is true, Fabius 'Not-Yet-Allobrogicus' had the advantage of service under a skilled and illustrious commander. He would have learned a thing or two about siege warfare and battles in rugged terrain, both of which could have proved helpful in his future campaigns. He must have won the praetorship, because he was a governor in Spain in 123.[57] He cannot have held that praetorship any later than 124 BC, because the *Lex* (Law) *Villia Annalis*, passed in 180, dictated that two full years out of office had to pass before a former praetor could be elected consul, and Fabius won the consulship for 121.[58] His year as governor was only noteworthy in that he sent grain to Italy acquired from the Spanish, but the tribune Gaius Gracchus had the grain returned to the Spanish and Fabius reprimanded for oppressing the provincials.[59]

Fabius 'Almost-Allobrogicus' next appears in the accounts of yet another series of wars against the Gauls of northern Italy and the Alpine regions. For centuries now, the Republic had battled the Gauls. Momentarily on the ropes after the Senonian Gauls sacked the city in 390, the Republic recovered and steadily encroached on the lands of Gallic tribes in northern Italy, planting colonies and fighting many wars in the fourth and third centuries BC. The Romans had continued to push their influence northward and, as they did, encountered new tribes of Gauls, which sparked new conflicts. By the final quarter of the second century, Roman influence had reached beyond the Alps, and the Romans were in contact with Gauls on both sides of that massive mountain barrier.

Expanding influence on the other side of the Alps and in Iberia brought the Romans in contact with the important Greek coastal city of Massilia (modern Marseilles). The city had been an ally for quite some time and received Roman assistance against Ligurian raiders in 154. In 126, they petitioned the Romans for help against a Gallic tribe known as the Salluvii. A consul of 125, Marcus Fulvius Flaccus, led an army to aid Massilia and, in the process, defeated some Ligurian tribes who lived on the other side of the Alps and, presumably, the Salluvii.[60] The next year, the proconsul Gaius Sextius, battled the Salluvii again and solidified Roman control in the region of Massilia, east of the Rhône, by founding a colony named after him, Aquae Sextiae. The Salluvian king, however, escaped capture and took refuge with the Allobroges at the town of Vindalium. This, and the charge that the Allobroges had attacked Roman allies in that region, brought war to their door. Gnaeus Domitius Ahenobarbus, 'bronze beard', served as proconsul after his consulship of 122 and fought the Allobroges. He must not have won a decisive victory that year.

Livy's summarizer then notes that as consul in 121, Fabius Maximus, grandson of Aemilius Paullus, successfully campaigned against the Allobroges and also against the Averni.[61] Though several sources agree that Allobrogicus won a smashing victory, none gives much detail. According to Livy's summarizer, Fabius' forces killed a staggering number of Averni: 120,000 warriors. Given the proclivity of ancient sources to fabricate astonishing numbers of casualties, we should probably distrust the figures, but clearly the Romans saw it as a major victory. Bituitus, the king of the Averni, personally went to Rome to seek peace. The Senate apparently granted it.[62] Bituitus was kept, as a guest or a prisoner, at Alba because the Senate reasoned that he should not be sent back to Gaul. As for the Allobroges, the Senate accepted their surrender.[63]

For his victory, Fabius gained the *cognomen* Allobrogicus.[64] He had a trophy and two temples constructed at the battlefield where he had crushed the enemy. The first was to the war-god Mars, a clear enough patron for the military victory. The second was a temple to Hercules, continuing the centuries-long association the Fabii made with that legendary hero.[65] Nor was this all. To immortalize his victory over the Allobroges, Allobrogicus constructed a victory arch, the *fornix Fabianus*. It may have been the very first arch associated with a triumph; there would be many to come in the age of the emperors.[66] Somehow, he persuaded the Senate to allow him to set it up on the eastern end of the Roman Forum, a highly public spot. It was quite well known and came to be considered the eastern boundary of the Forum, the heart of Rome. If it was like the other monuments of its time, the arch was likely constructed with a core of tufa, an outer surface of travertine and gilded statues.[67] Nothing remains of the first arch, however, and only a foundation and a few bits of stone are left from a grandson's restoration or reconstruction some seven decades later. Some inscriptions associated with it were found during the Renaissance but subsequently lost. Still, what little evidence we have suggests Fabius decorated it with statues of family members. He did not restrict himself to those named Fabius Maximus, either, but apparently included statues of Aemilius Paullus and Scipio Africanus.[68] No doubt this latter association would have mightily disturbed the great Fabius Cunctator, but it had become an important part of the late second and first-century Fabius Maximus pedigree.

It was, in some ways, the last hurrah for the Fabii Maxii. Allobrogicus was the last Fabius Maximus to win the consulship through a legitimate election, and the last to vanquish a significant foreign foe and claim great glory for himself and his family line. He does not seem to have achieved anything subsequently nearly as noteworthy as defeating the Allobroges. He had a grandson, for that Fabius, as curule aedile in 57 BC, restored the arch of Allobrogicus.[69]

The Decline of the Fabii Maximi

Now we shift back to Allobrogicus' cousin, Fabius Maximus Eburnus, the son of Quintus Maximus Servilianus, the consul who lopped off Spanish hands in 142. Though he had a successful political career, judging from the fact that he was both consul in 116 and censor in 108, he seems to have achieved little of note. The architectural scholar Frontinus noted that he and his co-consul made it a law that quaestors should inspect any work carried out building and maintaining aqueducts, but this was hardly the stuff of epics.[70] Eburnus is better known, though only slightly, for executing his son during his censorship. Three sources comment that Eburnus killed his son for some grievous lapse in sexual mores, though what exactly the crime was, is lost to us. Apparently, Eburnus first convicted his son in court. Clearly his contemporaries did not all agree that the youth should have been slain, however, for Eburnus apparently later suffered exile for the deed.[71] This seems to be the end of the Servilianus contingent of the Fabii Maximi.

Nor did Allobrogicus' son fare much better when it came to building on the fame of the Fabii Maximi. The son did little for historians to note. Valerius Maximus comments that Fabius Allobrogicus was famed as both a good citizen and general, 'but what a spoiled, decadent life his son, Quintus Fabius Maximus led! Even if we ignore all his other vices, we can still fully expose his disgraceful character by the following story.' Valerius relates that the urban praetor of 91 BC, Quintus Pompeius Rufus, declared that Maximus could not inherit the property of his father, Allobrogicus. While we cannot corroborate it, the gossip that Valerius Maximus relayed is that at least Pompeius and perhaps others believed that Fabius Maximus would squander his father's wealth in immoral ways.[72] With such a grand family history, it must have stung more than a little for this Maximus to be judged a blight on the family tree. On the other hand, knowing the fate of his second cousin, son of Servilianus, perhaps he should have been grateful.

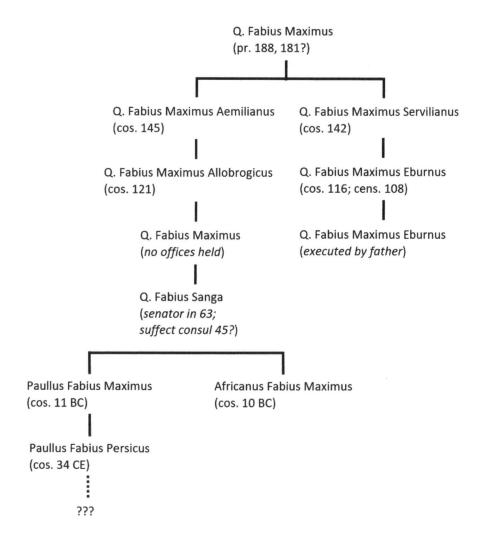

Q. Fabius Maximus
(pr. 188, 181?)

Q. Fabius Maximus Aemilianus
(cos. 145)

Q. Fabius Maximus Servilianus
(cos. 142)

Q. Fabius Maximus Allobrogicus
(cos. 121)

Q. Fabius Maximus Eburnus
(cos. 116; cens. 108)

Q. Fabius Maximus
(*no offices held*)

Q. Fabius Maximus Eburnus
(*executed by father*)

Q. Fabius Sanga
(*senator in 63;
suffect consul 45?*)

Paullus Fabius Maximus
(cos. 11 BC)

Africanus Fabius Maximus
(cos. 10 BC)

Paullus Fabius Persicus
(cos. 34 CE)

???

The next generation of Fabii Maximi was even more obscure to history. They were part of the last generation of the Roman Republic, living in a time marked by civil wars, murderous political rivalries and political street brawls. Eventually, Gaius Julius Caesar seized the dictatorship for life. His murder then initiated a final round of civil wars that brought the first of the Roman emperors, Augustus, to power. In this last generation of the Republic, several decades after Allobrogicus' son was denied his patrimony, two more Fabii Maximi appear fleetingly; or at least there seem to have been two. Sallust, a supporter of Caesar and a historian of the conspiracy launched by Lucius Sergius Catalinus to overthrow the Republic, mentions a Q. Fabius Sanga. He identifies him as a senator in 63 BC and a patron of the Allobroges in Gaul, a point confirmed by Appian in his history of the Civil War.[73] Since Roman patronage over a conquered people would pass down the generations as an inheritance, Sanga must have been Quintus Fabius Maximus

Sanga, direct descendant of Allobrogicus.[74] But we know no more of him. The second Fabius Maximus appears in the sources as a supporter of Julius Caesar's successful rebellion and as a suffect consul in 45 BC – elected to replace one of the original consuls who died in office. It has been suggested that Sanga was, in fact, the suffect consul of 45. It is also possible this second Fabius Maximus was the curule aedile who had restored his grandfather's arch and preserved the family honours. Both points have been argued, however, and certainty eludes, as it so often does in these investigations.[75]

Still, it is the suffect consul of 45 that we know the most about, as little as that is. What a different Republic he lived and competed in than that of his ancestors. The rivalry of the powerful consulars, Gaius Julius Caesar and Gnaeus Pompeius Magnus, had split the Republic, and its Mediterranean empire, in two on that fateful day when Caesar refused to terminate his military command and instead crossed with a small army into northern Italy and marched against Pompeius and his senatorial supporters. Civil war broke out across the empire for several years, Caesar and his supporters fighting his enemies, senators like Pompeius, Marcus Porcius Cato the Younger and many others. For the senatorial class, neutrality was not an option: each had to pick a side as best they could. This Fabius Maximus chose to serve Caesar.

The Second Civil War (49–45 BC) took place in various Mediterranean theatres. Fabius Maximus appears in the Spanish campaigns against the Pompeians as one of Caesar's trusted legates alongside a Quintus Pedius. According to an unknown author, who tried to pass himself off as Caesar and write an account of the Civil War in Spain, Fabius commanded at the siege of Munda, a Pompeian stronghold.[76] He successfully checked the enemy's attempt to break out of the besieged city and captured some 14,000 soldiers. He then targeted the town of Ursao.[77] For services in the Civil War, Caesar allowed Fabius and Pedius to celebrate their own triumph back at Rome. Unsurprisingly, this garnered some criticism. Dio Cassius notes:

'Although he had conquered no foreign nation, but had destroyed a vast number of citizens, [Caesar] not only celebrated the triumph himself, incidentally feasting the entire populace once more, as if in honour of some common blessing, but also allowed Quintus Fabius and Quintus Pedius to hold a celebration, although they had merely been his lieutenants and had achieved no individual success. Naturally this occasioned ridicule, as did also the fact that they used wooden instead of ivory representations of certain achievements together with other similar triumphal apparatus.'[78]

Caesar also named Fabius suffect consul (a replacement consul) for 45. This was no electoral achievement based on personal and family *dignitas* and *virtus*. Under Caesar, the consulship had become a reward for loyalty more than an office earned by the most successful aristocrats. Suetonius, the biographer of Caesar and the first emperors, records a public insult consul Fabius suffered. He had been consul for three months when he entered the theatre. His lictor followed protocol and instructed the theatre-goers to recognize his entrance. Apparently the crowd shouted 'He is no consul', an insult to Fabius' dignity to be sure.[79] His sense of shame, if he had any, cannot have lasted long; he apparently died after holding the office for only a few months.

For practical purposes, the Republic had ended. Caesar pushed too far, grasped for too much power. When he had himself named dictator for life in early 44 BC, a cabal of senators, most notably Brutus and Cassius, hatched a plot to assassinate him. So they did on the ides of March, stabbing him in the Senate twenty-three times. For a little over a decade longer, a series of civil wars and political machinations rocked the failing Republic. A final standoff came in 31 BC between Caesar's adopted son, Gaius Julius Caesar Octavianus, or 'Octavian' as he is generally called at this point in his career, and Caesar's trusted lieutenant, Marcus Antonius. Octavian claimed the victory; Antonius opted for suicide. Octavian went on to create and claim the position of *princeps*, 'first man', the first of those rulers of the Rome that historians call emperors. He would also receive from the Senate in 27 BC – a Senate now largely stripped of his opponents and filled with his supporters – the honorific name of Augustus, 'August One', which he held for the rest of his long life.

Augustus played a dangerous and deadly-serious game. He controlled most of the legions of the Empire, but the precedent of Julius Caesar's murder clearly showed that an untraditional grab for power would not serve him well. So Augustus sought to couch his position and rule within tradition and, at the same time, engage on a campaign to restore traditional Roman values that would cool tempers heated by the Civil Wars. He had the Capitoline *Fasti* chiselled in stone for all to see. He spoke of returning to the morality of the past. One of many physical illustrations of this traditional approach was the new Forum constructed and named after him. In it, Augustus had statues and elegies erected in a gallery of Roman heroes from the past. Fabius Maximus was one such hero who received a statue and inscription, though the statue is long gone.[80] But no living Fabius, nor even any recent Fabius, was deemed a hero of the Republic. Rather, the great Cunctator of the war against Hannibal was memorialized. The inscription reads thus:

'Q. Fabius Maximus, son of Quintus, Dictator twice; Consul five times; Censor; Interrex twice; Curule Aedile; Quaestor twice; Military Tribune twice; Priest; Augur. In his first consulate, he subdued the Ligurians and held a triumph over them. In his third and fourth, he tied down Hannibal, on the rampage after a string of victories, by following his every move. As Dictator, he came to the rescue of Minucius, the Magister of Horse, whose imperium the Roman people had brought level to the Dictator's imperium, and to the rescue of his routed army, and on that account he was saluted by Minucius' army as "Father". As consul for the fifth time, he captured Tarentum and held a triumph. He was regarded as the most cautious General of the age, and the most skilled in soldiering. He was chosen to be princeps senatus in two reviews.'[81]

A distinguished record to be sure, a record exceedingly few Romans of the Republic could match. In the days of Augustus and his successors, it was a record no Roman senator could match, for the political arena of the Republic was no more.

Conclusion – Living on the Legends of the Past

For better or for worse, the real distinction of the Fabius Maximus family in the early Empire was attached to the now-legendary deeds of their ancestors. Stories of the Fabii at Cremera, and more commonly the deeds of the great Cunctator, peppered the works of Augustan authors and their successors. Virgil's epic *Aeneid*, composed to provide a suitably grand tale of Roman foundation traditions, has its protagonist, Aeneas, the progenitor of Rome, travel to the underworld. There the ghost of his father, Anchises, shows him the spirits of the great heroes of Rome to come. For Virgil's contemporaries, of course, it is a list of heroes from the Republican past. Anchises says this about the Fabii: 'You Fabii, where do you rush me, all but spent? And you, famous Maximus, you are the one man whose delaying tactics save our Roman state.' And so the poet immortalizes the Fabii at the Cremera and the great Cunctator in one stroke.[1] Another famous Augustan poet, Ovid, wrote a literary calendar celebrating the customs, traditions and legends of the Roman people. Unsurprisingly, he devotes a space to the Fabii, but again it is the Fabii of old. For example, 13 February is remembered for the disaster at the Cremera, the better part of five centuries earlier:

'This was the famous day on which three hundred and thrice-two Fabii
fell to the weapons of Veii. One house had taken on itself the strength and
the burden of the city. That family's hands take up the weapons it has
volunteered.'[2]

And when Ovid has finished narrating the slaughter of the heroic Fabii that day, he connects the family to Hercules and the gods and praises Cunctator, all in one breath:

'And yet it is believable that the gods themselves took care that the seeds
of the race of Hercules should survive. For one boy of the Fabian house,

under-age and not yet ready to bear arms, had been left behind. Of course
– it was so that you, Maximus, might one day be born, you who would have
to save the state by delaying.'[3]

Ovid enjoyed the patronage of a Fabius Maximus, but when it came time to
aggrandize his patron, he felt compelled to draw on the past, for the present
condition of the Fabii Maximi must have presented no worthy material.

Inscriptions in the Forum, passages from the poets and chronicles from
Livy preserved what was conventional knowledge for the Roman aristocracy,
the traditions of their legendary ancestors, their pedigree. As noted before,
however, that pedigree was a blessing and a curse. For while it brought honour
and distinction, how could Romans at the start of the Empire help but draw
comparisons between the steely legends of the Fabii and their flesh-and-bone
descendants?

It seems that contemporaries could not resist. Paullus Fabius Maximus was the
son of the consul of 45 BC, an infant when his father died.[4] There is little in the
way of a connected story that can be told about him. The most immediate point
that arises is the irregularity, by Republican standards, of his *praenomen*. Giving
the child the *cognomen* Paullus as a wholly untraditional *praenomen*, instead of
the traditional Quintus, seems a clear attempt to revive and associate with the
dignity of Lucius Aemilius Paullus, the conqueror of Macedon from the second
century, whose biological son had become Quintus Fabius Maximus Aemilianus.[5]
Clearly, Paullus Fabius, when he came of age, attached himself to the cause of
the first emperor, Augustus, as all prudent aristocrats came to do when civil war
dissolved the Republic and the one-man rule of the Principate replaced it. In
10 BC, Augustus charged Fabius to govern the province of Asia as a proconsul,
and he may have spent a pair of years in that position. A letter attributed to him
offers a few pieces of information. Fabius seems to have cajoled the cities of Asia
to shift their calendar so that the new year began on Augustus' birthday, showing
a devotion to the emperor or at least a solid sense of good politics. Fabius also
managed to have a festival at Ilium, where the ancients believed Troy to have
been, dedicated to Augustus' name. These snippets, and the survival of some
Asian coins stamped with his profile, suggest that Fabius had Augustus' favour.
Paullus Fabius next surfaces in Spain a handful of years later. Around 3 BC, he
served as a legate there. Some locals apparently praised him by dedicating an
altar to Augustus on Fabius' birthday, praising the latter by association with the
ruler of the Mediterranean. That is about it. We really know little more than that
he played the game of politics in a monarchy well: ingratiating himself to the
emperor and gaining some power and prestige. It may be, however, that he lost
Augustus' favour, potentially tangled up in some way with Augustus' scandalous
daughter Julia and the equally scandalous poet, Ovid. Some rumours suggested
he was persuaded to take his own life in AD 14 when he died.[6] Of his brother,

Africanus Fabius Maximus, we know essentially nothing other than that he was consul in 10 BC.[7]

The recognition of the glorious lineage of the currently less-than-glorious. Fabii Maximi took a decidedly hostile turn in the next generation. Paullus Fabius Maximus had a son, Persicus-Paullus Fabius Maximus Persicus – and this *cognomen*, 'conqueror of Perseus', was assuredly meant to link him even more to Aemilius Paullus; Paullus named his daughter Numantina for similar reasons.[8] Persicus was awarded a pair of priesthoods, served as consul in AD 34 under the second emperor Tiberius, and, like his father, was a proconsul in Asia. Then he essentially disappears, dying in the reign of Claudius, the fourth emperor.[9]

But Fabius Persicus is probably best known, if he is known at all, as a target of the moralist Seneca's writings in the mid-first century AD. That stoic-minded senator blasted Persicus in a rant against inferior men who had achieved success solely due to the honours their ancestors had received. He saves some vitriol for Persicus, assaulting him by name:

> 'What recently made Fabius Persicus a priest in more than one college, a man whose kiss even the shameless counted an insult? What but a Verrucosus and an Allobrogicus and the famous three hundred, who, to save their country, blocked the invasion of the enemy with their single family?'

Then Seneca closes in words that make one wince: 'As filthy places become bright from the radiance of the sun, so let the degenerate shine in the light of their forefathers.'[10]

And as at least the political line of the Fabii died out with a few more minor office holders, if not the entire line, the satirist Juvenal drove a final nail in the coffin.[11] He lambasted in a poem either Persicus or those final Fabii but, in any event, any aristocrat still holding the name Fabius Maximus in the later first and early second century AD:

> 'Pedigrees now, what's their game?
>
> …
>
> What good are all the likenesses
> of warrior hosts, if it's all a game, a gamble through the night,
> With Numantines looking on, if your sleep starts when dawn
> Comes up, when Generals of old stirred troops and struck camp?
>
> Why should a son find joy in Allobrogics and High Altar,
> Born in the Fabian house, Hercules' shrine, if grasping, if
> Inane, and soppier as you please than any bien-né Venetian lamb,

If rubbed down with pumice Catinese, all succulent tenderloin,
He puts unkempt forefathers on parade, and as The Purchaser of Poison
His likeness merits smashing, he casts a pall on the stricken clan?'[12]

And here is where our account must end. The Fabii had persisted as politically prominent figures for as long as the Republic, but little longer. As the Republic rose, there were Fabii earning offices and distinction, commanding armies, wrangling with rivals and serving the Republic both in rhetoric and deed. In the intense game of aristocrat politics, the Fabius family relied not only on distinguished pedigree, but on a considerable measure of political success to maintain their family's distinction through most phases of the Republic. The heroic deed of the Fabii at the Cremera gave them the finest of aristocratic pedigrees. Over time, three became semi-legendary figures, noted more than any other Fabii for their exploits: Rullianus, Cunctator and Allobrogicus. But there was no room for such figures in the political landscape of the emperors, except as legends from a proud Republican past. They could ostensibly serve as a moral example, but never political ones, for the Empire. In the Empire, the Fabii Maximi, like so many other noble lines of the Republic, grew politically obsolete, their exploits, achieved only through the good will and favour of the emperors, ringing hollowly when the triumphs of their Republican ancestors shone for all to see. At the end of the line, the great deeds of the Fabii served as ammunition for detractors to throw at contemporary Fabii: 'You are nothing compared to your ancestors.' In this climate, the family disappeared. And so the practical end of the line of Fabius Maximus came, to borrow from T.S. Eliot, 'not with a bang, but a whimper'.[13]

Appendix A

Roman Names

Since all manner of Roman names appear in this book, a basic introduction to how Romans named themselves may be helpful. Unlike other Indo-European languages where the individual's name was the primary term of address, in Latin a family name, or *nomen*, was of far greater importance – family first in the Roman way of thinking. The masculine form of the *nomen* ended in '*ius*'; the *nomen* of the Fabian clan was Fabius, plural Fabii. It is worth noting that not all Romans with the same *nomen* were very likely to have descended from the same ancestor, but still the *nomen* was used by aristocrats to develop a distinguished lineage. Girls, even after marriage, kept their fathers' *nomina* in the feminine form ('*ia*'), so the daughter of a Fabius was named Fabia. For boys, a *praenomen* of secondary importance was added that identified the individual. Thrifty in using individual names for boys, in the Republic the Romans had a pool of only seventeen *praenomina* from which the vast majority of boys were named: names like Marcus and Quintus. Kaeso, used as a *praenomen* for some fifth-century Fabii, counted as an extraordinary *praenomen*. In official address, these *praenomina* were regularly abbreviated: M. for Marcus, Q. for Quintus and so on. *Praenomina* for women were much rarer and seem to have disappeared almost completely by the mid-fourth century BC. In public, the general practice was to address a person by his or her *nomen* alone, or by both *praenomen* and *nomen*: Fabia, Fabius, Quintus Fabius and so on.[1]

Over time, however, many aristocratic Romans of the Republic acquired a third name, the *cognomen*, often referred to as the nickname. These names existed for a few patricians as early as the fifth century BC, and seemingly for the first political Fabii, the Fabii Vibulani, but came into widespread use in the late second century.[2] Though often pejorative in origin – names like Verrucosus ('warty') and Brutus ('stupid') – these nicknames seem to have been adopted by elite Romans hoping to distinguish further their family line from the rest of those bearing the *nomen*.[3] So, over time, a number of branches of Fabii evolved, each with a different *cognomen*: Fabius Buteo, Fabius Maximus, Fabius Pictor, etc.

Appendix B

Glossary of Some Technical Terms

Aedile – One of two junior magistrates elected yearly to maintain the infrastructure of Rome, including roads, temples and other public buildings. Aediles also held public games and played a role in managing the grain market at Rome.

Annales Maximi – A list of important events for each year maintained by Rome's chief priest, the *pontifex maximus*. They were published in the second century BC. These were an important source of evidence for later writers.

Censor – One of two magistrates elected every five years whose primary task was to revise the list of Roman citizens, including those who had the status of senator.

Cognomen – The third name or nickname that many Roman aristocrats had, for example 'Maximus' in the name Quintus Fabius Maximus.

Consul – One of the two most powerful yearly magistrates. Consuls were the chief executive officials of the Republic and the chief commanders of the Roman armies.

Centuriate assembly – The assembly of Roman citizens organized according to wealth so that the wealthier citizens had more voting power. The centuriate assembly elected consuls and praetors, and declared wars, among other functions.

Cursus Honorum – The 'Course of Honours' or 'Course of Offices', the traditional hierarchy of offices the most successful Roman aristocrats would hold during their political careers: aedile, praetor, consul.

Dictator – A special magistrate selected by a consul to serve as supreme commander during a military crisis, or to hold elections when the consuls could not. A dictator had no colleague in office and, by convention, had to step down from office after six months.

Fasti – The chronological record of major office holders. Augustus preserved a public version of the consular *fasti* at the end of the Republic, inscribing it in stone.

Interrex – A special magistrate selected to hold elections when consular elections did not take place within the normal time frame.

Latin colonies – Colonies of Roman citizens and others planted by Rome to extend Roman power and to provide land for citizens and allies. The inhabitants of Latin colonies possessed Latin rights.

Latin rights – The core rights for those Italians that had Latin status, including the legal right to trade and intermarry with Roman citizens and the right to move to Rome and adopt full Roman citizenship.

Master of Horse – The lieutenant of a dictator, traditionally charged with command of the dictator's cavalry forces.

Military tribunes with consular powers – A special kind of magistrate in the early Republic that had the command powers of a consul, but was not technically a consul. Used during the Conflict of the Orders, it seems, as a way to give plebeians high office without actually granting them the consulship.

Nomen – The second name and family name for a Roman, for example 'Fabius' in Quintus Fabius Maximus.

Praenomen – The first name and personal name for a Roman, for example 'Quintus' in Quintus Fabius Maximus.

Praetor – A magistrate, second in power to the consuls, created in 367 BC. Praetors served as judges, as lesser military commanders and, in time, as governors of provinces. Their number increased over time, from one in 367 to eight by the end of the Republic.

Quaestor – The lowest major elected official, a junior magistrate who commonly served as a treasurer to a consul.

Appendix C

Glossary of Major Sources for the Republic

Good online overviews of most of these sources can be found on www.livius.org and these glossary entries are drawn from there, except for those on Dionysius of Halicarnassus and Valerius Maximus (basic online information for these can be found on Britannica. com; the source of the entry for Dionysius is W.R. Roberts (ed.), Dionysius of Halicarnassus: The Three Literary Letters (Cambridge, 1901)), pp. 1–2; for Valerius Maximus, the source of the entry is H.J. Walker, Valerius Maximus, Memorable Deeds and Sayings (Indianapolis, 2004) p. xiii. All dates for authors are approximate.

Appian of Alexandria (AD 95–165): A historian who wrote Roman histories in Greek. He was born a Roman citizen in the city of Alexandria, Egypt, part of the Roman Empire. He practised law in the city of Rome and became a minor Roman government official for a time. He wrote histories on a number of Roman subjects, from the earliest history of the city to the reign of the Emperor Trajan in the early second century AD.

Cassius Dio (AD 164–235): A Greek with Roman citizenship who wrote a history of Rome in Greek. He became a Roman senator and served as a consul and a governor in the imperial administrations of the Severan Emperors of the early third century. His *Roman History* now exists only in fragments, and many parts are known only through much later Byzantine historians who quoted his work extensively.

Diodorus Siculus (active between 60–30 BC): A Greek historian, born in Sicily, who wrote a universal history, i.e. a history of the Greek-speaking world, essentially the Mediterranean region. Written in forty books, only fifteen survive in full. The full history extended from the legendary and mythic past of Greek history to the mid-first century BC. He seems to have visited both Alexandria in Egypt and Rome itself. Diodorus includes details about the Roman Republic in his history, though his main focus is on the Greek-speaking world of the Mediterranean.

Dionysius of Halicarnassus: A first-century BC Greek historian who wrote a history of the Roman monarchy and Republic. Dionysius came from the Greek city of Halicarnassus, in the south-west of modern Turkey. He lived more than twenty years in Rome, beginning in 30 BC. While there he taught rhetoric and wrote a history of early Rome from the prehistoric period to the start of the First Punic War in 264 BC. Of the twenty books, the first nine survive complete, most of ten and eleven survive, and the rest exist only in pieces.

Plutarch (AD 46–122): A Greek in the early Roman Empire. Trained in philosophy and history like the educated of his day, Plutarch wrote a variety of works on ancient Greek and Roman history, including the *Lives of Greeks and Romans*, biographies of important figures in history. Plutarch resided in Greece, though he seems to have travelled extensively. He eventually became a Roman citizen and served as a minor official in the second-century Empire. His biographies are an important source of information about key figures in the Roman Republic.

Livy (59 BC–AD 17): Titus Livius, or Livy as he is more commonly known, lived from c. 59 BC to AD 17. He wrote *Ab Urbe Condita*, 'From the Founding of the City', a massive history of Rome from its origins to his own day. Originally 142 books, only thirty-five survive today. Like many ancient historians, Livy considered himself a moralist, whose history could serve to educate contemporary Romans.

Polybius (200–118 BC): A Greek from the city of Megalopolis, Polybius served as both a government official and military commander in the Achaean League. When the League ran afoul of the Roman Republic, Polybius was taken hostage along with 999 other Greeks and deported to Italy. There he became fast friends with Scipio Aemilianus and, as a result, had the ability to observe many of the political and military elements of the Republic first-hand. His *World History* covered the Mediterranean world from the First Punic War (264–241 BC) to the destruction of Carthage in 146 BC.

Valerius Maximus (first century AD): A Roman who wrote a collection of anecdotes from famous past Romans called the *Memorable Deeds and Sayings*. It was arguably intended to connect the Romans of the Empire with their Republican past and to emphasize moral subjects. He published the work in AD 31. Otherwise very little is known about him.

Velleius Paterculus (20 BC–AD 30): A Roman equestrian (the rank below senator) who wrote a history of Rome from earliest times until the early first century AD. His father and grandfather lived through the tumultous times of the end of the Republic. He served as a cavalry commander during the reign of Augustus and became a senator. He continued to serve as a military officer under Augustus' stepson, Tiberius. In AD 30 he published his history of Rome and the world. The first half deals with events up to the fall of Carthage (146 BC) and the second with the period up through the reign of the second emperor, Tiberius.

Online Sources of Ancient Authors
in Translation

Note: The best sources for public domain translations of ancient texts are the Perseus Digital Library (www.perseus.tufts.edu) and Lacus Curtius (penelope. uchicago.edu/Thayer/e/roman/texts/).

Abbreviation	*Full*	*Translations Online*
App. *B. Civ.*	Appian, *Bella Civilia*	Lacus Curtius: penelope.uchicago.edu/Thayer/E/Roman/Texts/Appian/home.html (Horace White trans.) Perseus: www.perseus.tufts.edu/hopper/text?doc=Perseus:text:1999.01.0232 (Horace White trans.)
App. *Iber.*	Appian, *Iberica* (sometimes called *Hispania*)	Lacus Curtius: penelope.uchicago.edu/Thayer/E/Roman/Texts/Appian/home.html (Horace White trans.) Livius.org: www.livius.org/sources/content/appian/ (Horace White trans.)
Caes. *B.Gall.*	Caesar, *Bellum Gallicum*	Lacus Curtius: penelope.uchicago.edu/Thayer/e/roman/texts/caesar/gallic_war/home.html (Henry John Edwards trans.) Perseus Digital Library: www.perseus.tufts.edu/hopper/text?doc=Perseus%3atext%3a1999.02.0001 (W.A. McDevitte and W.S. Bohn trans.)
Cass. Dio	Cassius Dio	Lacus Curtius: penelope.uchicago.edu/Thayer/e/roman/texts/cassius_dio/home.html (Ernest Cary trans.)
Cic. *Brut.*	Cicero, *Brutus*	Attalus.org: www.attalus.org/old/brutus1.html Project Gutenberg: www.gutenberg.org/cache/epub/9776/pg9776.html
Cic. *Cat. Mai.*	Cicero, *Cato Maiore*	Lacus Curtius: penelope.uchicago.edu/Thayer/E/Roman/Texts/Cicero/Cato_Maior_de_Senectute/home.html Perseus: www.perseus.tufts.edu/hopper/text?doc=Cic.%20Sen.
Diod. Sic.	Diodorus Siculus	Lacus Curtius: penelope.uchicago.edu/Thayer/e/roman/texts/diodorus_siculus/home.html
Dion. Hal. *Ant. Rom.*	Dionysius of Halicarnassus, *Antiquitates Romanae*	Lacus Curtius: penelope.uchicago.edu/Thayer/e/roman/texts/dionysius_of_halicarnassus/home.html (Ernest Cary trans.)
Flor.	L. Annaeus Florus	Lacus Curtius: http://penelope.uchicago.edu/Thayer/e/roman/texts/florus/epitome/home.html

Abbreviation	Full	Translations Online
Front. *Strat.*	Frontinus, *Strategemata*	Lacus Curtius: penelope.uchicago.edu/Thayer/E/roman/Texts/Frontinus/Strategemata/home.html
Hor. *Carm.*	Horace, *Carmina* (or Odes)	Perseus Digital Library: www.perseus.tufts.edu/hopper/text?doc=Perseus:text:1999.02.0025 (John Conington trans.)
Liv.	Livy, Ab *Urbe Condita*	Perseus Digital Library: www.perseus.tufts.edu/hopper/text?doc=Perseus:text:1999.02.0151:book=1 (Benjamin Oliver Foster, trans.) www.perseus.tufts.edu/hopper/text?doc=Perseus:text:1999.02.0157:book=25 (Frank Gardener Moore, trans.)
Liv. *Per.*	Livy, *Periochae*	Livius.org: www.livius.org/articles/person/livy/livy-the-periochae/
Ov. *Fast.*	Ovid, *Fasti*	Classical Texts Library: www.theoi.com/Text/OvidFasti1.html (James G. Frazer trans.)
Plin. *H.N.*	Pliny, *Historia Naturalis*	Perseus: http://www.perseus.tufts.edu/hopper/text?doc=Perseus:text:1999.02.0137 (John Bostock trans.)
Plut. *Aem.*	Plutarch, *Life of Aemilius Paullus*	Lacus Curtius: penelope.uchicago.edu/Thayer/E/Roman/Texts/Plutarch/Lives/Aemilius*.html (Bernadotte Perrin trans.)
Plut. *C. Gracch.*	Plutarch, *Life of Gaius Gracchus*	Lacus Curtius: penelope.uchicago.edu/Thayer/E/Roman/Texts/Plutarch/Lives/Caius_Gracchus*.html (Bernadotte Perrin trans.)
Plut. *Cam.*	Plutarch, *Life of Camillus*	Lacus Curtius: penelope.uchicago.edu/Thayer/E/Roman/Texts/Plutarch/Lives/Camillus*.html (Bernadotte Perrin trans.)
Plut. *Comp. Fab. Et Per.*	Plutarch, *Comparison of Fabius and Pericles*	Lacus Curtius: penelope.uchicago.edu/Thayer/E/Roman/Texts/Plutarch/Lives/Pericles+Fabius_Maximus*.html (Bernadotte Perrin trans.)
Plut. *Fab.*	Plutarch, *Life of Fabius*	Lacus Curtius: penelope.uchicago.edu/Thayer/E/Roman/Texts/Plutarch/Lives/Fabius_Maximus*.html (Bernadotte Perrin trans.)
Plut. *Marc.*	Plutarch, *Life of Marcellus*	Lacus Curtius: penelope.uchicago.edu/Thayer/E/Roman/Texts/Plutarch/Lives/Marcellus*.html (Bernadotte Perrin trans.)
Polyb.	Polybius	Lacus Curtius: penelope.uchicago.edu/Thayer/E/Roman/Texts/Polybius/home.html (William Roger Paton trans.)
Sall. *Cat.*	Sallust, *Bellum Catilinae*	Lacus Curtius: penelope.uchicago.edu/Thayer/E/Roman/Texts/Sallust/home.html (J.C. Rolfe trans.)
Sil. *Pun.*	Silius Italicus, *Punica*	Internet Archive Reader: archive.org/details/punicasi01siliuoft (James Duff trans.)
Suet. *Jul.*	Suetonius, *Life of Julius Caesar*	Lacus Curtius: penelope.uchicago.edu/Thayer/E/Roman/Texts/Suetonius/12Caesars/Julius*.html (J.C. Rolfe trans.)
Suet. *Tib.*	Suetonius, *Life of Tiberius*	Lacus Curtius: penelope.uchicago.edu/Thayer/E/Roman/Texts/Suetonius/12Caesars/Tiberius*.html (J.C. Rolfe trans.)
Tac. *Hist.*	Tacitus, *Historiae*	Lacus Curtius: penelope.uchicago.edu/Thayer/E/Roman/Texts/Tacitus/home.html (C.H. Moore trans.)
Vell. Pat.	Velleius *Paterculus*	Lacus Curtius: penelope.uchicago.edu/Thayer/E/Roman/Texts/Velleius_Paterculus/home.html (Frederick W. Shipley trans.)
Virg. *Aen.*	Virgil, *Aeneid*	Perseus: www.perseus.tufts.edu/hopper/text?doc=Perseus:text:1999.02.0054 (Theodore C. Williams trans.)

Notes

Chapter 1: Introduction

1. The main accounts of the Cremera campaign and the Fabian disaster are Liv. and DH.
2. Liv. 2.48–50 and Dion. Hal. *Ant. Rom.* 9.14–19 provide accounts of the Fabii disaster at the Cremera River.
3. Whether the earliest Republican magistrates were consuls and were paired is still a matter of hefty debate. For a discussion of some of the problems, see C. Smith, 'The magistrates of the early Roman Republic', pp. 19–40, G. Urso, 'The origin of the consulship in Cassius Dio's History', pp. 41–60, and A. Bergk, 'The development of the praetorship in the third century', pp. 61–74, all in Beck, H., Dupla, A., Jehne, M., Pina Polo, F. (eds) *Consuls and Res Publica: Holding High Office in the Roman Republic* (Cambridge, 2011).
4. Ov. *Fast.* 2.371–98 suggests that the Fabii were comrades of Remus, brother of Romulus. Plut. *Fab.* 1 adds the claim that the Fabius clan descended from Hercules. Sil. *Pun.* 6.627–36.
5. For discussion and analysis of the traditional accounts, see all of T.J. Cornell, *The Beginnings of Rome: Italy and Rome from the Bronze Age to the Punic Wars* (London, 1995), esp. pp. 1–26, 119–50, 215–39, and all of G. Forsythe, *A Critical History of Early Rome: From Prehistory to the Punic War* (Berkeley, 2005), esp. pp. 59–198.
6. For the development of the consulship, the chief republican office, see Smith, Urso and Bergk, in Beck, Dupla, Jehne, Pina Polo (eds), *Consuls and Res Publica*.
7. Polyb. 6.3–18.
8. For an excellent survey of the government of the Republic, see A. Lintott, *The Constitution of the Roman Republic* (Oxford, 1999).
9. Polyb. 6.11–18.
10. Cornell, *The Beginnings of Rome*, p. 248.
11. Festus p. 290 L. Quoted by Cornell, *The Beginnings of Rome*, p. 248.
12. Lintott, *Constitution of the Roman Republic*, pp. 121–26.
13. Smith, Urso, in Beck, Dupla, Jehne, Pina Polo (eds), *Consuls and Res Publica*.
14. Cornell, *The Beginnings of Rome*, p. 259; Lintott, *Constitution of the Roman Republic*, p. 121.
15. For excellent discussions of the Roman historians and their sources, see Cornell, *The Beginnings of Rome*, pp. 1–18; Forsythe, *A Critical History of Early Rome* (Berkeley, 2005), pp. 59–77.
16. Cornell, *The Beginnings of Rome*, pp. 13–15, 218; Forsythe, *A Critical History of Early Rome*, pp. 156–57.

17. Cic, *De or.* 2.52–3. Trans. in Forsythe, *A Critical History of Early Rome*, p. 69.
18. Cornell, *The Beginnings of Rome*, pp. 14–16; Forsythe, *A Critical History of Early Rome*, pp. 69–74.
19. Polyb. 6.53–54.
20. Cic. *Brut.* 62. Trans. in M. Crawford, *The Roman Republic* (London, 1978), p. 9.
21. Liv. 8.40. cf. 7.9.3–6 (Radice trans.).
22. Cornell, *The Beginnings of Rome*, pp. 10–12; Forsythe, *A Critical History of Early Rome*, pp. 75–77.

Chapter 2: Shadows of the Past: The Fabii and the Fledgling Republic
1. Sil. *Pun.* 6.625–37. Geryon: Eur. *HF.* 419, Lucr. 5.28, Hor. *Carm.* 2.14.7.
2. T.P. Wisemen, *Remus: A Roman Myth* (Cambridge, 1995), p. 10.
3. T.P. Wiseman, 'Legendary Genealogies in Late Republican Rome', *Greece and Rome* 21 (1974), p. 154.
4. When it comes to reconstructing the *fasti* of the early Republic, one can hardly do better than consult T.R.S. Broughton's great tomes, *The Magistrates of the Roman Republic* (New York, 1951–52). Broughton collected not only the references from the *fasti*, but all manner of references to magistrates and their time in office from the ancient sources. Vol. 1 of the *MRR* is accessible online at http://babel.hathitrust.org/cgi/pt?id=mdp.39015009351001;view=1up;seq=48.
5. Broughton, *MRR* Vol. 1, pp. 21–25.
6. C.J. Smith, *The Roman Clan: The Gens from Ancient Ideology to Modern Anthropology* (Cambridge, 2006), p. 291.
7. Liv. 2.41.1–3; Dion. Hal. *Ant. Rom.* 6.68–76. Forsythe, *A Critical History of Early Rome*, pp. 192–95.
8. Liv. 2.41.9–12; Dion. Hal. *Ant. Rom.* 8.77–78.
9. Dion. Hal. *Ant. Rom.* 8.78.
10. Dion. Hal. *Ant. Rom.* 8.82.2–3 (Cary trans.).
11. Dion. Hal. *Ant. Rom.* 8.82.1–4.
12. Liv. 2.42.1–2.
13. Dion. Hal. *Ant. Rom.* 8.84 (Cary trans.).
14. Dion. Hal. *Ant. Rom.* 8.82.4–86.9.
15. Liv. 2.42.2–7.
16. Cornell, *Beginnings of Rome*, pp. 242–71; Forsythe, *A Critical History of Early Rome*, pp. 157–66. K-J. Holkeskamp, 'Conquest, Competition and Consensus: Roman Expansion in Italy and the Rise of the "Nobilitas"', *Historia* 42 (1993), pp. 12–39.
17. Cornell, *Beginnings of Rome*, pp. 242–71; Forsythe, *Critical History of Early Rome*, pp. 157–66.
18. Dion. Hal. *Ant. Rom.* 8.89.1–2 (Cary trans.).
19. J. Rich, 'Warfare and Army in Early Rome', in P. Erdkamp (ed.), *A Companion to the Roman Army* (Malden, MA., 2007), pp. 16–17.
20. H. Van Wees, *Greek Warfare: Myths and Realities* (London, 2004), especially pp. 45–86; Rich, 'Warfare and Army in Early Rome', in Erdkamp (ed.), *A Companion to the Roman Army*, p. 17.

21. Van Wees, *Greek Warfare: Myths and Realities*, especially pp. 45–86.
22. Rich, 'Warfare and Army in Early Rome', in Erdkamp (ed.), *A Companion to the Roman Army*, p. 17; Forsythe, *A Critical History of Early Rome*, pp. 26–27; M. Sage, *The Republican Roman Army: A Sourcebook* (New York, 2008), p. 19.
23. Forsythe, *A Critical History of Rome*, p. 190.
24. Dion. Hal. *Ant. Rom.* 8.87–89.5.
25. Liv. 2.42.7–10.
26. Dion. Hal. *Ant. Rom.* 8.90–91.
27. Liv. 2.43.1.
28. Broughton, *MRR*, Vol. 1, p. 24.
29. Dion. Hal. *Ant. Rom.* 9.1–3; Liv. 2.43.3–11.
30. Dion. Hal. *Ant. Rom.* 9.9.1–9.10.1.
31. Liv. 2.44–48.3; Dion. Hal. *Ant. Rom.* 9.5.1–13.4
32. Liv. 2.47.9–11.
33. Liv 2.42–48; Dion. Hal. *Ant. Rom.* 8.81–91, 9.1–14.
34. Forsythe, *A Critical History of Early Rome*, pp. 186–90.
35. Forsythe, *A Critical History of Early Rome*, pp. 189–91.
36. Liv. 2.48.5–10.
37. Dion. Hal. *Ant. Rom.* 9.15.2; Liv. 2.49.1–9.
38. Dion. Hal. *Ant. Rom.* 9.15.4–6; Liv. 2.49.9.
39. Dion. Hal. *Ant. Rom.* 9.19.103; 9.20.1–4; Liv. 2.50.1–7.
40. Liv. 2.50.7–11.
41. Dion. Hal. *Ant. Rom.* 9.21.2–6 (Cary trans.).
42. Liv. 2.50.11.
43. Dion. Hal. *Ant. Rom.* 9.22.1–7.
44. Diod. Sic. 11.53.6 (Loeb trans.).
45. Sil. *Pun.* 2.3–6; Plut. *Cam.* 19; Tac. *Hist.* 2.91.
46. E. Pais, 'The Fabii at the River Cremera and the Spartans at Thermopylae', in Richardson and Santangelo, *The Roman Historical Tradition: Regal and Republican Rome*, pp. 167–86. Ettore Pais wrote about the Fabii at the beginning of the twentieth century.
47. Liv. 3.1; Dion. Hal. *Ant. Rom.* 9.59.3.
48. Liv. 3.2–3.
49. Dion. Hal. *Ant. Rom.* 9.60.
50. Dion. Hal. *Ant. Rom.* 9.61.
51. Liv. 3.8; Dion. Hal. *Ant. Rom.* 9.69. Note that Dionysius seems to mistakenly call Fabius 'Furius' in this section (9.69.2).
52. Liv. 3.9–21.
53. Liv. 3.22.
54. Liv. 3.23.7 (Warrior trans.).
55. Dion. Hal. *Ant. Rom.* 10.20–21.
56. Liv. 3.31–46; Dion. Hal. *Ant. Rom.* 10.50–11.44.
57. See the articles 'Ambustus, Fabius' and 'Vibulanus' in W. Smith, *A Classical Dictionary of Biography, Mythology and Geography* (London, 1891), pp. 43, 814.
58. Liv. 4.17–19.

59. Liv. 4.26.
60. Liv. 4.27–29.
61. Liv. 4.25–28, 37.
62. Liv. 4.37–40.
63. Liv. 4.40.
64. Again, see Smith for the family tree, as best as it can be reconstructed, *A Classical Dictionary of Biography, Mythology and Geography*, pp. 43, 814.
65. Liv. 5.10, 12, 24.
66. Liv. 5.36; Dion. Hal. *Ant. Rom.* 13.12; Diod. Sic. 14.113. All three have a slightly different version of whom exactly the Gauls wanted handed over: Quintus Fabius, Quintus Fabius and his brother (which one?), or all three Fabii.
67. Liv. 5.36; Diod. Sic. 14.113; Dion. Hal. *Ant. Rom.* 13.12.
68. Liv. 5.36–40; Diod. Sic. 14.113; Dion. Hal. *Ant. Rom.* 13.12
69. Liv. 5.40–49, 6.

Chapter 3: The First Fabius Maximus – Rullianus and the Samnite Wars

1. M. Stone, 'The Genesis of Roman Imperialism', in D. Hoyos (ed.), *A Companion to Roman Imperialism* (Leiden, 2013), pp. 25–28.
2. Liv. 7.1.
3. Liv. 7.1.
4. Liv. 7.11.
5. Liv. 7.11.
6. Liv. 7.12.
7. Liv. 7.15 (Yardley trans.).
8. Liv. 7.17 (Yardley trans.).
9. Liv. 7.19.
10. Liv. 7.22.
11. Forsythe, *A Critical History of Early Rome*, pp. 281–83.
12. Stone, 'The Genesis of Roman Imperialism', in Hoyos (ed.), *A Companion to Roman Imperialism*, pp. 26–28.
13. Forsythe, *A Critical History of Early Rome*, pp. 284–89.
14. Forsythe, *A Critical History of Rome*, pp. 289–92.
15. Liv. 8.18. See D. Hoyos' notes in Yardley trans. *Livy: Rome's Italian Wars* (Oxford, 2013), p. 310.
16. Forsythe, *A Critical History of Early Rome*, pp. 293–94.
17. Forsythe, *A Critical History of Early Rome*, pp. 294–95.
18. Forsythe, *A Critical History of Early Rome*, pp. 294–95.
19. Liv. 8.25.
20. Liv. 8.30–37; Val. Max. 2.7.8.
21. Liv. 3.29.
22. Liv. 1.7.
23. Val Max. 1.6–7.
24. Val. Max. 1.4.3.
25. Liv. 8.30; Val. Max. 2.2.9.
26. J. McCall, *The Cavalry of the Roman Republic: Cavalry Combat and Elite Reputations in the Middle and Late Republic* (London, 2002), pp. 21–22.

27. Liv. 8.30.
28. Liv. 8.32–33.
29. Cornell, *Beginnings of Rome*, pp. 276–77.
30. Liv. 8.33–34; quoted passage from Liv. 8.34.1–2 (Yardley trans.).
31. Liv. 8.6–8.
32. Liv. 8.36; Val. Max. 2.7.8; Front. *Strat.* 1.4.39.
33. Broughton, *MRR* Vol. 1, pp. 148–49.
34. P. Sabin, 'The Face of Roman Battle', *Journal of Roman Studies* 90 (2000), pp. 1–17.
35. Liv. 8.38–39.
36. Liv. 8.40.4–5 (Yardley trans.).
37. Broughton, *MRR* Vol. 1, pp. 149–50; see D. Hoyos' notes in Yardley trans. *Livy: Rome's Italian Wars*, pp. 336.
38. Liv. 9.1–6.
39. See Forsythe, *A Critical History of Early Rome*, pp. 297–99; Cornell, *The Beginnings of Rome*, p. 353.
40. Liv. 9.7.13–15.
41. Cornell, *The Beginnings of Rome*, pp. 353–54.
42. Broughton, *MRR* Vol. 1, p. 156.
43. Liv. 9.22.
44. Liv. 9.22.
45. Liv. 9.22; Liv. 9.23.5 (Yardley trans.).
46. Diod. Sic. 19.66.1.
47. Diod. Sic. 19.72.3–9.
48. Diod. Sic. 19.72.3–9.
49. Broughton, *MRR* Vol. 1, p. 156.
50. Liv. 9.23.4–5.
51. See Hoyos' notes to Liv. 23 in Yardley trans. *Livy: Rome's Italian Wars*, p. 336.
52. Liv. 9.24.
53. Liv. 9.26.
54. Liv. 9.26.
55. Liv. 9.26.
56. Liv. 9.26.
57. Diod. Sic. 19.73.1.
58. Diod. Sic. 19.76.1–5 ; Liv. 9.28.
59. Diod. Sic. 19.101.1 (Loeb trans.).
60. Diod. Sic. 19.101.1–3.
61. Liv. 9.28.
62. Broughton, *MRR* Vol. 1, p. 158.
63. The only two examples that readily come to mind are Papirius Cursor and Fabius Maximus Cunctator, who was dictator in 221 and 217.
64. Liv. 9.29; Cornell, *The Beginnings of Rome*, p. 354.
65. Diod. Sic. 19.105.1–5.
66. K. Olson, *Masculinity and Dress in Roman Antiquity* (New York, 2017), pp. 19, 84–85.

67. F.X. Ryan, *Rank and Participation in the Republican Senate* (Stuttgart, 1998), pp. 72–87.
68. Liv. 9.30. Cornell, *The Beginnings of Rome*, p. 354.
69. Ineditum Vaticanum translation in Cornell, *The Beginnings of Rome*, p. 170; see also Forsythe, *A Critical History of Early Rome*, p. 304–05.
70. Sall. *Cat.* 51.37–8.
71. Polyb 6.22 (Paton trans.).
72. Polyb. 6.23 (Paton trans.).
73. Polyb. 6.22.1–5.
74. A. Goldsworthy, *The Roman Army at War 100 BC to AD 200* (Oxford, 1996), pp. 209–12.
75. M.C. Bishop and J.C.N. Coulston, *Roman Military Equipment: From the Punic Wars to the Fall of Rome* (Oxford, 2006), p. 92.
76. Polyb. 6.22 (Paton trans.).
77. Bishop and Coulston, *Roman Military Equipment*, pp. 50–52.
78. Bishop and Coulston, *Roman Military Equipment*, p. 78.
79. Polyb. 2.30, 6.23; see also G. Webster, *The Roman Imperial Army* (Totowa, NJ, 1985), pp. 128–29; Bishop and Coulston, *Roman Military Equipment*, pp. 54–56.
80. Polyb. 6.20; Liv. 8.8.
81. Polyb. 6.25.
82. McCall, *Cavalry of the Roman Republic*, pp. 51–52.
83. Polyb. 6.26.
84. Polyb. 6.21.5.
85. Polyb. 11.23 on the definition of a cohort. For some examples of allied soldiers operating in cohorts, see Liv. 23.14, 17, 24.1, 20, 33.36.10, 41.1.8.
86. McCall, *The Cavalry of the Roman Republic*, pp. 54–55.
87. Figures from Polyb. 6.21, 26, Liv. 22.36.
88. Discussion in D. Hoyos' appendix, 'Livy on the Manipular Legion' in Yardley trans. *Livy: Rome's Italian Wars*, pp. 291–93.
89. Liv. 8.8 (Foster trans.; I used 'maniples' to replace 'companies', and 'standard' to replace 'banners').
90. Polyb. 15.9.7–9.
91. See Sabin, 'The Face of Roman Battle', *Journal of Roman Studies* 90 (2000), p. 7.
92. A. Eckstein, *Senate and General: Individual Decisions Making and Roman Foreign Relations, 264–194 BC* (Berkeley, 1987).
93. Polyb. 6.19.
94. Polyb. 6.19.
95. McCall, *Sword of Rome: A Biography of Marcus Claudius Marcellus* (Barnsley, 2012), pp. 125–27.
96. Diod. Sic. 20.26.3–4.
97. Liv. 9.31.1–5.
98. Liv. 9.31.
99. Liv. 9.32.
100. Liv. 9.32.
101. Liv. 9.32.11.

102. Diod. Sic. 20.35.1–2. On this last point, see Oakley, *A Commentary on Livy, Books VI-X*, Vol. 3, p. 457.
103. Liv. 9.35.1–37.12 is the account. Oakley, *A Commentary on Livy, Books VI-X*, Vol. 3, pp. 451–60, provides the critical discussion of the problems in Livy.
104. Liv. 9.35.2.
105. Diod. Sic. 20.27.1 lists Fabius and Marcius as consuls. His account of the year for 20.35 essentially agrees with Livy, though he suggests that both Fabius and Marcius defeated the Etruscans, then Marcius went south to Samnium.
106. On this last point, see Oakley, *A Commentary on Livy, Books VI-X*, Vol. 3, p. 457.
107. Liv. 9.36.
108. See Hoyos' notes in Yardley trans. *Livy: Rome's Italian Wars*, p. 336.
109. Liv. 9.36.
110. Liv. 9.37.1–3.
111. Liv. 9.37.
112. See Hoyos' notes in Yardley trans. *Livy: Rome's Italian Wars*, p. 336.
113. Liv. 9.37.11–12 (Yardley trans.).
114. Again, a critical analysis comes from Oakley, *A Commentary on Livy, Books VI-X*, Vol. 3, pp. 485–86.
115. Liv. 9.38.10 (Yardley trans.).
116. Oakley, *A Commentary on Livy, Books VI-X*, Vol. 3, pp. 489–90.
117. Oakley, *A Commentary on Livy, Books VI-X*, Vol. 3, p. 461.
118. Liv. 9.38–39.
119. Liv. 9.41.1; Broughton, *MRR*, Vol. 1, p. 164.
120. Liv. 7.42.1.
121. Liv. 9.41.
122. Diod. Sic. 20.44.8–9.
123. Oakley, *A Commentary on Livy, Books VI-X*, Vol. 3, p. 531.
124. Oakley, *A Commentary on Livy, Books VI-X*, Vol. 3, p. 532.
125. Liv. 9.42.1–2.
126. Liv. 9.42.4 (Foster trans.).
127. Oakley, *A Commentary on Livy, Books VI-X*, Vol. 3, pp. 549–50.
128. For a brief discussion of Appius Claudius Caecus, see M.H. Crawford, *The Roman Republic*, Second Edition (Cambridge, MA, 1993), pp. 43–45.
129. Liv. 9.45.
130. Liv. 9.46. See also Hoyos' notes in Yardley trans. *Livy: Rome's Italian Wars*, p. 336.
131. Liv. 9.46.14–15 (Yardley trans.).
132. McCall, *The Cavalry of the Roman Republic*, pp. 53–77.
133. Note Dion. Hal. *Ant. Rom.* 6.13, who says it began in 496 BC.
134. M. McDonnell, *Roman Manliness: 'Virtus' and the Roman Republic* (Cambridge, 2006), pp. 186–88, 216.

Chapter 4: The Battle of Sentinum
1. Liv. 7.42.
2. Liv. 10.6–9.
3. Liv. 10.9.10.

4. Oakley, *A Commentary on Livy, Books VI-X*, Vol. 4, pp. 139–41.
5. Liv. 10.11.9–10. Oakley, *A Commentary on Livy, Books VI-X*, Vol. 4, p. 141.
6. Liv. 10.11–12.
7. Oakley, *A Commentary on Livy, Books VI-X*, Vol. 4, p. 180.
8. Liv. 10.13.
9. Liv. 10.14.9.
10. Liv. 10.14.
11. On this point, A. Zhmodikov, 'Roman Republican Heavy Infantrymen in Battle (IV-II Centuries BC)', *Historia* 49 (2000), pp. 67–78.
12. McCall, *The Cavalry of the Roman Republic*, pp. 21–22.
13. Liv. 10.14 (Yardley trans.).
14. Liv. 10.14.15–16.
15. Liv. 10.14.
16. Liv. 10.15.
17. Liv. 10.17. See Oakley, *A Commentary on Livy, Books VI-X*, Vol. 4, p. 198.
18. Liv. 10.18–19.
19. Liv. 10.20.
20. Liv. 10.20–21.
21. Though Oakley, *A Commentary on Livy, Books VI-X*, Vol. 4, p. 231, suggests this might have been a rhetorical device.
22. Liv. 10.21.
23. Liv. 10.23; see McCall, *Sword of Rome*, pp. 133–34.
24. Liv. 10.24.
25. Liv. 25–26.
26. Liv. 10.26.
27. Liv. 10.26.
28. Liv. 10.27.1–8.
29. Polyb. 2.19; Diod. Sic. 21.6; Front. *Strat.* 1.8.3; Val. Max. 5.6.5–6; Oros. 3.21.
30. Liv. 10.27.
31. McCall, *The Cavalry of the Roman Republic*, pp. 53–77.
32. Liv. 10.28.
33. Liv. 10.28.15–18 (Yardley trans.).
34. Liv. 8.10–11.
35. Polyb. 6.55.
36. M. McDonnell, *Roman Manliness*, pp. 199–200.
37. Liv. 8.9 (Foster trans.).
38. Liv. 8.8.
39. Liv. 10.29.1–7.
40. Liv.10.29.
41. Liv. 10.29.
42. Liv. 10.30.
43. Liv. 10.30.10 (Yardley trans.).
44. Forsythe, *A Critical History of Early Rome*, p. 330.
45. Macr., Sat. 3.13.
46. Liv. 10.31.9. Aediles imposing fines: Liv. 10.23, 10.33, 27.6, 31.50, 33.25, 33.42.

47. Liv. Per. 11 in J.D. Chaplin trans., *Livy. Rome's Mediterranean Empire: Books Forty-One to Forty-Five and the Periochae* (Oxford, 2007), p. 232.
48. Eutrop. 2.9.3.
49. Zonar. 8.1.
50. Liv. 27.6.8.
51. Dion. Hal. *Ant. Rom.* 17–18.4.
52. Cass. Dio Fragment 36.31 and Zonar. 8.1.
53. Liv. Per. 11; Broughton *MRR*, Vol. 1, p. 183
54. Note that Broughton *MRR*, Vol. 1, p. 182, does give Postumius Megellus a triumph.
55. Broughton *MRR*, Vol. 1, pp. 183–84, for sources.
56. A main point of N. Rosentein, *Imperatores Victi: Military Defeat and Aristocratic Competition in the Middle and Late Republic* (Berkeley, 1990).
57. Broughton *MRR*, Vol. 1, p. 195.
58. Val. Max. 9.1 ext. 2; Flor. 1.16; Zonar. 8.7. See Broughton *MRR*, Vol. 1, p. 201.
59. See Broughton *MRR*, Vol. 1, p. 202, for a brief review of the arguments.
60. Plut. *Fab.* 1.
61. Plut. *Fab.* 2.1.
62. Plut. *Comp Fab.et Per.* 2.1.
63. McDonnell, *Roman Manliness*, p. 216.
64. Broughton *MRR*, Vol. 1, p. 227.

Chapter 5: Fabius Maximus Cunctator and the War against Hannibal

1. D. Hoyos, *Mastering the West: Rome and Carthage at War* (Oxford, 2015), pp. 97–126, offers an excellent overview.
2. Polyb. 3.65.1–4. Liv. 21.40–47 describes the encounter at the Ticinus and includes lengthy speeches from Cornelius and Hannibal.
3. McCall, *The Cavalry of the Roman Republic*, pp. 53–77.
4. Polyb. 3.65.6. McCall, *The Cavalry of the Roman Republic*, pp. 34–35, 39.
5. Polyb. 3.65 (Paton trans.).
6. Liv. 21.46.6 (Foster trans.).
7. Polyb. 3.65.9–11.
8. Liv. 21.46.7–10.
9. Polyb. 3.66; Liv. 21.47.2–8.
10. Liv. 21.47.7.
11. Polyb. 3.68.
12. Polyb. 3.69.1–4; Liv. 21.48.8–10.
13. Polyb. 3.69.5–14; Liv 21.52.
14. Polyb. 3.70.1–8; Liv. 21.53.
15. Polyb. 3.71.1 (Paton trans.).
16. Polyb. 3.71–72; Liv. 21.54–55.
17. Polyb. 3.72.10 (Paton trans.); Liv. 21.55.
18. Polyb. 3.73.1–8.
19. Polyb. 3.72–74.
20. Hoyos, *Mastering the West*, pp. 109–12.

21. Polyb. 18.28–32 gives the classic comparison of the Roman manipular army with the Macedonian phalanx.
22. Hoyos, *Mastering the West*, p. 113.
23. Polyb. 3.86.
24. Polyb. 3.86.7 (Paton trans.).
25. Hoyos, *Mastering the West*, p. 114.
26. Polyb. 3.87.6 (Paton trans.); Liv. 22.8.
27. Liv. 22.8; Plut. *Fab.* 3–4.
28. Though Plut. *Fab.* 4 asserts he did pick his Master of Horse. Polybius and Livy disagree.
29. Polyb. 3.88.7.
30. Liv. 22.9–10; Plut. *Fab.* 4–5.
31. Dion. Hal. *Ant. Rom.* 4.62.
32. Liv. 22.9.
33. Liv. 5.13.5–8 in M. Beard, J. North and S. Price (eds), *Religions of Rome: A Sourcebook* Vol. 2, p. 130 (adaptation in the brackets from the author).
34. R. Miles, *Carthage Must Be Destroyed: The Rise and Fall of an Ancient Civilization* (New York, 2010), p. 274.
35. Miles, *Carthage Must Be Destroyed*, p. 273.
36. Liv. 22.11.
37. A central point of P. Erdkamp, 'Polybius, Livy, and the Fabian Strategy', *Ancient Society* 23 (1992), pp. 127–47.
38. Polyb. 3.86–87.
39. Liv. 22.11.
40. Liv. 22.9.2.
41. Polyb. 3.88.
42. Polyb. 3.89.5–90.5 (Paton trans.).
43. Liv. 22.12.1–9; see also Plut. *Fab.* 5 for a more general take.
44. Note Erdkamp, 'Polybius, Livy, and the Fabian Strategy', p. 137.
45. Polyb. 3.92; Liv. 22.14.
46. J. Lazenby, *Hannibal's War: A Military History of the Second Punic War* (Norman, OK, 1998), p. 69.
47. Polyb. 3.92.6–8.
48. Plut. *Fab.* 5.
49. Polyb. 3.90.5–6; Liv. 22.14.3–15.
50. Polyb. 3.92.
51. Liv. 22.15.2–3; Erdkamp, 'Polybius, Livy, and the Fabian Strategy', pp. 132–37, 145.
52. Lazenby, *Hannibal's War*, p. 70.
53. Polyb. 3.93–4; Liv. 22.16–17; Plut. *Fab.* 6–7. Lazenby, *Hannibal's War*, p. 71.
54. Polyb. 3.94.7; Liv. 28.18.8; see Plut. *Fab.* 7.2.
55. Polyb. 3.94.7; Liv. 22.18.8; see Plut. *Fab.* 8.1.
56. Argued in passing by Lazenby, *Hannibal's War*, p. 71.
57. Liv 22.18.
58. Liv. 22.23; Plut. *Fab.* 7

59. Polyb. 3.100–101.
60. Polyb. 3.101; Liv. 22.24.
61. Polyb. 3.102; Liv. 22.24.
62. Liv. 22.24–26; Plut. *Fab.* 7–10.
63. Liv. 22.25.1–16.
64. Liv. 22.25.12–16.
65. Plut. *Fab.* 9.
66. Liv. 22.25; Plut. *Fab.* 8–9.
67. Polyb. 3.103.7–8; Liv. 22.27.8–11; Plut. *Fab.* 10.3–5.
68. Polyb 3.104–105; Liv. 22.28.3–13; Plut. *Fab.* 11.
69. Liv. 22.29.1–2 (Foster trans.).
70. Polyb. 3.105.
71. Liv. 22.29.7–11 (Foster trans.); Plut. *Fab.* 13.
72. Liv. 22.31 (Foster trans.).
73. Erdkamp, 'Polybius, Livy, and the Fabian Strategy', p. 143.
74. Liv. (Foster trans., Yardley trans., Roberts trans., Evans trans.).
75. Liv. 22.32 (Yardley trans.).
76. Polyb. 3.1.
77. Polyb. 3.106.2–11.
78. Erdkamp, 'Polybius, Livy, and the Fabian Strategy', pp. 143–47, provides a critical comparison.
79. Polyb. 3.89.5–90.5.
80. Polyb. 3.106.1.
81. Liv. 22.34–35; see also Plut. *Fab.* 14.
82. Liv. 22.34.2.
83. E. Gruen, 'The Consular Elections for 216 BC and the Veracity of Livy', *California Studies in Classical Antiquity* 11 (1978), pp. 61–74, offers an important analysis of the election for 216.
84. A point noted by Gruen, 'The Consular Elections for 216 BC and the Veracity of Livy', pp. 61–74.
85. Liv. 22.34–35.
86. Polyb. 3.107.1–4.
87. Polyb. 3.107.8–15.
88. Polyb. 3.107.7–13.
89. Liv. 22.36.
90. Liv. 22.36.6.
91. Liv. 22.39; Plut. *Fab.* 14.
92. Noted by Erdkamp, 'Polybius, Livy, and the Fabian Strategy', pp. 143–47.
93. Liv. 22.41–43.
94. Polyb. 3.107. Again, see Erdkamp, 'Polybius, Livy, and the Fabian Strategy'.
95. Polyb. 3.108–109.
96. Polyb. 4.1–2.
97. A. Goldsworthy, *Cannae: Hannibal's Greatest Victory* (London, 2007), p. 74.
98. Polyb. 3.110.
99. Polyb. 3.110.1–11.

100. Polyb. 3.111–112.
101. Polyb. 3.112.1–5.
102. Goldsworthy, *Cannae*, p. 84.
103. Polyb. 3.113. (Waterfield trans.); Liv. 22.45–46 omits this detail, but Polybius is more credible here.
104. Polyb. 3.113.
105. Polyb. 3.113; Liv. 22.46.
106. Polyb. 3.113; Liv. 22.47 notes the protrusion of the Carthaginian line.
107. Accounts of Cannae: Polyb. 3.113–117; Liv. 22.45–49; Plut. *Fab*. 15–16.
108. Polyb. 3.116 (Waterfield trans.).
109. Polyb. 3.117; see Liv. 22.49.
110. Liv. 22.55–56; Plut. *Fab*. 17–18.
111. Liv. 22.57 (Foster trans.).
112. Liv. 22.57.
113. Liv. 22.57.
114. Liv. 23.22.
115. Liv. 22.57–23.23; quotation from Liv. 23.23 (Yardley trans.).
116. Liv. 23.18.
117. Hoyos, *Masters of West*, p. 149.
118. Liv. 23.23 (Yardley trans.).
119. Liv. 23.24.
120. Liv. 23.31 (De Selincourt trans.).
121. McDonnell, *Roman Manliness*, p. 188.
122. Liv. 23.21.
123. Liv. 23.32.
124. McCall, *Sword of Rome*, p. 52.
125. Liv. 23.36.
126. Liv. 23.46.
127. Liv. 23.46.

Chapter 6: The Fabian Strategy and the End of the War

1. Hoyos, *Mastering the West*, pp. 132–33; Lazenby, *Hannibal's War*, pp. 88–94.
2. Liv. 24.7.10–11.
3. Liv. 24.8 (Yardley trans.).
4. Liv. 24.8.1–20.
5. See F.K. Drogula, *Commanders and Command in the Roman Republic and Early Empire* (Chapel Hill, NC, 2015), pp. 92–97, for an excellent discussion of the fasces and imperium.
6. Liv. 24.9.10–11 (De Selincourt trans.).
7. Liv. 24.10.6–13 (Moore trans., with a few word changes by the author).
8. Liv. 24.11.
9. Liv. 24.13.1–5.
10. Liv. 24.13.6–7.
11. Liv. 24.12.5.
12. Liv. 24.13.8–14.1.

13. Liv. 24.17.1–8.
14. Liv. 24.19.1–8.
15. Liv. 24.19.9–11.
16. Liv. 24.20.1–6.
17. Liv. 24.20.9–16.
18. Liv. 25.43.5.
19. Liv. 24.44.1–9; Liv. 24.44.10 (Yardley trans.).
20. Liv. 24.45.1–3.
21. Liv. 24.45.1–14.
22. Liv. 24.46.1–7.
23. Liv. 24.47.1–15; Polyb. 3.117.
24. Liv. 25.1, 7.
25. Liv. 25.7.10 (Roberts trans.).
26. Liv. 25.7.9–14.
27. Liv. 25.8.1–8.
28. Liv. 25.8.9–9.7; Polyb. 8.26.
29. Liv. 25.9.9–17; Polyb. 8.27–29.
30. Liv. 25.9.16–10.6; Polyb. 8.30–31.
31. Liv. 25.10.6–10; Polyb. 8.31–32.
32. Liv. 25.11.1–20; Polyb. 8.32–34.
33. Liv. 25.15.4–5.
34. Liv. 26.5.1–3.
35. Liv. 26.5.1–6.17.
36. Liv. 25.7.1–4.
37. Liv. 26.8.1–11.
38. Liv. 26.8.9–9.6.
39. Liv. 26.9–12.
40. Liv. 26.22.1–9 (Roberts trans.).
41. Liv. 26.22.14–15 (Yardley trans.).
42. Liv. 26.37–40.
43. Liv. 27.3.8–9.
44. Liv. 27.5.1–19.
45. Liv. 27.6.1–18.
46. Liv. 27.6.9–17 (Roberts trans.).
47. Liv. 27.7.2–3.
48. Liv. 27.1.
49. Liv. 27.9.1–10.10.
50. Liv. 27.11.1–6 (De Selincourt trans.).
51. See Ryan, *Rank and Participation in the Republican Senate*, pp. 226–27.
52. Ryan, *Rank and Participation in the Republican Senate*, pp. 102, 170, 280.
53. Liv. 27.11.9–12.
54. Liv. 27.12–15.
55. Liv. 27.15.4–8.
56. Liv. 27.15.9–12; Plut. *Fab.* 21 also notes some divergent stories.
57. Liv. 27.15.12–19; Plut. *Fab.* 22.

58. Liv. 27.16.1 (Moore trans.).
59. Liv. 27.16.1–3.
60. Liv. 27.16.5–6; Plut. *Fab*. 22.4.
61. Plut. *Fab*. 22.4.
62. Liv. 27.16.6.
63. Liv. 27.16.6 (Roberts trans.).
64. See A. Ziolkowski, '*Urbs Direpta* or How the Romans Sacked Cities', in J. Rich and G. Shipley (eds), *War and Society in the Roman World* (London, 1993), pp. 69–91.
65. Liv. 27.16.7–8 (Roberts trans.).
66. McDonnell, *Roman Manliness*, p. 217.
67. Polyb. 9.10; Liv. 25.40.2–4; Plut. *Marc*. 21. McCall, *Sword of Rome*, pp. 89–91.
68. Liv. 25.40.2–4 (Moore trans.).
69. Plut. *Marc*. 21 (Perrin trans.).
70. Strab. *Geog*. 6.31; Plin *H.N.* 34.18.
71. Plut. *Fab*. 22 (Perrin trans.).
72. Liv. 27.22.1.
73. See Ryan, *Rank and Participation in the Republican Senate*, pp. 293–305; Ryan notes that the first eight references in Livy to the *princeps senatus* speaking first involve Fabius Maximus Cunctator, our current subject.
74. Hoyos, *Mastering the West*, p. 153.
75. Liv. 27.25.1.
76. Liv. 27.25.1–3.
77. McCall, *Sword of Rome*, pp. 19–23.
78. McDonnell, *Roman Manliness*, pp. 217–21.
79. McCall, *Sword of Rome*, pp. 116–22.
80. Liv. 27.34.1–10.
81. Val. Max. 4.2.2; Suet. *Tib*. 3.
82. Liv. 27.34.11–15.
83. Val. Max. 4.2.2.
84. Liv. 27.35.5–8.
85. Liv. 27.35.7–9.
86. Liv. 28.9.
87. Hoyos, *Mastering the West*, pp. 192–95.
88. Liv. 27.51.12–13.
89. Liv. 28.9.18–10.2.
90. Liv. 28.11.8–12.
91. Liv. 28.12.1–8.
92. Hoyos, *Mastering the West*, pp. 164–85; Miles, *Carthage Must Be Destroyed*, pp. 298–302.
93. Hoyos, *Mastering the West*, pp. 164–85; Miles, *Carthage Must Be Destroyed*, pp. 298–302.
94. Hoyos, *Mastering the West*, pp. 164–85; Miles, *Carthage Must Be Destroyed*, pp. 298–302.
95. Liv. 28.38.1–9.

96. Liv. 28.38.13–14.
97. Liv. 28.38.1–21.
98. Hoyos' notes in Yardley trans. *Livy: Rome's Italian Wars*, p. 689.
99. Liv. 28.40.3–10.
100. Liv. 28.40.12–14.
101. Liv. 28.42.
102. Liv. 28.42.13–14.
103. Liv. 28.42 (Roberts trans.).
104. Liv. 28.43.1.
105. Liv. 28.43.
106. Liv. 28.45.1–8.
107. Liv. 28.45.8–13.
108. Liv. 28.45.14–46.1. Miles, *Carthage Must Be Destroyed*, p. 305.
109. Liv. 28.46.7–13.
110. Liv. 28.46.13.
111. Liv. 29.1.1–19.
112. Liv. 29.2.1–3.6.
113. Liv. 29.6.1–7.10.
114. Liv. 29.8.7–9 (Yardley trans.).
115. Liv. 29.9.1–7.
116. Liv. 29.9.11–12 (Roberts trans.).
117. Liv. 29.16.4–7.
118. Liv. 29.17.15–16 (Yardley trans.).
119. Liv. 29.18.7–8.
120. Liv. 29.19.
121. Liv. 29.19.
122. Liv. 29.20.
123. Liv. 29.21.
124. Liv. 28.9.
125. Cic. *Cat. Mai* 4; Plut. *Fab.* 1.3.
126. Hoyos, *Mastering the West*, pp. 199–219.
127. Liv. 30.26 (De Selincourt trans.).
128. Liv. 33.42.

Chapter 7: Spanish Wars, Gallic Wars, Civil Wars and the End of the Line

1. Liv. 33.42.
2. Liv. 39.29.4; Broughton, *MRR*, Vol. 1, pp. 365–66.
3. Liv. 40.36.13; *MRR* 1, p. 388
4. Liv. 40.26.7, 40.28.9; Broughton, *MRR*, Vol. 1, p. 384
5. Plut. *Aem.* 5.
6. A. Eckstein, 'Hegemony and Annexation beyond the Adriatic', in Hoyos (ed.), *A Companion to Roman Imperialism*, pp. 89–90.
7. Nick Sekunda, *Macedonian Armies after Alexander 323–168 BC* (Oxford, 2012), p. 6.
8. Plut. *Aem.* 15–17; Liv. 44.35.

9. Liv. 45.40.
10. Liv. 45.41; Diod. Sic. 31.8; Plut. *Aem.* 32–34.
11. Polyb. 31.28; Plut. *Aem.* 35.
12. Polyb. 31.23.
13. Polyb. 31.24.
14. Polyb. 31.28; Plut. *Aem.* 39.
15. Polyb. 31.28.
16. Polyb. 36.5.
17. J.L.L. Castro, 'The Spains, 205–72 BC', in Hoyos (ed.), *A Companion to Roman Imperialism*, pp. 67–69.
18. Castro, 'The Spains, 205–72 BC', in Hoyos (ed.), *A Companion to Roman Imperialism*, p. 70; Diod. Sic. 31–42; App. *Iber.* 66.
19. Castro, 'The Spains, 205–72 BC', in Hoyos (ed.), *A Companion to Roman Imperialism*, p. 70; see App. *Iber.* 59–60.
20. Liv. *Per.* 52 (Chaplin trans.).
21. Diod. Sic. 33.1; Broughton, *MRR*, Vol. 1, pp. 464–65.
22. Diod. Sic. 33.1.
23. App. *Iber.* 64; Castro, 'The Spains, 205–72 BC', in Hoyos (ed.), *A Companion to Roman Imperialism*, p. 71.
24. App. *Iber.* 65.
25. App. *Iber.* 65.
26. Val. Max. 6.4.2.
27. Vell. Pat. 2.5.3 (Loeb trans.).
28. App. *Iber.* 65; Castro, 'The Spains, 205–72 BC', in Hoyos (ed.), *A Companion to Roman Imperialism*, p. 71.
29. App. *Iber.* 66.
30. Castro, 'The Spains, 205–72 BC', in Hoyos (ed.), *A Companion to Roman Imperialism*, p. 71; App. *Iber.* 78.
31. App. *Iber.* 70; S.J. Northwood, 'Q. Fabius Maximus Servilianus', in T.J. Cornell (ed.), *The Fragments of the Roman Historians* (Oxford, 2014), Vol. 1, p. 227.
32. Liv. *Per.* 53.
33. App. *Iber.* 67.
34. App. *Iber.* 68.
35. App. *Iber.* 68.
36. Val. Max. 2.7.11 (Walker trans.).
37. Front. *Strat.* 4.1.42.
38. Oros. 5.4.12.
39. App. *Iber.* 68.
40. Liv. *Per.* 54 (Chaplin trans.).
41. Liv. *Per.* 54 (Chaplin trans.); Diod. Sic. 31.1; App. *Hisp.* 70.
42. S.J. Northwood, 'Q. Fabius Maximus Servilianus', in Cornell (ed.), *The Fragments of the Roman Historians*, Vol. 1, pp. 227–29.
43. Val. Max. 7.1; Liv. *Per.* 57.
44. App. *Iber.* 90.
45. App. *Iber.* 91.

46. Josh Levithan, *Roman Siege Warfare* (Ann Arbor, MI, 2013), pp. 112–14.
47. App. *Iber*. 93.
48. App. *Iber*. 94.
49. App. *Iber*. 95 (White trans.).
50. App. *Iber*. 95 (White trans.).
51. App. *Iber*. 96.
52. Liv. *Per*. 57 and 59 also relate a compressed version of Scipio at Numantia.
53. Liv. *Per*. 59.
54. Val. Max. 8.15.4.
55. App. *Iber*. 84.
56. Broughton, *MRR*, Vol. 1, p. 491.
57. Plut. *C. Gracch*. 6.2; Broughton, *MRR*, Vol. 1, p. 512.
58. Broughton, *MRR*, Vol. 1, p. 512.
59. Plut. *C. Gracch*. 6.2.
60. Liv. *Per*. 60; App. *B. Civ*. 1.34; see Broughton, *MRR*, Vol. 1, p. 510.
61. H.H. Scullard, *From the Gracchi to Nero 133 BC to AD 68*, Fifth Edition (London, 2003), pp. 39–40; Liv. *Per*. 61.
62. Caes. *BGall*. 1.45.2.
63. Liv. *Per*. 61; Cic. *Font*. 36; Strab. *Geog*. 1.4.11.
64. Vell. Pat. 2.10, 2.39.
65. Strab. *Geog*. 1.4.11.
66. F. Kleiner, *Arch of Nero in Rome* (Rome, 1985), pp. 16–17.
67. S. Platner, *A Topographical Dictionary of Ancient Rome* (Oxford, 2002), pp. 211–12; L. Richardson, *A New Topographical Dictionary of Ancient Rome* (Baltimore, 1992), p. 154.
68. Platner, *A Topographical Dictionary of Ancient Rome*, p. 211.
69. Richardson, *A New Topographical Dictionary of Ancient Rome*, p. 154
70. Broughton, *MRR*, Vol. 1, pp. 530, 548–49.
71. Oros. 5.16.8; Val. Max. 6.1.5–6; Ps. Quint. *Decl*. 3.17.
72. Val. Max. 3.5.2 (Walker trans.).
73. Sall. Cat. 41.4; App. *B. Civ*. 2.4.
74. Ryan, *Rank and Participation in the Republican Senate*, pp. 210–11.
75. Ryan, *Rank and Participation in the Republican Senate*, pp. 210–11.
76. App. *Iber*. 41.
77. App. *Iber*. 41.
78. Cass. Dio 43.42.1–2.
79. Suet. *Jul*. 80.3.
80. M. Roller, 'The Consul(ar) as exemplum', in H. Beck, A. Dupla, M. Jehne and F. Pina Polo (eds), *Consuls and Res Publica: Holding High Offices in the Roman Republic* (Cambridge, 2011), p. 207.
81. See Roller, 'The Consul(ar) as exemplum', in *Consuls and Res Publica: Holding High Offices in the Roman Republic*, p. 207; the inscription in the Augustan Forum is fragmentary; a full copy was found at Arretium (CIL. 1.1828; base translation J. Henderson, *Figuring out Roman Nobility: Juvenal's Eighth Satire* (Exeter, 1997), pp. 52–53; adapted slightly to be more formal and to keep a few of the terms in Latin).

Conclusion: Living on the Legends of the Past

1. Virg. *Aen.* 973–75 (Fagles trans.).
2. Ov. *Fast.* 2.195–99 (Wiseman trans.).
3. Ov. *Fast.* 2.240–44 (Wiseman trans.).
4. These final shoots of the Fabius Maximus tree are documented by R. Syme, *Augustan Aristocracy* (Oxford, 1989), pp. 403–20.
5. B. Salway, 'What's in a Name? A Survey of Roman Onomastic Practice from c. 700 BC to AD 700', *Journal of Roman Studies* 84 (1994), p. 130.
6. Syme, *The Augustan Aristocracy*, pp. 403–15.
7. See the family tree in Syme, *The Augustan Aristocracy*, Table 27.
8. Henderson, *Figuring out the Roman Nobility*, p. 53.
9. Syme, *The Augustan Aristocracy*, pp. 416–17.
10. Sen. *Ben.* 4.30.1–4 (Basore trans.).
11. Syme, 418–19.
12. Juv. *Sat.* 8.1, 8.9–18; translation and commentary by John Henderson, *Figuring out Roman Nobility*, pp. 48–50
13. T.S. Eliot, 'The Hollow Men'.

Appendix A: Roman Names

1. Salway, 'What's in a Name? A Survey of Roman Onomastic Practice from c. 700 BC to AD 700', pp. 125–27.
2. Salway, 'What's in a Name? A Survey of Roman Onomastic Practice from c. 700 BC to AD 700', p. 127
3. A. Corbeill, *Controlling Laughter: Political Humor in the Late Roman Republic* (Princeton, 1996), pp. 57–67.

Bibliography

Beard, Mary, North, John, and Price, Simon (eds), *Religions of Rome, Volume 2: A Sourcebook* (Cambridge, 1998).

Bergk, Alexander, 'The development of the praetorship in the third century', in H. Beck, A. Dupla, M. Jehne and F. Pina Polo (eds), *Consuls and Res Publica: Holding High Offices in the Roman Republic* (Cambridge, 2011), pp. 61–74.

Bishop, M.C., and Coulston, J.C.N., *Roman Military Equipment: From the Punic Wars to the Fall of Rome* (Oxford, 2006).

Broughton, Thomas R.S., *The Magistrates of the Roman Republic Volume 1* (New York, 1951). Available online at http://babel.hathitrust.org/cgi/pt?id=mdp.39015009351001;view=1up;seq=48.

Castro, Jose L.L., 'The Spains, 205–72 BC', in Hoyos (ed.), *A Companion to Roman Imperialism*, pp. 67–69.

Chaplin, Jane D. (trans.), *Livy. Rome's Mediterranean Empire: Books Forty-One to Forty-Five and the Periochae* (Oxford, 2007).

Corbeill, A., *Controlling Laughter: Political Humor in the Late Roman Republic* (Princeton, 1996).

Cornell, Timothy J., *The Beginnings of Rome: Italy and Rome from the Bronze Age to the Punic Wars* (London, 1995).

Crawford, Michael, *The Roman Republic* (London, 1978).

Drogula, Fred K., *Commanders and Command in the Roman Republic and Early Empire* (Chapel Hill, NC, 2015).

Eckstein, A., 'Hegemony and Annexation beyond the Adriatic', in Hoyos (ed.), *A Companion to Roman Imperialism* (Leiden, 2012), pp. 89–90.

Eckstein, Arthur, *Senate and General: Individual Decisions Making and Roman Foreign Relations, 264–194 BC* (Berkeley, 1987).

Erdkamp, Paul, 'Polybius, Livy, and the Fabian Strategy', *Ancient Society* 23(1992), pp. 127–47.

Forsythe, Gary, *A Critical History of Early Rome: From Prehistory to the Punic War* (Berkeley, 2005).

Goldsworthy, Adrian, *Cannae: Hannibal's Greatest Victory* (London, 2007).

Goldsworthy, Adrian, *The Roman Army at War 100 BC to AD 200* (Oxford, 1996).

Gruen, Erich, 'The Consular Elections for 216 BC and the Veracity of Livy', *California Studies in Classical Antiquity* 11(1978), pp. 61–74.

Henderson, John, *Figuring out Roman Nobility: Juvenal's Eighth Satire* (Exeter, 1997).

Holkeskamp, Karl-J., 'Conquest, Competition and Consensus: Roman Expansion in Italy and the Rise of the "Nobilitas"', *Historia* 42 (1993), pp. 12–39.

Hoyos, Dexter, 'Appendix 2. Livy on the Manipular Legion', in Yardley (trans.), *Livy: Rome's Italian Wars*, pp. 291–93.

Hoyos, Dexter, *Mastering the West: Rome and Carthage at War* (Oxford, 2015).

Hoyos, Dexter, Notes in J.C. Yardley (trans.), *Livy: Rome's Italian Wars* (Oxford, 2013).

Kleiner, Fred, *Arch of Nero in Rome* (Rome, 1985).

Lazenby, John, *Hannibal's War: A Military History of the Second Punic War* (Norman, OK, 1998).

Levithan, Josh, *Roman Siege Warfare* (Ann Arbor, MI, 2013).

Lintott, Andrew, *The Constitution of the Roman Republic* (Oxford, 1999).

McCall, Jeremiah, *The Cavalry of the Roman Republic: Cavalry Combat and Elite Reputations in the Middle and Late Republic* (London, 2002).

McCall, Jeremiah, *Sword of Rome: A Biography of Marcus Claudius Marcellus* (Barnsley, 2012).

McDonnell, Myles, *Roman Manliness: 'Virtus' and the Roman Republic* (Cambridge, 2006).

Miles, Richard, *Carthage Must Be Destroyed: The Rise and Fall of an Ancient Civilization* (New York, 2010).

Northwood, S.J., 'Q. Fabius Maximus Servilianus', in T.J. Cornell (ed.), *The Fragments of the Roman Historians* (Oxford, 2014), Vol. 1, pp. 227–29.

Oakley, Stephen P., *A Commentary on Livy, Books VI-X*, 4 vols (Oxford, 1997–2005).

Olson, Kelly, *Masculinity and Dress in Roman Antiquity* (New York, 2017).

Pais, Ettore, 'The Fabii at the River Cremera and the Spartans at Thermopylae', in J.H. Richardson and F. Santangelo (eds), *The Roman Historical Tradition: Regal and Republican Rome* (Oxford, 2014), pp. 167–86.

Pina Polo, F., *et al* (eds.), *Consuls and Res Publica: Holding High Office in the Roman Republic* (Cambridge, 2011), pp. 61–74.

Platner, Samuel B., *A Topographical Dictionary of Ancient Rome* (Oxford, 2002).

Radice, Betty (trans.), *Livy. Rome and Italy: Books VI-X of the History of Rome from its Foundations* (London 1982).

Rich, John, 'Warfare and Army in Early Rome', in P. Erdkamp (ed.), *A Companion to the Roman Army* (Malden, MA, 2007), pp. 7–23.

Richardson, Lawrence, *A New Topographical Dictionary of Ancient Rome* (Baltimore, 1992).

Roberts, W.R. (trans.), *Dionysius of Halicarnassus: The Three Literary Letters* (Cambridge, 1901).

Roller, Matthew, 'The Consul(ar) as exemplum', in H. Beck, A. Dupla, M. Jehne and F. Pina Polo (eds), *Consuls and Res Publica: Holding High Offices in the Roman Republic* (Cambridge, 2011), pp. 182–210.

Rosentein, Nathan, *Imperatores Victi: Military Defeat and Aristocratic Competition in the Middle and Late Republic* (Berkeley, 1990).

Ryan, Francis X., *Rank and Participation in the Republican Senate* (Stuttgart, 1998).

Sabin, Philip, 'The Face of Roman Battle', *Journal of Roman Studies* 90 (2000), pp. 1–17.

Sage, Michael, *The Republican Roman Army: A Sourcebook* (New York, 2008).

Salway, B., 'What's in a Name? A Survey of Roman Onomastic Practice from c. 700 BC to AD 700', *Journal of Roman Studies* 84 (1994), p. 130.

Scullard, Howard H., *From the Gracchi to Nero 133 BC to AD 68*, fifth edition (London, 2003).

Sekunda, Nick, *Macedonian Armies after Alexander 323–168 BC* (Oxford, 2012), p. 6.

Smith, Christopher J., *The Roman Clan: The Gens from Ancient Ideology to Modern Anthropology* (Cambridge, 2006).

Smith, Christopher, 'The magistrates of the early Roman Republic', in H. Beck, A. Dupla, M. Jehne, and F. Pina Polo (eds.) *Consuls and Res Publica: Holding High Office in the Roman Republic* (Cambridge, 2011), 19–40.

Smith, William, "Ambustus," "Fabius," and "Vibulanus" in *A Classical Dictionary of Biography, Mythology and Geography* (London, 1891).

Stone, Martin, "The Genesis of Roman Imperialism," in D. Hoyos, ed., *A Companion to Roman Imperialism* (Leiden, 2013), 23–38.

Syme, Ronald, *Augustan Aristocracy* (Oxford, 1989), pp. 403–420

Urso, Gianpaolo, "The origin of the consulship in Cassius Dio's History," in H. Beck, A., Dupla, M. Jehne and F. Pina Polo (eds), *Consuls and Res Publica: Holding High Office in the Roman Republic* (Cambridge, 2011), pp. 41–60.

Van Wees, Hans, *Greek Warfare: Myths and Realities* (London, 2004).

Walker, Henry J. (trans.), *Valerius Maximus, Memorable Deeds and Sayings* (Indianapolis, 2004).

Warrior, Valerie M. (trans.), *Livy. The History of Rome Books 1–5.* (Indianapolis, 2006).

Waterfield, Robin (trans.), *Polybius. The Histories* (Oxford, 2010).

Webster, Graham, *The Roman Imperial Army* (Totowa, NJ, 1985).

Wiseman, Anne and Peter (trans.), *Ovid. Fasti* (Oxford World's Classics) (Oxford 2013).

Wiseman, Timothy P., 'Legendary Genealogies in Late Republican Rome', *Greece and Rome* 21 (1974), pp. 153–64.

Wiseman, Timothy P., *Remus: A Roman Myth* (Cambridge, 1995).

Yardley, J.C. (trans.), *Livy. Hannibal's War: Books 21–30* (Oxford, 2006).

Yardley, J.C. (trans.), *Livy. Rome's Italian Wars: Books 6–10* (Oxford, 2013).

Zhmodikov, Alexander, 'Roman Republican Heavy Infantrymen in Battle (IV–II Centuries BC)', *Historia* 49 (2000), pp. 67–78.

Ziolkowski, A., '*Urbs Direpta* or How the Romans Sacked Cities', in J. Rich and G. Shipley (eds), *War and Society in the Roman World* (London, 1993), pp. 69–91.

Index

Note: individuals are listed alphabetically according to their family name (nomen)

216 Consular Elections, 101–103
300 Fabii, 2, 22–4

Aediles, 3, 37, 68, 80, 171
Aemilius Paullus, L., (cos. 216), 102–103
Aemilius Paullus L., (cos. 168), 150–1, 157, 162, 167–8
Aequi, 1, 12–13, 19–29, 33
Allia River, Battle of, 32–3
Allies, Italian, 54, 89, 104
Allobroges, 159–63
Annales Maximi, 7, 18, 22, 171
Antium, 13, 25, 27–8
Appeal to the people, 32, 41
Appian Aqueduct, 49
Appian Way, 49, 119
Ap. Claudius Caecus (Censor 312), 49–50, 63–6, 72–4
Apulia, 36, 43–4, 93–4, 97, 102, 104, 109, 113, 117–18, 120, 129
Aquae Sextiae, 161
Arpi, siege of in Second Punic War, 120–2
Arrenius, G. and L., tribunes who vetoed 210 elections, 127
Augurs, 68, 84, 111–12
Auspices, problems with, 39, 41, 67, 111–13

Baetis River (Spain), 138, 153, 156
Banquet singers, as a source of historical information, 8
Battle with pauses in fighting 71, 43, 76

Campania, 33, 36–8, 44, 47–9, 73–4, 78–9, 95–6, 109–11, 113–15, 117–19, 124
Cannae, Battle of, 103–14, 115, 120, 138, 150
Capua, 33, 36–7, 47–9, 110, 113, 118–19, 124–5, 128–9, 134, 141
Capua, siege of in Second Punic War, 124–5, 134

Carthage, 83–4, 123, 143, 146–7, 150, 152, 154
Casilinum, 113, 119
Cassian Treaty, 21
Cato the Elder, 84
Caudine Forks, Samnites defeated Romans at, 44
Cavalry;
    association with Fabii, 64–5, 111–12
    census class, 17, 64–5
    dismount in combat, 65, 87, 107
    equipment, 54
    in battle, 19, 29, 40, 42–3, 45, 51, 57, 59, 71, 75–6, 78–9, 86–9, 99–100, 106–108
    Parade of, 65, 85
    size of force, 54, 74, 104
Censors, 3–4, 17, 49–50, 63–5, 110, 129, 134, 136, 171
Centuriate Assembly, 4, 17, 18, 65, 69–70, 111, 115, 139, 171
Ciminian Forest, 59–60
Cincius Alimentus, L., historian, 64–5, 75, 84
Civitas sine suffragio, 37
Clastidium, supply depot for Hannibal, 87, 89
Claudius Marcellus, M., (cos. 222), 109–10, 111–13, 116–19, 126–7, 129, 131–6, 143
Claudius Nero, G., co-commander at the Metaurus, 135–8
Cohort, 54
Comitia centuriata, *see* Centuriate Assembly
Commander, role of in Roman battles, 56–7
Conflict of Orders, 13–15, 26, 34, 103
Constitution, flexibly interpreted, 73–4, 128–9
Consulship;
    coveted office, 67
    law requiring 10 years between each holding of, 62, 67, 70
Consuls, powers of, 3

Cornelius Cethegus, M., (cens. 209), 129
Cornelius Scipio, P., (cos. 218), 86–7, 138
Cornelius Scipio Aemilianus, P., (cos. 147) 3, 150–2, 154, 160
Cornelius Scipio Africanus, P., (cos. 205), 139–46
Corsica, 85
Cremera River, Battle of, *see* 300 Fabii

Dasius Altinius, defector from Arpi, 120–1
Decemviri, drafters of the 12 tables, 28
Decius Mus, P.;
    challenges provincial assignments 73–4
    devotio at Sentinum, 76–9
Decrees/edicts of Fabius Cunctator, 113
Devotio ritual, 76–9
Diodorus Siculus, 6, 24, 31, 38, 45, 173
Dionysius of Halicarnassus, 6, 11, 82, 173–4

Elections of 215, 110–13
Equites, see Cavalry, census class, 64–5
Equites Equo Publico, 65
Etruscan War, (311–309), 57–62
Etruscans, 12, 16, 19–20, 22, 29, 33, 35, 50, 67, 73–9, 83

Fabii;
    origins of cognomens
        Allobrogicus, 159
        Ambustus, 5, 30–1
        Cunctator, 100
        Gurges, 80
        Maximus, 64, 91
        Ovicula, 84
      Rullianus, 5, 37
      Verrucosus, 84
      Vibulanus, 5, 11
    origins of family, 10–11

Fabius Ambustus Vibulanus, K., N., and Q., role in the sack of Rome, 31–2
Fabius Ambustus Vibulanus, Q., (cos. 485), 30–1
Fabius Buteo, M. (dict. 216), refills senate after Cannae, 110
Fabius Maximus Aemilianus, Q. (cos. 145), 150–7
Fabius Maximus Allobrogicus, Q. (cos. 121), 159–62
Fabius Maximus Cunctator, Q., 83–148
    dictatorship, 91–101

legacy of, 149–50, 159, 165–9
ransomed troops, 97
Fabius Maximus Eburnus, Q. (cos. 116), executed his son, 162
Fabius Maximus Gurges, Q. (cos. 292), 80–4
Fabius Maximus Rullianus, Q. (cos. 322), 5, 33–84
investigates poison plot, 37, 39
Fabius Maximus Servilianus, Q. (cos. 142), 155–62
Fabius Sanga, Q. (sen. 63), 163–4
Fabius Vibulanus, K. (cos. 484), 12–13, 18–20, 22–3
Fabius Vibulanus, M. (cos. 483), 10, 13, 15–16, 19–20
Fabius Vibulanus, M. (cos. 442), 28–30
Fabius Vibulanus, Q. (cos. 485), 11–12, 18–19
Fabius Vibulanus, Q., survivor of the Cremera disaster, 23–8
Falernum, 95–7
Family histories, in form of eulogies, 7–8
Fasti Capitolini, 6, 79
Fasti Consulares, 6
Fasti Triumphales, 44
Fetial priests, 69
First Punic War, 50, 92, 128
Flavius, Gn. (aed. 304), 64
Fornix Fabianus, 161
Flaminius, G., (cos. 217), 90

Gauls, 31–4, 72–9, 88, 90, 111, 134, 137, 143, 159–62
Gentes Maiores, 10–11
Gereonium, supply depot for Hannibal, 97–8
Gladius, 53–4
Gloria, 67, 88, 91, 139

Hannibal, 86–148
Hastati, 52, 54–6, 59, 71
Hercules;
    association with the Fabii, 2, 10, 93, 154, 161, 166, 168, 177 n. 4
    colossal statue of in Tarentum, 133, 150
Hernici, 1, 11–13, 25, 34
Honos and Virtus, Temple, 111–12, 132, 134
Honos, Temple, 85, 111–12, 132, 134
Hoplite panoply, 16–18
Hostilius Mancinus, G. (cos. 137), 39

Imperium, 3, 5, 116, 139, 165–6
Ineditum Vaticanum, 50–1
Infantry in battle, 3–4, 17, 20, 40, 43, 50–7, 65, 71, 75–6, 78–9, 86–7, 89, 99–100, 107–108
Interrex, 18, 30, 82, 172

Lake Regillus, Battle of, 21
Latin colonies, refused to provide troops in 209, 127–8
Latin League, 33, 36
Latin Rights, 36–7, 177
Latin War, 36–7, 41
Latins, 1–2, 21, 36–7, 77, 109
Lautulae, battle near, 45–7
Lectisternium, 92
Lex Ovinia, see Ovinian Law
Lex Villia Annalis, 160
Lictors, 41, 78, 93, 116, 120, 144
Livius Macatus, M., prefect of Tarentum citadel, 120, 123, 134, 136
Livius Salinator, M. (cos. 207), 135–7
Livy, as a historian, 6–9
Lusitanian war, 153–5

Marcellus, *see* Claudius Marcellus, M.
Metilius, M. (tr. pl. 217), 98–9
Minucius Felix, M. (dict. 217), 91, 93, 95–100
Manipular army, 50–7
Massilia, 161
Metaurus River, Battle of, 136–7
Military Tribunes with Consular Powers, 29–32, 172
Mount Cimino, 60

Nail, driven into the temple of Jupiter, 37–8
Names, Roman, 170
Neapolis, 38, 96, 110, 113
Nico, leads Tarentum revolt, 122–3, 131
Nola, 48–9
Numantine War, 155–9
Numidian cavalry, 86, 88–9, 98, 106–108, 123, 156

Ogulnius (tr. pl. 300) 68
Omens in Livy, 104, 117, 119, 128
Ovid, poet, 166–7
Ovinian Law, 4, 49

Papirius Cursor, L. (cos. 326), 39–42, 45–6, 48, 61–2, 67
Patrician, 8, 12–15, 28, 34–5, 68, 72–3, 103, 112, 135

Pax deorum, 93
Phalanx, 16–17, 18, 50–2, 90
Phileas, Tarentine exile at Rome, 122
Philemenus, leads Tarentum revolt, 122–3, 131
Pilum, 51, 53
Placentia, 87, 89, 137
Plebeian, 4, 11–15, 19, 25, 28, 34–5, 63, 68, 73, 103, 111–12, 127, 135
Pleminius, G., fiasco at Locri, 143–6
Polybius, as a source, 3–4, 158
Pontiffs, 7, 64, 68, 77, 112, 134–5
Postumius Megellus, L., (cos. 291), 82
Praetors, 3–5, 17
Princeps Senatus, 129, 134, 137, 141, 145, 150, 166,
Principes, 52, 54–6, 59, 71, 78–9
Prorogation, 38
Provocatio ad populum, see appeal to the people
Puteoli, 114–15, 118
Pyrrhus, King of Epirus, 83, 122, 145

Quinctius, K., plotted *coup d'etat*, 26

Republic, government of, 2–5
Resting during battle, *see* Battle with pauses in fighting
Roman Army, Early Republic, 16–18
Roman Army, manipular, 51–7
Roman Kings, 2–5

Sack of Rome, 31–2
Sack of Tarentum, compared to sack of Syracuse, 129–33
Samnites, 36
Samnite Wars;
    First, 36–7
    Second, 37–63
    Third, 69–82
Sardinia, 85
Saticula, 44–6
Scutum, 51–4
Secession of the Plebs, 14
Sempronius Tuditanus, P. (cens. 209), 129
Senate, 3–5, 14
Senones, Gallic tribe that sacked Rome, 32, 37
Sentinum, Battle of, 66–85, 95
    Devotio, *see* Decius Mus, P., devotio at Sentinum
    Omen before, 75
Servilius Geminus, Gn. (cos. 217), 90, 93–4, 101–104

Sicily, 84–5

Socii, 54

Sora, 45–6, 48–9

Sora, battle with Samnites near in 297, 45–6

Spurius Cassius (cos. 502), 7, 11

Sutrium, battle with the Etruscans near, 58–60

Sword and Shield, epithets for Marcellus and Fabius Cunctator, 116

Sibylline books, 92, 104, 109

Tarentum, 33, 83, 118–120, 122–6, 129–36

Tarpeian Rock, 11, 120, 122

Tarquinii, sacrifice captured Romans, 34–5, 62

Terentius Varro, G., commander at Cannae, 98, 103–108

Tibur, 33–6, 93

Ticinus, cavalry battle at, 86–7

Titus Manlius Torquatus (cos. 347), as dictator executed his son, 41–2

Titus Manlius Torquatus (cos. 235), role in elections for 210, 125–6, 129

Toga, 49, 77

Transvectio Equitum, *see* Cavalry, Parade of

Trasimene, Battle of, 90–1

Trebia, Battle of the, 88

Triarii, 41, 52, 54–5, 78

Tribunes of the Plebs, 4, 14, 29, 70, 142

Veii, 1–2, 12, 19, 22–4, 28, 31, 33

Velites, 51–2, 54, 57, 88–9, 100

Venus Erycina, 92

Vestal Virgins, 18

Vestini, 39

Viriathus, 154–7

Volsci, 7, 12–13, 15, 20–2, 24–8, 30, 33

Volsini serf revolt, 83–4